# LED ZEPP

## ALL THE ALBUMS
## ALL THE SONGS

### EXPANDED EDITION

# MARTIN POPOFF

# ELIN

chartwell
books

# CONTENTS

Introduction  6

Led Zeppelin  10

II  36

III  62

Untitled  90

Houses of the Holy  116

Physical Graffiti  140

Presence  180

In Through the Out Door  204

Coda  222

Over the Hills and Far Away:
16 Essential Rarities  248

Acknowledgments  282

About the Author  282

Image Credits  283

Index  285

# INTRODUCTION

**"T**HE VERY FIRST TIME I HEARD 'I WANNA HOLD YOUR HAND,' IN THE FRONT SEAT OF MY DAD'S CAR—I WAS PROBABLY FOUR OR FIVE YEARS OLD—IT WAS LIKE, I DON'T KNOW. WHEN 'NOWHERE MAN' CAME OUT AND I WAS ABOUT SIX OR SEVEN, THAT WAS THE SONG. IT WAS LENNON'S VOICE, HIS MELODIES. IT'S JUST THAT HIS VOICE CUTS THROUGH, AND WHAT HE SAYS, IT'S JUST HARD TO EXPLAIN. HE'S INCOMPREHENSIBLE TO ME, AND NOW THAT HE'S DEAD IT'S MORE SO. LIKE I CAN'T EVEN BELIEVE HE WAS HERE."

Those are the amusing words of Eric Wagner, lead singer for Chicago doom band Trouble, and I've never forgotten them, ever since he uttered them to me something like twenty years ago. Now, I couldn't give a damn about the Beatles, but Wagner's words are kind of how I feel about Led Zeppelin (the Clash too, but that's another matter)—I can't even believe they were here.

There was this idea when I was growing up that Led Zeppelin existed on another plane and that the usual rules didn't apply to them. And now here I am, presenting to you exactly the kind of book that I've long wanted to write about Led Zeppelin. Why? Well, the biographies have all been done. And indeed, there have even been two books done this way, song by song: one by Chris Welch and one by Dave Lewis. But oddly, in the months before this project was proposed to me by Dennis Pernu at Voyageur Press, I had been walking to work, listening to my iPod, and thinking I should start writing deep analyses of Zeppelin's songs for something that I thought I would probably end up self-publishing.

This was all spurred by 2014's deluxe reissues. Somehow I got it in my head that I wanted to write all my thoughts about every last Led Zeppelin song: every recording detail I could hear, my theories on the lyrics—basically album review–length pieces on every song.

Now, I mentioned "every last Led Zeppelin song" there, didn't I? I must explain that the analyses that follow represent an expanded edition of the original *Led Zeppelin: All the Albums, All the Songs*—the volume you hold in your hands hauls into the discussion an additional sixteen tracks not included

Chateau Marmont,
West Hollywood,
May 1969.

on the nine official Led Zeppelin studio LPs. (There's a further gray area here, for we could talk about *The Song Remains the Same* as official, albeit live, and *Coda* as official, but a posthumous compilation.)

The idea of adding these sixteen closely curated tracks was to nail a revised definition of "all the albums, all the songs." Because, folks, there really is no such thing as "all" with Led Zeppelin. Where do you stop? Do you include pieces of studio jams later given names by fans? Every live cover? Every *snippet* of a live cover? Every officially released live song, even if a version was on one of the first nine records? Every alternate mix or demo version given a name by Jimmy and stuck on one of the reissues? It gets a little silly.

We could debate all this 'til the cows come home, but after deep consideration, here's what we've gone with: *Led Zeppelin: All the Albums, All the Songs* now includes every song, instrumental or not, given a name by Jimmy and included on the individual reissues that is *not* a close variant of an eventual LP track. We have also included every non-LP track officially released on *The BBC Sessions*, *The Complete BBC Sessions*, the (badly named or unnamed) two-part box sets, and *DVD* (this last would be "C'mon Everybody"—I know it's a video package, but it's official and the audio is of standalone audio quality).

Also included is every selection from the individual expanded reissues that is not an alternate version of another song. Arguably, "Jennings Farm Blues" breaks this rule, but it is substantially different enough from its sister track to stand on its own. So this book now covers, with those caveats, every song across all official studio albums, live albums, and compilations, save "LA Drone" on *How the West Was Won*, which, to be sure, is Jimmy naming something, but I think we can sensibly disqualify it for what it is: fourteen seconds of impromptu, live monotone guitar as introduction to "Immigrant Song" (there, I reviewed it!).

Additionally, beyond these qualifications, I couldn't resist one stunning live cover in "As Long as I Have You" and one unreleased studio track in "Swan Song." The former qualifies, as it was a regular in the set, and although it's a medley track it sits at the front of said medley structure and is returned to at the end. In other words, this isn't some old, rote blues embedded and briefly sampled all over the place. Besides, most of the old, rote blues Zeppelin played live are indeed addressed on the following pages as an official studio LP song, as a BBC session song, or as some sort of drift in and out with the band's fringe acoustic rarities. "Swan Song" gets in on the technicality that it was a named and defined piece of music in Jimmy's mind.

Now, for those who don't know, this sort of project isn't out of character or out of my comfort zone. Apparently (and pathetically), by any tallies that I've seen, I've written more record reviews than anybody ever throughout all space and time—currently about 7,900. (I'm sure someone will have more one day, but for now, my to-do list includes trying to get an official Guinness record for that.)

Anyway, that's one reason that I suppose I was half-qualified to do this. Another reason is that one of my jobs, besides writing books, has been to comb album credits and listen very carefully to their corresponding recorded tracks for their instrumentation and other performances—backing vocals, handclaps, tambourine, you name it—on certain albums to help a nonprofit group in Canada mete out certain accruing performance royalties. It's a long story, but that training, along with trying to figure out where the damned differences were on these tracks that Jimmy was sticking on the deluxe editions' companion discs . . . well, that got me set down this path even before this project was proposed to me.

And once the idea was proposed, I still wasn't completely onboard, knowing that the songs had already been written about, in fact twice song-by-song (see page 6) and then, of course, elliptically across all the other books about Led Zeppelin. A good deal of information was already out there, much of it gleaned from the same few interviews the band ever gave where they actually talked about the songs (I've never seen more column inches spent on playing live—*zzz*). But as I started thinking about it, I thought, hey, it was time for another look, a new book, given new information that has arisen, given the unearthed music included on new deluxe releases, given any extra trivia I could pick up and disseminate from my own listening, and given the fact that, as an opinionated reviewer, I hell an' gone just wanted to say my piece.

Additionally, I knew I could provide a drummer's perspective, which with many bands wouldn't matter much. But given the importance of Bonham to Zeppelin, well, I hope that in this book I help a bunch of non-drummers appreciate Bonzo more than they might have by pointing out his many genius bits across the catalog. I also heeded the wise words of a few of my guitar and bass buddies about a few things to ensure we were adding something to the body of knowledge already out there.

And there was one other subtle reason for taking on this project. I got to framing this book as essentially a listener's guide to Led Zeppelin. I've lately quite fancied the whole concept of a listener's guide. In this day and age when so much music is coming out all the time, and with hundreds of thousands of albums completely accessible to us through streaming services, I increasingly value an educated opinion as to what to listen to (and for) and the various reasons why listening will be an enriching experience.

If you think about it, take some twenty-year-old kid and throw on a Led Zeppelin record, and there's a pretty good chance he or she is going to think it sounds like crap. And bloody ancient. Underwritten or barely written. Heck, these debates were going on even in the '70s. I certainly never wanted to hear another blues song as long as I lived, or as long as Tank and Raven and Witchfinder General were lurking around the corner.

On sound alone (let's forget how many guitar players think Page is sloppy), yeah, by some measures, most Led Zeppelin albums sound, variously, distorted, lacking in low end, midrange-y, flat. This is a long discussion that will be touched upon throughout the following pages. I really don't want to go there right now, but I've spent my whole life wrestling with the idea of Led Zeppelin as overrated in so many ways—but how can you *not* be overrated when you are "rated" the way Led Zeppelin are rated, as gods who walk the earth? Who can live up to that?

On the pages that follow, I propose to you a few hundred very specific reasons why Zeppelin should be greatly admired and lauded as artists and craftsmen and poets, even. In that respect, I do what every DJ loves to do: try to turn you one to something you might not know well, or if you do know it, point out myriad subtleties deep inside, many of which will have you digging out those headphones you have stashed away somewhere and listening intently for squeaky bass drum pedals and ringing telephones.

Enough said. Thanks again to all who have written about Zeppelin, in book form and in all corners of the internet. And thanks to those experts who shared their opinions (and sometimes best guesses) with me. I've certainly regurgitated many of the factoids others have unearthed, which is not normal for me and a bit uncomfortable. But with a band this mysterious, especially when it comes to their recordings, I'd venture a guess that every Led Zeppelin scholar is guilty. And so, without further ado, let's dive down the rabbit hole of an action-packed nine-record catalog that's long been baffling to some, thrilling to millions more, and sometimes a little of both.

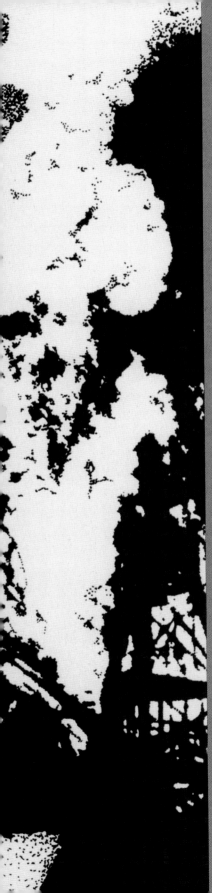

SIDE

# 1

**Good Times Bad Times**

**Babe I'm Gonna Leave You**

**You Shook Me**

**Dazed and Confused**

SIDE

# 2

**Your Time Is Gonna Come**

**Black Mountain Side**

**Communication Breakdown**

**I Can't Quit You Baby**

**How Many More Times**

Recorded
September–October 1968
Olympic Studios, London

Release Dates
January 12, 1969 (US, Atlantic SD 8216)
March 28, 1969 (UK, Atlantic 588171)

Produced by Jimmy Page
Director of Engineering: Glyn Johns

RIAA Certification: 8x Platinum
Top Billboard Position: No. 10

1969

LED ZEPPELIN

# LED ZEPPELIN

**ROBERT PLANT**
lead vocals,
harmonica

**JIMMY PAGE**
electric guitar,
acoustic guitar,
pedal steel guitar,
backing vocals

**JOHN PAUL JONES**
bass, organ,
backing vocals

**JOHN BONHAM**
drums, timpani,
backing vocals

**VIRAM JASANI**
tabla drums on
"Black Mountain
Side"

The story of *Led Zeppelin* begins with the rapid-fire dismantling of the Yardbirds in August 1968, with their leader Jimmy Page forming the New Yardbirds to fulfill Scandinavian touring obligations (as well as the guitar legend's vaulted ambitions to take over the world).

One can divine a more detailed history of the band from countless other sources, but since our focus here is the songs, suffice to say that our history of the band per se begins and ends with the lineup of the New Yardbirds, soon to be renamed Led Zeppelin: Jimmy Page, the last standing Yardbird; session bassist John Paul Jones; and two mates from Birmingham in different bands, both essentially unknowns—Robert Plant, the hippie, and John Bonham, the loudest drummer in town.

It must also be said that the story of *Led Zeppelin*, and notably its rapid conception and capable assembly, is necessarily linked to the myriad blues and folk influences woven through Jimmy's career in the '60s, as well as bits and pieces of writing he had done with the Yardbirds.

The nine songs on *Led Zeppelin* were recorded essentially live (engineer Glyn Johns, a pal of Jimmy's from teenage years, presiding), a procedure not particularly uncommon for the time. Jimmy was inclined to keep overdubs to a minimum so that the band could reproduce the material faithfully on stage afterward. Against the norm of the day, the album was recorded in stereo only, not stereo and mono versions.

Setting the situation up for success was the fact that Led Zeppelin, just two and a half weeks old, recorded immediately following fifteen hours of rehearsal and that fourteen-date Scandinavian tour. The band hadn't even been signed to Atlantic yet, with Jimmy and manager Peter Grant financing the record. Zeppelin worked at Olympic Studios in West London in October 1968, completing the sessions in thirty to thirty-six hours over the course of about nine days, with Jimmy chuckling that he remembers the number of hours because he paid the bill, reported to be 1,782 pounds.

The record deal would come quickly and pretty much effortlessly when Jerry Wexler and Ahmet Ertegun at Atlantic won a bidding war, paying an advance of two hundred thousand dollars (the same amount that they had recently paid for the Bee Gees).

As for the album's iconic cover art, it portrays Luftschiff Zeppelin 129 *Hindenburg* moments after exploding into flames in New Jersey on May 6, 1937.

The final George Hardie design replaced his original line art concept, which can be seen in miniature on the album's back cover, which is dominated by a gauzy photograph taken by ex-Yardbird Chris Dreja, soon to become a lifelong professional photographer.

With respect to the band's name, various stories exist, but it's most likely a variation of the old show biz expression "went over like a lead balloon." The most popular account has it that "Led Zeppelin" was cooked up by the Who's John Entwistle, possibly as a band name he might use when he finally had enough and left the Who. Entwistle surmised that the idea might have gotten over to Page through road manager Richard Cole, who worked for the Who before Zeppelin—Entwistle even laid claim to the idea for the album cover.

Zep at Chateau Marmont, West Hollywood, May 1969.

# GOOD TIMES
## BAD TIMES

**PAGE/JONES/BONHAM/2:46**

There is no better action-packed sequence of sounds in the Led Zeppelin canon with which to open the band's historic debut record than the prevocal pound of "Good Times Bad Times." "Communication Breakdown" might be the more explosive song, but the slamming stacked chords that introduce "Good Times Bad Times" included a canny statement of intent that this was going to be a dramatic, world-beating band worth watching.

What's more, with the combination of E major barre chords and licks marbled betwixt, Jimmy builds an early, proto-metal version of a note-dense riff. And before we even hear the singer, we know that his Black Country mate, John Bonham, is every bit worthy to stand shoulder to shoulder with the band's session-bred guitarist of note.

Quickly we are introduced to Plant, and not one line is out of his mouth before we realize that the veteran bassist is the equal of both Page and Bonham. For Robert's part, he doesn't join the ranks as equal until he peels off some of his patented high screams late in what is a very short song—so short that it doesn't even seem quite complete.

In fact, most of Robert's singing on "Good Times Bad Times" supports his claim that at twenty-one years old and up against two seasoned big-city studio session veterans (although neither is much his senior), he was unsure of himself, singing tentatively, not taking as many chances as he might have later, with his confidence emboldened.

Fact is, all around the horn, "Good Times Bad Times" is a hard rock tour de force for late 1968, with tasty appointments such as Bonham's quick grace note–style triplets on a single bass drum. All manner of drummers would later try to decipher how he did it, and whether in fact it can be done on anything fewer than two bass drums, as he had. Bonham apparently picked up the trick from Vanilla Fudge's Carmine Appice, who also inspired his use of very large Ludwigs, most notably a twenty-six-inch bass drum.

In any event, Bonzo waits until the second line to lay it on us, then waits until the more casual second verse and last verse—oddly, after both the break and the guitar solo passage—to bring it back, and for double the duration to

OPPOSITE: Jones, Plant, Bonham, and Page, 1968.

boot. None other than Jimi Hendrix was impressed by Bonzo's quick right foot, likening the effect to castanets.

Then there's Jimmy's guitar solo, which finds his custom-painted Fender 1959 Telecaster (dubbed Dragon, a gift from Jeff Beck) driven through a Leslie speaker, a piece of equipment whose dizzying effect created by its rotating speaker was usually reserved for Hammond organs. Jimmy very carefully tried mics around the room, not only in front of the amps but as far as twenty feet away, to achieve an ambient live feel and reveling in the bleed between instruments (although remaining somewhat less enamored with the resulting vocal bleed).

"Good Time Bad Times" features artful fingerpicked flights of fancy from Jones during the chorus, the break, the guitar solo, and even the verse lick, where he mirrors Jimmy's notable guitar hero sequence. Jonesy, who could generally stake a writing claim to Zeppelin songs with lots of notes in them, was in his milieu here. He later cited this track as an example and one of the hardest for him to play. Indeed, Page gives Jones the verse and takes the chorus himself, also using Bonham's bass drum part for inspiration.

Lyrically, "Good Times Bad Times" is classic ambiguous handwringing of the blues variety (also signature is the call and response between vocal and lead guitar). Robert asserts his experience despite having little, reminisces about the days of his youth, and seems about to tell us how to deal with women. But he's quickly self-deprecating, relating bad times along with the good, getting into "the same old jam," getting dumped, and losing "another friend," who smartly could be interpreted as a guy friend betrayed or as a conquest who, now seduced, is something other than a friend. By the last verse, less formal than the first to the point of sounding nearly improvised, the sense of defeat is conveyed in an admission of loneliness and a longing for home—although there's also the inference that the speaker's lovemaking sessions with his latest lover are enough to drive the neighbors crazy.

"Good Times Bad Times" was issued as Zeppelin's first single (Atlantic 45-2613 in the US; not issued in the UK), backed with "Communication Breakdown," the two tidy tracks on this album touted most vehemently by those who argue that Led Zeppelin invented heavy metal.

OPPOSITE: Zeppelin visit the studio of San Francisco photographer Herb Greene in January 1969 on the band's first trip to the States. "Good Times Bad Times" gave notice that this was going to be a world-beating band.

# BABE I'M GONNA LEAVE YOU

**TRAD. ARR. PAGE/6:40**

With "Babe I'm Gonna Leave You," Jimmy Page serves notice that Led Zeppelin won't stand for being tagged yet another British blues-boom band. In polar contrast to the record's hard rock opener, this torrid folk classic is the first in an acoustic canon from Page that largely is over and done four albums later.

Since 1990, the writing credit on this track has read "Anne Bredon/Page/Plant." American folkie Bredon wrote the original in the late '50s. Joan Baez had picked it up from one Janet Smith, who had heard Bredon, thirty years old at this point, perform the track on Berkeley, California, radio station KFPA in 1960. By the time folk boom prodigy Baez had gotten around to her ethereal version, she was erroneously crediting it as traditional and included it on her *In Concert Part 1* album in 1962 (the tablature version in *The Joan Baez Songbook* from 1964 credits correctly). This is the version Jimmy Page had heard and liked, toying with it on six-string while playing with Marianne Faithfull. Both Page and Plant greatly admired Baez for her near magical grasp of folk's

Paris, October 1969. The transformative vocal melodies on "Babe I'm Gonna Leave You" could have come only from Plant.

charms, especially compared to the academic vibe then
coming from men operating within the idiom.

Of note, in 1968 Quicksilver Messenger Service
covered the song (credited to Bredon and two others)
in a manner closer to the Plebs' jaunty rock 'n' roll
version from 1964 (credited "Trad. arr. Dennis"). In
between is the nearly proto–power ballad version by
the Association (1965), credited to Anne H. Bredon,
arranged by Terry Kirkman and Bob Page(!).

Hence the credit on *Led Zeppelin* was later
amended to include Bredon as well as Robert,
with Bredon receiving substantial royalties. Now
disputed is how much Robert had to do with the
song and, indeed, the originals on the first album, having
been left off the credits wholesale. It has been theorized this was due to Robert's
contractual ties to CBS or because Jimmy still had him on "probation," unlike
Jones and Bonham, in whom he was confident.

What one *can* surmise, given how vastly altered the song is from both the
Bredon and Baez versions, is that the guitar changes are Page's and the very
transformative vocal melodies could only have come from Plant. Page, for his
part, has said he came up with the arrangement years earlier and played it for
Robert the first time the two met, in July of 1968 at Jimmy's Pangbourne home.
Plant, meanwhile, has expressed fond memories of "rearranging" the song in the
studio with Page and marveling at their efficient creative connection.

In any event, in the hands of Led Zeppelin, the A minor–based song was much
more structured, enforced by repetition and dramatic Spanish-style flourishes
from Page, rarely to be revisited. The guitar Jimmy played here was a Gibson
J-200 with heavy-gauge strings and owned by Big Jim Sullivan, perhaps the only
1960s English session guitarist more famed than Jimmy.

For that warm tone, Jimmy used plate reverb and his dual mic technique. There
are also more recurring overdubs than most elsewhere on the album (including
acoustic on acoustic and an eerie electric slide), and a bashing heavy section utilizing
a descending bass line, constant crash cymbals, and electric guitar massaged with the
ever-present acoustics. At 1:41 the famed "ghost" vocal from Robert ("I can hear it
calling me") is the result of vocals bleeding into nonvocal mics.

A gorgeous track that foreshadows the light-and-shade structure of "Over the
Hills and Far Away" and "Stairway to Heaven," "Babe I'm Gonna Leave You"
ends with a poignant descending finale made all the more special in its formality
by the fact Led Zeppelin never again played the song live after the 1969 tour.

Page first heard "Babe
I'm Gonna Leave You"
on Joan Baez's 1962
LP, *In Concert,* where
it was initially and
erroneously credited
as "Traditional."

# YOU SHOOK ME

**DIXON/6:30**

Alas, how extra-spicy *Led Zeppelin* would have been had the band included sparkplug "Sugar Mama" from these sessions rather than tired ol' twelve-bar blues "You Shook Me," first recorded by Muddy Waters and credited to his bassist Willie Dixon and later also J. B. Lenoir. It is said that Earl Hooker should be credited as well, given the song was based on his instrumental, "Blue Guitar."

In May of 1968, the Jeff Beck Group recorded a version of the song that would show up on the *Truth* album, issued in August 1968, two months before the *Led Zeppelin* sessions. Although Jimmy claims to have been unaware of the recording, his own bassist, John Paul Jones, had played keyboards on the session, a role he would repeat on the Led Zeppelin version. The Jeff Beck version includes piano by Nicky Hopkins and is much shorter although, in the end, just as dull. Beck was crestfallen that the song showed up on *Led Zeppelin*, but there's been some degree of consolation in that many critics have posited that *Truth*, crudely stated, is the fist Led Zeppelin album.

In any event, "You Shook Me"—or at minimum, the act of including it on an album at the time—illustrates all that was claustrophobic and restrictive about the British blues boom. In the pudding, especially with so much other derivative material on the record, Led Zeppelin come off as mere mortals not particularly removed from the imagination-lacking pack, in stark contrast to the excitement they would inject just a few tracks later with "Dazed and Confused" and even on a second Willie Dixon track, "I Can't Quit You Baby," which at least features Bonham modestly unchained. Chucking in a nod to Robert Johnson's "Stones in My Passway" only goes to show how so much of this music was interchangeable and thus in need of the type of makeover Zeppelin would execute in fine fashion over the course of nine albums, though not on this track.

Bonham decides to play it sparse here, straight and uncharacteristically clunky, the band choosing a crushingly slow tempo spread over six and a half minutes. Page, Plant, and Jones make the best of a bad situation with some interesting yet small individual victories.

At Plant's end, there's torrid singing for miles, some rote call and response, and nice blends with Page's "singing" Earl Hooker–styled guitar work throughout, as well as lots of harmonica, neither exemplary nor clumsy.

Jones pulls double duty, playing bass and, in a rare move, a Hammond M-100 without a Leslie speaker, utilizing instead the instrument's built-in vibrato. As for Page, "You Shook Me" is the album's only track on which his electric is not his Telecaster—here he's using a Gibson Flying V, borrowed from someone who was trying to sell it to him. The guitar's big humbuckers caused his amp to break up a bit in the middle of the track, but Jimmy liked to hear an amp having a hard time of it.

Elsewhere, Jimmy employs a backward echo technique, first unveiled all over the Yardbirds' single-only cover of Harry Nilsson's "Ten Little Indians." Here he applies this technique at the end, mostly to Robert's vocal and a bit to his guitar. The effect is a somewhat ghostlier version of feedback mixed with bleed and not loud in the mix—it's overpowered by the call and response, an idea later made more famous by Ian Gillan and Ritchie Blackmore in Deep Purple. Jimmy had argued with engineer Glyn Johns over being able to make the effect work, winning in the end, as Johns meekly turned up the faders and accepted the sonic evidence.

All told, "You Shook Me" betrays Zeppelin as rushed (a typical occurrence at the time), unwilling, or too pressed to respect their own creative instincts and wait for more of the superlative writing that was waiting inside this band like a caged dragon.

OPPOSITE: The inclusion of the derivative "You Shook Me" on Zep's debut album illustrates all that was claustrophobic and restrictive and about the British blues boom. John Paul and Bonzo lock in at the Teen Club, Gladsaxe, Denmark, March 15, 1969.

# DAZED AND CONFUSED

**PAGE/6:27**

"Dazed and Confused" originated as a song written by Jake Holmes that showed up on his debut album, 1967's *"The Above Ground Sound" of Jake Holmes*. Jake had opened for the Yardbirds at the Village Theatre in New York, and Yardbirds drummer Jim McCarty was struck by the harrowing song, causing him to buy the otherwise fairly upbeat album the next day. Yardbirds vocalist Keith Relf adjusted the lyrics and the lads worked up a new arrangement for full band (Jake's was sans drums), Jimmy driving a guitar stake through it, and entered the song into their set list.

The song was never recorded by the Yardbirds, but did show up on an exploitative posthumous release called *Live Yardbirds Featuring Jimmy Page*, notably as "I'm Confused" and without writing credit.

Holmes eventually attempted to contact the Zeppelin camp in the early 1980s. Initially he got no reply but settled out of court in 2012 after bringing suit in 2010. Recent releases of the song credit it as written by Jimmy Page and "inspired by" Jake Holmes.

Jimmy bows the whiteguard 1959 Tele gifted to him by Jeff Beck. Copenhagen, March 1969.

By the time of the Yardbirds' nexus, the song was essentially the same song Zeppelin would record, right down to the rhythmic call-and-response section (which had occurred in the Jake Holmes version, albeit in an quieter form). Also featured on the Yardbirds version was Jimmy's famed work with a violin bow (regular bow, more tension and more rosin) and frankly each and every hammer-and-tongs section that would appear on *Led Zeppelin*. And at 6:47, the album version would certainly prove to be the most succinct take the band would perform.

It's difficult to defend the original "Page" credit to this song, and difficult to fathom that Jimmy had no clue as to the song's origin.

Beyond that, it really does seem that Jimmy is the engine rewriting this song beyond its original framework, Relf lyrics notwithstanding. The song is transformed from what can be described as proto-wyrd folk, injected first with the power of the blues boom and then with something new: this idea of proto-metal. Many have called the result the first doom metal song, the litmus test being that "Dazed and Confused" wouldn't seem out of place on Black Sabbath's first album. Add to that the auras of raga, drone, and Eastern mysticism, and you have the first classic in a Zeppelin subplot that cuts through "Friends," "No Quarter," and "Kashmir" en route to "Achilles Last Stand."

"Dazed and Confused" was the second song the band recorded at Olympic, Jimmy using his '59 Telecaster plus, for the psychedelic jam, the aforementioned bow, thus reviving a technique pioneered by guitarist Eddie Phillips in his band Mark Four and on his two 1966 hit singles with the Creation, "Making Time" and "Painter Man." Of note, Pink Floyd frontman Syd Barrett had also used a bow, and in 1990, Jimmy said session violinist David McCallum Sr. first suggested the idea.

The bow would return on this record for "How Many More Times" and then for "In the Light" on 1975's *Physical Graffiti*. Jimmy was very serious about the technique and quick to defend against accusations of gimmickry. For the "Dazed and Confused" solo, Jimmy revisited and then plundered his solo from the Yardbirds' proto-metal classic, "Think About It," later covered by Aerosmith.

Over time, "Dazed and Confused"—played live nearly 440 times, over 100 more than the band's second-most traveled live song, "Whole Lotta Love"—sometimes grew into a monster forty-five minutes in length and was immortalized a second time as a twenty-seven-minute entire side on *The Song Remains the Same*, the band's 1977 live album. But the grinding memory of the song as an egregiously gratuitous jam shouldn't sully the tight and eventful original, which crawls into existence before being fired up by numerous rhythmic exercises, including a frenzied proto-thrash. As the song returns to its eerie murk, we are reminded of Led Zeppelin's pedigreed blues roots but also the creative acumen with which they gainfully moved beyond. We are also reminded how blues, hard rock, and the seemingly incongruous folk all spring from the same primordial well—and in the right hands can be forced to coexist.

TOP: Page adapted "Dazed and Confused" from Jake Holmes, who had opened for the Yardbirds. The song appeared on Holmes's 1967 LP, *"The Above Ground Sound" of Jake Holmes*.

ABOVE: Page plundered the "Dazed and Confused" solo from his own work on the Yardbirds' "Think About It," released as the B-side of "Goodnight Sweet Josephine."

# KICKING OFF THE '70s
# WITH ZEPPELIN

It's no great revelation that Led Zeppelin's first record resulted in a firestorm of interest and changed the way fans and musicians alike thought about rock 'n' roll's prospects for the 1970s.

"*Led Zeppelin* did influence me a lot," muses Deep Purple bassist Roger Glover, "because I was in a pop group called Episode Six and we were trying to get heavier and weren't making it because we were just playing the same music but louder. When the album first came out, you could tell it wasn't the loudness so much as a feeling, what you felt about the music rather than how they played it. Episode Six, as we were, weren't the right combination of people to be heavy, and I gradually gained the impression that heavy music wasn't for me because I didn't like what we were playing: loud pop music. And I decided for a time to go into folk music.

"I've never been so struck by an album as I was by *Led Zeppelin*. It really left me open-mouthed. What they were playing was very simple stuff, loud and exciting, and it moved me. I suddenly wanted to be in a club playing that music—loud, straightforward, with simple guts. And by pure coincidence, just about that time I was offered a job with Deep Purple! But for Zeppelin, I might never have been in Deep Purple."

"I remember Jimmy playing me the first Led Zeppelin album," says Yardbirds drummer Jim McCarty. "There was 'Dazed and Confused' and there was a Howlin' Wolf–type thing, 'How Many More Times,' which is very similar to the stuff we'd been playing—it was similar to 'Smokestack Lightning,' I thought. . . . It was

Jimmy as a young session musician, circa 1966. Even before Zep, Page and Jones made an impression on their peers with their studio work.

very well done, the first Zeppelin album; I thought it was very good. You can see the links, how easy it was to go from us to them."

Years later, multiplatinum titans Foreigner would utilize a few Led Zeppelin lessons, perhaps via Bad Company, to great success. But as a nascent rocker trying to make it in the business, Foreigner founder Mick Jones could see the value in Jimmy and his "project" straightaway.

"At the time, I was cutting my teeth in France. Don't ask me how, but I'd become sort of the musical director and producer of Johnny Hallyday, who's sort of the French Elvis, as it were," Jones begins. "We would go over to England to record, and we ended up with an engineer named Glyn Johns, who at that time had worked with Steve Miller and later the Eagles. I think he had been working with the Eagles even before their record came out. But he had worked a lot with John Paul and Jimmy when they were session musicians. And they happened to be session musicians on the stuff that I was doing for Johnny Hallyday. And so I was fully aware of who they were.

**Jones as a session player fiddles with a Fender Bass VI in 1966. Jones says he was responsible for the riffs with "lots of notes." The lurchy and chordy stuff was all Page.**

"And Jimmy Page, he blew me away every time we went into the studio. I had so much respect for him as a guitar player, and a friendship developed. He would even come over to Paris with Glyn Johns and cut tracks over there. In fact, some of the music that we were doing with Johnny Hallyday provided the opportunity for Jimmy to work closely with Glyn Johns in preparing the first Zeppelin album. And I remember the day that Glyn took me into the studio, the back of Olympic Studios in London, and he said, 'I'm going to play you a couple things on Jimmy's project.' And he sat down and played me 'Communication Breakdown' and it just blew me away. Just blew my mind. I couldn't believe it. I had never heard anything as mean and powerful in my life. It just left me staggered."

But Led Zeppelin wasn't entirely "of the future," per se. On this first record, John Paul Jones could see ties to the past, in particular, the Yardbirds and Jeff Beck's *Truth*, on which both he and Jimmy played.

"But it soon took off from there," Jones adds. "Most of the songs we had done on the first album had been done by Jimmy and the Yardbirds as well. It was only things like 'Good Times Bad Times,' which was a riff I brought in, that I wrote in the studio. That's got John's famous drum part, of course. John never used double bass. He did in fact bring in a double bass drum for rehearsal, and we played a couple of songs with it, but then we hid it when he went for lunch. When he came back, it was gone.

"We didn't move into a style; I think we kind of created it," concludes Jones. "And if you would have asked me in 1969, as people did, what sort of band I was in, I would have said a progressive rock band. But then that came to mean something else. There you go banging up against categories again. And then it was just sort of like blues rock, because the band was quite blues-oriented. And it was just the style, the way the members of the band played together. But in terms of actual riffs, well, anything with notes [*laughs*], lots of notes, like 'Black Dog,' 'Good Times Bad Times' . . . those were my riffs. And anything that was kind of lurchy and chordy were Page's riffs. That's how you tell them apart."

TOP: In Led Zeppelin, Jones saw ties to Jeff Beck's *Truth* LP, on which both he and Page had appeared as session musicians.

ABOVE: The back cover of *Led Zeppelin* featured a gauzy Chris Dreja photo of the lads and, in a miniature inset, the line art originally intended for the front sleeve.

# YOUR TIME IS GONNA COME

**PAGE/JONES/4:41**

Counted among the less derivative songs on the album, "Your Time Is Gonna Come" is a pop song evocative of easy-drinking San Francisco psych, distinguished by the fact that Jimmy plays laid-back acoustic lines on a Fender ten-string steel guitar that he has since stated he fears was slightly out of tune. The sessions for the album marked the first time Page had played the instrument. Marbled into the track presaging southern rock are sinewy slide guitar notes and Jones's bluesy, pervasive organ parts, which in fact open the song in an elegiac minute-long church organ solo—which Bonzo commences to crash in on with a heavy but behaved midtempo beat, an odd fit to such slight music.

Jones layers two Hammond M-100 tracks, first clean and then turning on the vibrato for the chorus. With such a strait-laced display of classical organ music, Zeppelin created a moment of post-psych/proto-prog, aligning themselves with Procol Harum, Yes, Genesis, and the Moody Blues, the latter of whom came from Plant's and Bonham's northern industrial home turf.

The song's chorus features the rest of the band on backing vocals behind Robert, and its simplicity—the title over and over—reinforces the naïve pop of the thing, even if Bonzo tries to spice it up with convoluted bass drum work. The lyrics find the song's protagonist defiantly washing his hands of his cheating woman; the refrain would be menacing if not for the sheer hook-laden idyll of its musicality. Perhaps the message is that revenge is no longer a consuming desire, and that nothing more than a life lesson, an illumination, is wished upon the female philanderer.

The band never played the song live, offering only a brief section during one show in Tokyo in 1971 amid the band's "Whole Lotta Love"–anchored medley. One final side note: Sandie Shaw became the first artist to cover Led Zeppelin on record when "the barefoot pop princess of the 1960s" worked up a faithful version of "Your Time Is Gonna Come" for her fifth album, *Reviewing the Situation*, issued by Pye Records in late 1969. Side side note: Drumming on the track was the very capable Ian Wallace, later of King Crimson.

# BLACK MOUNTAIN SIDE

**PAGE/2:06**

Page relied on his 1961 Danelectro 3021 for the solo on "Black Mountain Side." Bath Festival of Blues, Somerset, England, June 28, 1969.

"Black Mountain Side" began life as a traditional Irish folk tune called, with variations, "Down by Blackwaterside." It received a major facelift when Bert Jansch, who learned the song from collaborator Anne Briggs and covered it as "Blackwaterside" on his 1966 album, *Jack Orion*. Briggs marveled at Jansch's "freedom from chords," and his transformation of the song from sleepy to complex and Middle Eastern–flavored was a perfect example of Jansch's development. Scottish folkie Al Stewart, who had hired Page for his debut album session, claims to have taught Page Jansch's version, though his guitar was mistakenly tuned to the modal D-A-D-G-A-D instead of the drop-D tuning Jansch had used, hence a further evolution. Jimmy nicknamed this "CIA" tuning (for Celtic, Indian, and Arabic).

Most of the notable licks in Page's instrumental version can be found in the earlier Jansch version, with Page additionally mimicking Jansch's vocal melodies on guitar. Lo and behold, we're ripe for another debate over credit appropriation. Although nuanced.

Today, after decades of debate over such matters, there's a clearer understanding through hundreds of precedents on the very specific issue of songs and their evolution from traditional to modern versions (usually involving the blues). But in 1969, with Jansch crediting the song as traditional, it would have seemed sensible that Page could perform it and not assign credit, particularly to Jansch. Although crediting it to himself is another matter, not to mention the material change to the title.

But, again, these things were murkier and less defined back in 1969. To be sure, in today's world, with the level of research available at our fingertips, one could more easily see how much Jansch transformed earlier versions, to the point where an appropriate and morally cogent credit on *Jack Orion* might have read: "Trad., arr. by Jansch," and on the Zeppelin album "Trad./Jansch, arr. by Page." Jansch's legal action sputtered—clearly, the song was in the public domain, most notably its melody.

That issue dispelled, "Black Mountain Side" joins "Babe I'm Gonna Leave You" on *Led Zeppelin* in terms of supporting the argument for the band as striving, exploring folkies, not dispensed with the finer academics of the now-waning folk boom, just as they hadn't entirely given up on the similarly past-expiry blues boom, even if Jimmy liked to call what they were doing at the time "contemporary blues."

Connecting to "Dazed and Confused" is the Eastern or Arabic subplot, reinforced here through a guest performance on tabla by Viram Jasani, as well as Page's own simulation of sitar on the same Gibson J-200 borrowed from Big Jim Sullivan heard on "Babe I'm Gonna Leave You." Jimmy didn't know Jasani and the session was rushed, but he later surmised that Jasani figured out what to do quickly because he was a sitar player as well. Even this short acoustic instrumental includes a furious though brief "Dazed"-like storm of noise, here the effect evoking images of Whirling Dervishes. Live, the song was often paired with Page's more raga-like "White Summer" instrumental from his Yardbirds days. Jimmy had gone to India with the Yardbirds and instantly became enamored with the country's music. For this intimate sit-down moment in the band's set, Page created a solo guitar tour de force on a 1961 Danelectro 3021, the band's light- versus-shade credo represented by the two song titles paired in natural opposition. Both songs are played in D-A-D-G-A-D tuning, as is "Kashmir."

An additional touch is how on the record the song's beginning cross-fades with the outro to "Your Time Is Gonna Come." There's something of a message here, an attention to detail, a knowing wink between creator and listener that such bells and whistles are to be used soberly and sparingly.

TOP: "Black Mountain Side" began life as a traditional Irish folk tune called "Down by Blackwaterside," which Scottish folkie Bert Jansch adapted on his 1966 album, *Jack Orion*.

ABOVE: Another Irish folkie, Al Stewart, claims to have taught Page Jansch's version of "Blackwaterside" when the session guitarist played on Stewart's debut, *Bedsitter Images*.

# COMMUNICATION BREAKDOWN

**PAGE/JONES/BONHAM/2:26**

For a band that didn't mind taking credit, curiously no one in Zeppelin wanted dibs on inventing heavy metal. To be fair, neither did members of the Who, Deep Purple, or even Black Sabbath. But with this aggressive, almost punky rocker, along with another half-dozen songs throughout their first two albums, Led Zeppelin did their contributing (slight and still rooted in '60s idioms as it was). With *Led Zeppelin* and *II*, they were still forging their irons in 1968 and 1969, in advance of *Black Sabbath* and Deep Purple's monumental fourth album *In Rock*.

Ergo, "Communication Breakdown" matters, with its brisk, no-nonsense 4/4 beat, Plant's heavy metal howling, and most pertinently, the muted staccato chug of Page's downstroked D-A-D machine-gun riff. The song essentially is Zeppelin's "Paranoid," almost two years before that classic of up-tempo metal might, elevated bpm being the interesting distinction with the likes of "Dazed and Confused," "No Quarter," "Black Sabbath," and "Iron Man." Page has said the riff is hard to play due to the rapid downstrokes, so it makes sense that Andy Shernoff from the New York punk band Dictators says that his friend and the king of the punk rock downstroke, Johnny Ramone, used the song obsessively for practicing.

Adding to the urgency of the track is Page's trashy and immediate manner of achieving distortion: plugging his Telecaster into a Vox wah pedal and then into a tiny Supro amp. The result is a cruddy yet conspicuous riff that cuts through and sits absolutely dead center at the heart of the song, with everybody else involved crowding around it like a campfire: Jonesy has no choice but to follow Jimmy in unison (for the verse, but not the blues resolution chorus) and Bonham does nothing much more than goad the riff while Plant seems to have been sent to the roof to either mumble or yelp helplessly.

Heavy as it is, the song was decipherable enough, short enough, and thus "pop" enough for radio play. With the band rocking out, listeners didn't have to think about the lyrics, because they were barely there, Plant in a flash celebrating girlkind like a berserk teenager, while Page turns in a rare backing vocal, taunting his love-struck singer. Thanks to the song's charm, Zeppelin played it live often and enthusiastically, usually either opening shows with it or using it as an encore number.

OPPOSITE: Plant and Page offered heavy metal howling and a machine gun-riff, respectively, on "Communication Breakdown."

# I CAN'T QUIT YOU BABY

**DIXON/4:42**

The other straight blues on *Led Zeppelin*, "I Can't Quit You Baby" is a Willie Dixon composition written for Otis Rush in 1956. Better executed than their rendition of Dixon's "You Shook Me" on the album's previous side earlier (but half the song and performance of the band's own "Since I've Been Loving You" on *III*), "I Can't Quit You Baby" is a showcase first for Robert and second for Page, both exercising their acumen for light-and-shade dynamics, in this case more whisper to roar.

By the time Otis Rush had got to the 1966 Vanguard version of the song, he had added the two pairs of verse-ending doom chords, which of course, Led Zeppelin would have to stomp hard in their aggressive rock band rendition. Zeppelin's version is actually bluesier as well, dropping the pop lilt of the original and leaning deep into the groove.

Other than that, Zeppelin behave in reverence of their blues masters until Bonzo exercises his itchy bass drum foot. Jimmy plays some fluid runs and there's a pause in the guitar solo before yet more soloing (which is where Bonham gets busy), as we work our way toward a final verse sung laid-back by Robert interspersed with call-and-response with Page. For his part, Page decried the number of mistakes in the track. At the very end, Plant lets out some of his highest screams of the album, but he's so far back in the mix it's all for naught.

Irrespective of whether they were both written by Willie Dixon, including two quite similar rulebook slow blues on the record seems gratuitous. Again, one wonders why "Sugar Mama" or even the balladic "Baby Come Home" from the same sessions didn't make the cut instead.

**LED ZEPPELIN**

JIMMY PAGE

ROBERT PLANT

JOHN BONHAM

JOHN PAUL JONES

**SUNDAY, MAY 11, 1969**
**Aqua Theatre - Seattle**
7:30 P.M. · $4.50 advance $5.00 at door

OPPOSITE: Zep behaved in reverence of their blues masters on "I Can't Quit You Baby."

# HOW MANY
## MORE TIMES

**PAGE/JONES/BONHAM/8:28***

In the hands of the Allmans, "How Many More Times" and "Dazed and Confused"—and, for that matter, "Whipping Post"—represent distinct examples of the blues merging into hard rock and thus nascent heavy metal. Zeppelin did the same on this particular track, but also took the progression further. A funky yet flowing walking bass line is emboldened by authoritative swing drumming and a riff up top in unison, over which Plant drapes a straight blues melody.

After a pile of noise, the band crane up at the three-and-a-half-minute mark, giving a nod to "Beck's Bolero," on which both Jimmy and John Paul had guested. In fact, Jimmy is credited as the song's sole writer on every printing of the album *Truth* after the first issue. Jimmy indeed has said that much of "How Many More Times" was made up of leftover Yardbirds bits, but Plant also included elements from his days with Band of Joy. A murky psychedelic passage presages that of "Whole Lotta Love" with less studio trickery, though panned stereo is utilized along with Jimmy's violin bow.

As the track continues deconstructing, at the five-and-a-half-minute mark we're into a catchy Mardi Gras beat on Bonzo's Ludwig snare, at which time the band throws in a nod to "The Hunter," written by Booker T & the M.G.s and first recorded by Albert King in 1967. Significantly, "The Hunter" was covered by Free and Blue Cheer, both in 1968, the latter on their second album *Outsideinside* (another candidate for first heavy metal album, if one considers that band's predecessor, *Vincebus Eruptum,* too derivative).

Plant has admitted paying tribute to Howlin' Wolf's "How Many More Years" in the title and in some of his vocal choices, although the connection is flimsy at best—there's a closer match to Howlin' Wolf's "No Place to Go," with respect both to vocal line and a lyric placed over a less similar riff, but one that could be considered an associated inversion. Robert delivers an in-joke with the line, "I got another child on the way, that makes eleven," referring to the fact that he did have a child on the way (though not his eleventh).

Live, the band's further disassembly of an already freeform song allowed the band to chuck in bits of additional songs they admired, such as "Travelin' Little Mama," "Boogie Chillin'," "That's Alright Mama," and Neil Young's recent "On the Way Home."

*\*Note: Amusingly, "How Many More Times" is clocked at 3:30 on the back cover of the album, but is in fact 8:28 (the record centerpiece says 8:30). Jimmy did this to trick radio stations into playing a song that they otherwise wouldn't have accommodated.*

OPPOSITE: Plant draped a straight blues melody over a funky yet flowing walking bass line emboldened by authoritative swing drumming.

**II**

SIDE

# 1

**Whole Lotta Love**

**What Is and What Should Never Be**

**The Lemon Song**

**Thank You**

SIDE

# 2

**Heartbreaker**

**Living Loving Maid
(She's Just a Woman)**

**Ramble On**

**Moby Dick**

**Bring It on Home**

Recorded
April–August 1969
Morgan Studios, Mayfair Studios, and Olympic Studios, London
Mirror Studios, Mystic Studios, A&M Studios, Quantum Studios,
and Sunset Studios, Los Angeles
A&R Studios, Groove Sound, and Juggy Sound,
New York City
Ardent Studios, Memphis
R&D Studios, Vancouver

Release Dates
October 22, 1969 (US, Atlantic SD 8236)
October 31, 1969 (UK, Atlantic 588198)

Produced by Jimmy Page
Director of Engineering and Mixing: Eddie Kramer
Engineers: Eddie Kramer, George Chkiantz,
Andrew Johns, Chris Huston

RIAA Certification: 12x Platinum
Top Billboard Position: No. 1

**1969**

**LED ZEPPELIN II**

# LED ZEPPELIN II

**ROBERT PLANT**
lead vocals,
harmonica

**JIMMY PAGE**
electric and
acoustic guitars,
backing vocals,
theremin

**JOHN PAUL
JONES**
bass, organ

**JOHN BONHAM**
drums

Hard to believe the Frankenstein's monster that is Led Zeppelin's *II* came together let alone cohered as well as it did. Issued to effusive praise, it went on to sell three million copies in three months and eventually notch twelve-times platinum status in the United States. Now revered as one of the great albums of all time, all of it—all of it—is played regularly on classic rock radio.

Indeed, success flew at the band from all directions. *II* would unseat *Abbey Road* from the number-one slot on the charts, and during the album's whirlwind recording, venue capacities and the band's asking price rose exponentially. Amid recording in New York in July, the band found themselves taking a short break to receive gold records from Atlantic Records' Ahmet Ertegun for the first album. Then it was directly back into the studio for further work on the album.

Topographically, *II* is very much a fortified, focused update of the debut, matching up track for track through styles, save for one important advancement: no blues covers. Still not completely unchained from reworking old songs, Page nonetheless gets into much less trouble here, mostly just getting on with the business of writing with his suddenly successful mates: muscled-up blues/hard rock hybrids and equally road-hardened folk/rock hybrids.

It's easy to put too much emphasis on the record's bizarre recording schedule, the guys essentially making the album in bits and pieces on the road to and from wherever, striking while the iron was red-hot and cashing in on the Zeppelin mania sweeping America. Yet, the record doesn't sound loose-fitting or raw, particularly, especially when up against the album before it and fully three afterward. What it does sound is accomplished, confident, the work of busy achievers, a band being told at every turn that they must be doing something right. Jimmy, however, famously lost confidence in the record through its chaotic process and was apprehensive that *II* would not be received well.

Yet if there's one negative, one could argue that the band was still rooted in the past, still making the best Brit blues boom records imaginable, though many progressive, hard rock, and underground bands, certainly by 1970, had modernized.

Of course, this all reflected a choice on Zeppelin's part, not lack of talent: serving a deliberate reverence of roots music, an idea that didn't seem to be hurting the Stones none either. And so "Whole Lotta Love," "The Lemon Song," "Heartbreaker," and the trick start to "Bring It on Home" each pummel us with riff-bolstered blues, but blues all the same. Even the album's flash, modern

The band arrives in Honolulu, Hawaii, in May 1969 with the master tapes for *II* in hand.

proto-metaller "Living Loving Maid (She's Just a Woman)" can't completely shake time-worn chord progressions, which, frankly, represent rules—and wasn't Led Zeppelin made to break all the rules? Or maybe it was just attendance records and terms and conditions of contracts.

Nay, with Zep *II*, the beauty is in the folk and pop and light and shade in the songs that are unhurried and unclassifiable . . . in "What Is and What Should Never Be," with its light jazz verses against James Gang chords; in "Thank You," the band's first fully original ballad; in the wonderful "Ramble On," which sets idyllic faerie folk against explosive rhythm; and in the thorny funk metal of "Bring It on Home," which again sounds like Joe Walsh givin' 'er. Coincidentally, Jimmy had met Walsh at the Fillmore in April 1969 and bought his second Les Paul off him, a 1959 'Burst for $1,200, instantly falling in love with the guitar, which would come to be known as "Number One."

Little did the band know that electric expectations had now been set, and nothing less than more of them stacked power chords were going to keep the band's high-as-a-kite blue jean army from mass revolt.

# WHOLE LOTTA LOVE

**PAGE/BONHAM/PLANT/JONES/5:33**

"Whole Lotta Love" was one of the more considered and rehearsed songs in the harried process that would result in *II*, and to be sure, it was worthy of its pole position on the album thanks to its instantly modern heavy metal riff, Plant's torrid performance, a counter full of ear candy delights in the chewy center, and an easy-drinking, almost meditative repetition. Considering this orderliness, it's not surprising that the song was recorded at Olympic, although additional overdubs and engineer Eddie Kramer's mix were conducted over the course of two days in August at A&R in New York, on a twelve-channel Altec board (plus a 3M eight-track and Ampex 440 reel-to-reels), with Mystic Studios in Hollywood being used for overdubs as well.

Built on the chassis of an old blues tune, in this case Willie Dixon's "You Need Love" (recorded by Muddy Waters in 1962 and issued as a single the following year), the song is a proto-metal barnstormer. Dixon was credited on issues of the album after suit was brought in 1985. The similarity is most obvious on Robert's lyric, which picks up further direction from the Small Faces' "You Need Loving," which, incidentally, was credited to Ronnie Lane and Steve Marriott. Passed through this song, in effect, are lifts from Dixon's "Back Door Man" and "Shake for Me."

However, without Plant's lyric, phrasing, and vocal melody, the song is the frame of an early heavy metal song preceding and superseding the pioneering work in that area by Black Sabbath, Uriah Heep, and indeed Led Zeppelin themselves, or stateside, Mountain and Cactus. Page vehemently defended his riff (cooked up on his houseboat on the Thames), but ceded to the buffet of old blues phrasings coming out of Robert.

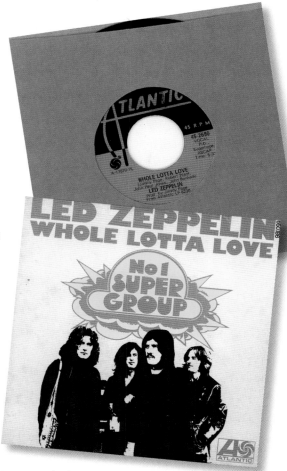

OPPOSITE: Zeppelin was essentially a guitar-centric band, with the all-hands-on-deck riff worship of "Whole Lotta Love" being prime evidence. K. B. Hallen, Copenhagen, February 28, 1970.

To get a little technical, the song's iconic riff makes aggressive use of an E chord, played on the seventh fret. The four notes that precede the E chord at the opening (right after the three count) are B, D, B, D, with the E chord landing on the one beat. The riff, played on Jimmy's trusty sunburst '59 Les Paul Standard, is spiced by John Bonham's choppy 4/4 beat until he drops out for a high hat and cymbal solo that quickly dissolves into chaos.

For the unexpected and quite nightmarish break section, Jimmy and engineer of Hendrix fame, Eddie Kramer, take over, knob-jobbing a firestorm of sounds, capturing Robert's sexual moans while John beats on congas. Jimmy directs the traffic on his rapidly panned hippie-fried theremin (detuned to create "evil" growls) and revives his backward echo technique from the first album, albeit a fair bit that was recorded was subsequently removed. Further touches include Page's recurring panned dive-bomb effect (accomplished with metal slide and more backward reverb) and his subtle use of wah-wah for his punctuated guitar solo. In the mix, Jimmy and Eddie utilized low-frequency oscillators on the tape machines to confound the recorded sounds further.

The song's internal aural sculpture diverts from the fact that the song is a one-trick pony all the way through, with Robert keeping up the ruse by remaining in the throes of his Golden God-ness once the band returns for another hurrah, after a stark, stopped section on which we get a ghost vocal even more pronounced than that on "Babe I'm Gonna Leave You." On what is essentially the song's reprise, Bonham's congas return for a second drum track, an idea later used by both Uriah Heep and Deep Purple.

But really, as Jimmy stresses, Zeppelin was a guitar-centric band, and when in heavy metal mode, that necessarily meant an all-hands-on-deck riff worship, "Whole Lotta Love" being a prime example. At the time, Jimmy mused that the song had a Rolling Stones feel but was just a "basic rock tune." To underscore the point, Jonesy and Robert virtually stay out of the way. Amusingly, Robert barely comes up with a lyric, almost conversationally paraphrasing earlier recorded versions in the spirit of a vocal placeholder as he waits for inspiration or crawls off to the corner to properly write.

Live, the song replaced "How Many More Times" as the expandable receptacle for tossed-off blues references. And it was always long, with the official live version issued on 1977's *The Song Remains the Same* clocking in at 14:25.

"Whole Lotta Love" was another single for the band, backed with "Living Loving Maid" in the United States (sadly, non–picture sleeve). It was issued worldwide, essentially, except for in the United Kingdom, meaning that Peter Grant could say that his no singles policy remained in force, his strategy being that he'd rather have the punters buy the whole album. Over a million copies of the small rounder were sold in the United States, vaulting the record to gold status. On later pressings the psychosexual interlude was cleaved and an early fade imposed, both of which resulted in second life for a song that lives ever on regardless, no crash diet necessary.

"Whole Lotta Love" was built on the chassis of an old blues tune, Willie Dixon's "You Need Love," which was recorded by Muddy Waters in 1962.

# WHAT IS AND WHAT SHOULD NEVER BE

**PAGE/PLANT/4:47**

With "What Is and What Should Never Be," Robert put pen to paper to create a small stack of love letters as seductive as they are abstract and vague. Indeed, what he's on about here could have been stitched to the front of "Stairway to Heaven" and we'd double our oohing and ahhing over the cryptic message of the band's most famous song.

As it is, Robert, in floral print, one suspects, sounds like he's leaning over a waif that looks like a young, prefame Stevie Nicks and whispering sweet nothings (emphasis on "nothing").

Musically, the song alternates harshly between the bluesy bass line and soft strummery of the verse and the crunching chords of the chorus, where the band's developing chemistry really comes to the fore. "What Is and What Should Never Be" was one of the first songs worked for the album—Jimmy wrote this and "Ramble On" on his Harmony acoustic—and it was considered a bold experiment, receiving much attention for its craft against the likes of, say, "Moby Dick."

Bonham's announcing fills to the hard rock chorus are simple and memorable. After an unexpected long harmonized vocal, it's back to the psychedelic amble, over which Jimmy throws in some slide (in standard tuning, something most guitarists find tougher than open tuning), which continues through the return of the trundle. There's also much messing about with a stereo panning effect on Jimmy's Les Paul Number One. Robert's vocal is then put through a tape-phasing process using dual reel-to-reel decks (one track correct, the other slowed and warbled) until it's back to his strong high singing. A new funky riff is introduced late in the sequence, celebrated by a Chinese gong smash from Bonzo, after which Robert free-associates and contradicts any gelling understanding of the song before it ends with the jarring words "I move like hell."

Method to the madness or meaning behind the mess? Apparently, the song is about the sister of Robert's wife Maureen, whom he had dated before marrying Maureen. There's definitely complex emotion in the lyric.

Ultimately, what is commendable about "What Is and What Should Never Be" is that the band has moved squarely into the realm of original material and simultaneously left blues structures behind. Sure, there's an R&B feel and echoes back to the Summer of '67, but for the quiet bits, the band explores new territory beyond, say, acoustic folk, and with its heaviness, the song contributes to the overall embattled traveling band vibe of the rest of the surround-sounding record.

Of note, Zeppelin was not afraid to reveal material for public consumption prior to official release. "What Is and What Should Never Be" had been recorded twice long before the album came out, once on June 16, 1969, at Aeolian Studios for broadcast the following week on BBC's *Tasty Pop Sundae* and a second time at BBC's Maida Vale for broadcast on John Peel's *Top Gear*, June 29, at which time they also worked up "Whole Lotta Love."

# THE LEMON SONG

**PAGE/BONHAM/PLANT/JONES/6:20**

"The Lemon Song" is the band performing at their peak, especially John Paul Jones, whose complex parts work off his mates' behemoth blues work.

Adding to the impression that *II* is a "virile" record, as Page put it, "The Lemon Song" is both bludgeoning (but still blues-based, which can only sound so heavy) and sexually charged.

The track was recorded at engineer Chris Huston's four-track Mystic Studios in Hollywood, with the band forever on the run from the GTOs, quipped Page, referring to an infamous rock band comprising groupies gadding between the bands then gravitating to the Sunset Strip. The song's road-hardened feel is abetted by the fact that it was recorded virtually live with no effects (other than a bit of tape echo) in a sixteen-by-sixteen foot room with wooden walls and low ten-foot ceilings, the band performing at their peak, especially John Paul Jones, who plays complex parts against his mates and their behemoth blues work. Jimmy recalled that the only overdub was an extra guitar track at the bridge. Robert was recorded with a hand-held mic in the middle of the room, adding to the echo and ambiance. To get Bonham's notoriously fat sound, Huston placed him on a platform in the corner and used only four mics on his kit: two overhead, one for the snare, and a ribbon mic placed two feet from his kick. The result was, as Huston puts it, the actual sound of the drums in the room.

"The Lemon Song" evolved out of Howlin' Wolf's "Killing Floor," which the band regularly played live well into the tour for the first album. A suit brought in December 1972 by publisher Arc Music was soon settled out of court, with Howlin' Wolf (Chester Arthur Burnett) receiving a check for $45,123 from Arc and the settlement amount remaining

undisclosed. Subsequent issues of the album credit the song to the four members of Zeppelin plus Burnett.

The song also contains echoes of Albert King's "Crosscut Saw," and Page's chords on the rave-up section feel like a tribute to James Brown, but at this trace level, any opposition is drowned out by Jimmy's blobulous riff. In this respect, there's a parallel to "Whole Lotta Love": Howlin' Wolf's song, "Killing Floor," from only five years earlier, is an integrated performance of an original, while Jimmy's song (even as the band's earlier live rendition of "Killing Floor") is dominated by a new riff that becomes the song's focal point—and here we are back to the previously discussed central tenet of heavy metal.

The most (in)famous feature of the song, however, is its scandalous "squeeze my lemon" lyric, later added to the "Whole Lotta Love" medley live. Even this could be heard elsewhere previously, in two songs from 1937: Roosevelt Sykes's "She Squeezed My Lemon" and Robert Johnson's "Travelling Riverside Blues," which Zeppelin covered. Taking it one step further, Sykes was known as the Honeydripper, and in 1984, of course, Robert formed a short-lived project named the Honeydrippers in tribute to Sykes, scoring hits with "Sea of Love" and "Rockin' at Midnight."

"The Lemon Song" was *II*'s most derivative churn of a song, essentially blurred into existence from a standard the band knew well, and thus brought surly and kicking into the white man's blues realm without much effort at all, even if John Paul Jones decides to take charge and distinguish himself, perhaps cognizant that another "You Shook Me" just won't do this time 'round.

ABOVE: "The Lemon Song" evolved out of Howlin' Wolf's "Killing Floor," which the band regularly played live well into the tour for the first album.

BELOW: The scandalous "squeeze my lemon" lyric could be heard previously in Roosevelt Sykes' "She Squeezed My Lemon" and Robert Johnson's "Travelling Riverside Blues," the latter of which Zep had covered.

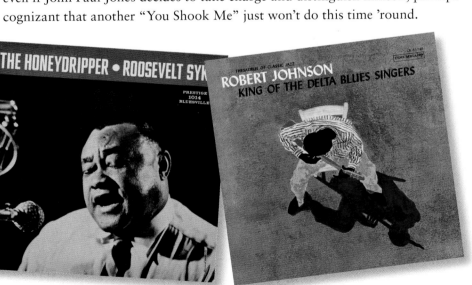

# THANK YOU

**PAGE/PLANT/3:50**

The only ballad on *II* is a gorgeous song, again, not purely folk and fairly rocked up by John Bonham's forceful drumming. Recorded in June 1969 at Morgan in North London (where the band also worked on "Living Loving Maid"), the song is one of Robert's earliest almost fully original lyrics (save for Jimmy's "Little drops of rain" and a contribution to the bridge), Jimmy encouraging his new singer who now looks as if he's neither going to be fired nor quit due to the demands set upon him. Page, none too confident in his own lyric-writing, was in fact glad to see Robert take over, citing his work here and on "What Is and What Should Never Be" as proof that the vocalist could take over and leave Page to concentrate on music and production.

Lyrically, "Thank You" is a simple paean to Robert's wife Maureen, set to a fairly ambitious arrangement that finds John Paul Jones contributing ample Hammond C-3 organ, and in fact, a protracted solo evocative of the "Your Time Is Gonna Come" intro, on both passages, John drawing on his experience playing organ in church as a boy. The sound is not typical Hammond—there's no vibrato or distortion, just a bit of echo provided by tape delay.

But there was a problem with the slow-fading false ending twenty seconds before close when it came to radio play: stations had to decide whether to allow the dead air or to call it a day early. Some even ginned up their own edited versions. But really, what comes after the false ending isn't much—more or less just the faders turning back up for a second organ passage ending on a resolution chord.

Jimmy plays a Vox twelve-string on the track, highlighted by a rare acoustic guitar solo from Page. An extra treat is Jimmy as backing vocalist during the "little drops of rain" section. Also, the first and the third lines are nearly identical matches to the first and third lines of Jimi Hendrix's 1967 mind-bender "If Six Was Nine," demonstrating that Zeppelin was capable of shout-outs to contemporaries as well as early influences.

OPPOSITE: Lyrically, "Thank You" is a simple paean to Robert's wife Maureen, set to a fairly ambitious arrangement.

# HEART**BREAKER**

**PAGE/BONHAM/PLANT/JONES/4:15**

"Heartbreaker," another example of Zeppelin forging heavy metal from the blues boom opens with Jimmy amusingly adding a disorienting extra note, but the band finds the pocket quickly. Fillmore East, New York City, 1969.

"Heartbreaker," like "Whole Lotta Love" a side earlier, is another example of Zeppelin forging heavy metal from the blues boom by piling a big riff onto a frame made of blues tropes like scale, modulation, and vocal phrasings and idioms. At the heart of the song is a blues lyric, Robert bemoaning the return to town of a heartbreaker named Annie, who evidently not only caused him years of anguish, but plopped the cherry on top by calling out another guy's name when he tried to make love to her.

Furthermore, on a musical front, as with "How Many More Times" and "Dazed and Confused" from the first album, there's a doominess to the shotgun marriage of blues and Jimmy's rock guitar that wouldn't sound out of place on *Black Sabbath*, yet, significantly, would pale as dated by the time of *Paranoid* (1970) and *Master of Reality* (1971) . . . or *Physical Graffiti*.

The song opens with Jimmy amusingly adding a disorienting extra note, but they find the pocket quickly, as Bonzo enters with his simple beat and slightly odd high hat signature. Also noteworthy is Jones's usually snarling bass sound, accomplished in part through the playing of chords, and Jimmy's improvised solo guitar performance, after which the band enters a speedy jam over a whole new riff and rhythm. Page's solo is slightly off pitch because it was recorded separately and parachuted in afterward.

As the song ends, "Living Loving Maid" begins immediately, and although radio stations often played the two together as a result, the band never played "Living Loving Maid" live. "Heartbreaker," however, was a concert favorite, indeed used often to kick off shows or as an encore number. Only this song and "Communication Breakdown" were played on every Led Zeppelin tour, albeit sometimes as parts of medleys. "Heartbreaker" was pliable, with the solo section a good place for Jimmy to throw in classical quotes, not to mention a nod to "I'm a Man," "That's All Right," and Simon & Garfunkel's "The 59th Street Bridge Song (Feelin' Groovy)."

"Heartbreaker" was recorded late in the *II* sequence, on the band's second tour of North America, at A&R Studios in New York. Jimmy's solo was recorded at Atlantic with Eddie Kramer presiding at both sessions. Eddie Van Halen has stated that Jimmy's hammer-ons and pull-offs on the song inspired his own famed tapping technique (although he also cites Steve Hackett and Billy Gibbons in that regard). But most notable guitar-wise is the rave-up section where Jimmy weaves three separate guitar tracks: two of slashing chords to the left and right, one of solo guitar down the middle, creating with Bonham and Jones the heaviest sound on what is often considered the heaviest record in the band's entire oeuvre.

# LIVING LOVING MAID (SHE'S JUST A WOMAN)

**PAGE/PLANT/2:40**

On this short, tight, fastback rocker, Robert tells a detail-rich story of a woman who is not a maid, but rather lives off alimony, owns a Cadillac, and once had a butler, "servants three," and a maid. The Cadillac is "aged," her hat's worth fifty cents, and there is a reference to "tall tales of how it used to be" and to a bunch of talk that nobody pays any mind. Page, who contributed the first verse and the chorus, summed it up as a "sarcastic" tale of an old socialite trying to hang onto her youth.

It's testimony to how when one roots around Led Zeppelin's lyrical canon, among a fair number of unapologetically sparse blues phrasings are ample examples of engaging storytelling.

On the musical front, the song serves as further grist for the corollary that much of *II* is the first album improved, in this case, "Living Loving Maid" being a better appointed, more event-filled version of "Communication Breakdown," with Zeppelin in an increasingly modern and focused heavy metal mood.

Also like its doppelganger on the first album, "Living Loving Maid" represents a commercial and radio-friendly Zeppelin, hitting the listener between the eyes and pricking their ears, the direct opposite of something like, say, "Dazed and Confused." The keys to its easy appeal are the electric-twelve-string-hardened riff and the repetitive and punchy rhythms of the line-ending title refrain, backing vocals courtesy of John Paul

OPPOSITE: Page famously disliked "Living Loving Maid," thus its banishment from the set list.

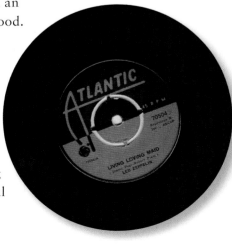

Jones. Page, however, famously disliked the song throughout Zeppelin's reign, thus its banishment from the set list.

The song indeed got some radio play, reaching No. 65 on the Billboard Hot 100, helped by its use as the B-side of "Whole Lotta Love." Curiously, on the centerpiece of the original UK pressing (but not inside the gatefold), the song was listed as "Livin' Lovin' Wreck (She's a Woman)."

# RAMBLE ON

PAGE/PLANT/4:35

Led Zeppelin continued to build their hippie-happy whisper-to-roar sound in this song that begins as a tribute to idyllic West Coast acoustic rock, starring Robert the romantic troubadour. Stick around long enough and the story becomes rather site-specific, with all this longing taking place in Tolkien's Middle-earth—Mordor, to be specific—the protagonist (in an event quite antithetical to what likely would occur in *The Lord of the Rings*) losing the fair maiden to Gollum and "the evil one." It's a strange reference that Plant and so fleeting it seems a metaphor.

And yet the music supports the reference, with Page's near-Renaissance feel (in E major) via up-the-fretboard open chords and Bonham's metronomic homespun percussion, tapped out on either a guitar case or possibly a pail, with either sticks or his bare hands (most cited is bare hands on a guitar case). In fact, it is up to Jones to play the dominant verse melody as Page jangles.

But this is *II*, so the band must rock out, which they most certainly do, Bonzo announcing the noise with the most exquisite snare whacks, spurred on by a prechorus on which Jimmy limbers up with a few soft electric licks. The band shifts around, leaving space and pregnant pause for each other. Indeed, the chorus sounds like a brutish bash, the listener misdirected by Plant's wail and Bonzo's simple percussion, but both Jimmy and John Paul are playing anything but the expected notes, again, most of them quite high, mirroring their performances on the verse.

Recorded at the rudimentary Juggy Sound in New York while on the band's second US tour, "Ramble On" was never played live in its entirety by the original band (it was always a tease), due to Jimmy's reluctance at reproducing the acoustic mixed with the electric, even as he pronounced it Plant's favorite track on the album. However, with Jason Bonham, the band finally gave this funky fan favorite a live debut at the historic O2 Arena show in 2007.

OPPOSITE: Zep . . . in the darkest depths of Mordor? Actually, just the lobby of the Boston Tea Party (sans Bonzo), Boston, Massachusetts, May 1969.

# MOBY DICK

**BONHAM/PAGE/JONES/4:25**

Referred to as "Pat's Delight" (in honor of Bonham's wife) at the band's genesis and "Over the Top" well after its immortalization on *II*, "Moby Dick" was often a much longer piece than it is here, at its heart really just a drop-D twelve-bar blues frame on which to post a drum solo.

The track is, of course, an instrumental, with the front and back played by the band sans Robert, and the middle left to Bonzo, playing his Ludwig thermogloss natural maple kit, which he used only on the *II* album. This was his first set of drums on his official endorsement deal with Ludwig, obtained after Carmine Appice rang up the company and told them that Bonzo wanted a kit exactly like his, which Bonzo saw when Zeppelin supported Vanilla Fudge in the United States back in December 1968.

Again, Led Zeppelin is playing dated, old-timey music, but with enough aggression, production heft, and pivot to the power of riff to drag the doom out of it—this is yet another Zeppelin track that could have served time on a double album version of *Black Sabbath*; one could even imagine Sabbath stick man Bill Ward conjuring and executing a similar solo, on his similarly sized—and sounding—kit.

"Moby Dick" turned out to be an edit job, with Page capturing Bonzo pounding away whenever he could as the band gadded about from studio to studio all over the UK and North America, with Mystic being the primary space. The song had evolved quickly from unused BBC session track "The Girl I Love She Got Long Black Wavy Hair," but it's also considerably similar to Bobby Parker's V-Tone Records single "Watch Your Step" in terms of its riff and blues progression. But once the vocals and the added arrangement ensue, the similarities begin to recede.

Although the spirit of "Moby Dick" was there every time Bonzo broke into his live drum solo (a regular occurrence, it ranged wildly in length, and sometimes featured Bonham playing with his bloody hands), in the case of the North American *Presence* tour, the solo emerged from "Out on the Tiles" and then ended in that famous white blues whale of a riff, which in itself symbolized that this was a drummer worthy of having a song written in tribute.

"Moby Dick" was an edit job, Page capturing Bonzo pounding away whenever he could as the band gadded about from studio to studio all over the UK and North America.

# LIKE CANNONS GOING OFF

**L**ed Zeppelin II is of course the record that gave us "Moby Dick," the ultimate love letter to John Bonham from the rest of his band—and the ultimate love letter from Bonzo back to the fans. Here are a few more love letters, this time from a few of Bonzo's fellow rock stars, who seem to agree on one thing: John Bonham was loud.

**Quartz guitarist, fellow Brummie and early Bonham bandmate Mick Hopkins:** He was always loud. Years ago, I don't know if they had them in Canada, but they used to have these special sound things, where if you played above a certain level, it would cut you off and cut the power off. And you could bet your life, if John was playing, he could knock it off on his own. He was so loud. There was nobody who could touch him. A booming drummer.

**Black Sabbath guitarist Tony Iommi:** We knew Zeppelin well because they were friends of ours in the early days and we were from the same town, so we used to see them a lot, certainly Robert Plant and John Bonham. We were very familiar with what they were doing. When they started Zeppelin, I remember Bonham saying, "We've got this band we're joining with Jimmy Page." He started telling us about it. And I remember the days from before he joined Zeppelin, he used to play in different bands around Birmingham and he was always getting fired because he was too loud. . . . Bill and myself from Sabbath had another band and Bonham was with various bands. So we used to see him every other week playing at this place called the Midland Red Club in Birmingham, and he'd be there one week, and the week after that, he wouldn't be there. "What happened?" "Oh, he was too loud. We fired him."

**Ted Nugent guitarist and lead vocalist Derek St. Holmes:** John had the biggest drum groove known to mankind, and playing as loud as he plays, when you stand next to a drummer playing loud, it makes you play loud. And then if the whole band is playing loud, you bring it to a level of intensity that is hard to match. It's hard to beat. I know that's what he did for Led Zeppelin, and I think that's what he did for many, many drummers in the rock industry, because they just went, "Well, he's such a powerhouse, we have to be like that."

**Cheap Trick drummer Bun E. Carlos:** John Bonham had the best beat, he had the feel, he had the big fat backbeat, and the big fat high-hat sound and bass drum sound. And so when you look back on, like, 1980s rock drums, where it sounded like cannons going off and guns getting shot, that's all John Bonham come to fruition, basically, after the '70s. Everybody could be John Bonham in the 1980s and all the drums sounded like cannons. But he was the guy who kind

Bonham at the Bath Festival in Shepton Mallet, England, June 28, 1970.

of invented that and the guy who did it the best. And there's no matching his pocket. I mean, anything, certain tempos come to mind, it's John Bonham all the way for a lot of rock drummers, myself included.

**Grand Funk drummer Don Brewer:** The first time I saw John Bonham play this huge twenty-six-inch bass drum, it was like, "Wow, I gotta get a bigger bass drum than a twenty-one." There were twenties too and it was like a cocktail kit. So I started playing the twenty-four. Not only did it sound better, but it looked cool.

**Savoy Brown and Foghat drummer Roger Earl:** I remember once, we were playing with Led Zeppelin in 1969. Savoy Brown and Jethro Tull were doing some dates with Led Zeppelin. And a couple of times, during soundchecks, John would be playing, [Tull drummer] Clive Bunker would be playing, and I would play. And whatever guitar player was around would play. . . . All the drum kits were just set around the stage and we would just start to play. John Bonham was louder than everybody else, including the guitarist and the other two drummers. You could hear him above everything. Yeah, he was a monster. He wrote the book on the attitude of rock 'n' roll drums. And it's not easy standing out in a rather crowded field. There've been some great drummers, but John was special. He was unique in his approach. He played sort of a rudimentary style, but he would do things with his feet that you're only supposed to do with your hands [*laughs*]. He was spectacular. I met him a couple of times afterward; we hung out and had a few beers together. One night we were down in the Village in New York City with bunch of people sitting around a table at a bar, and he starts playing on the table with two empty Heineken bottles. He was something else.

**John Paul Jones:** He was a very sophisticated musician, a very sophisticated drummer. And he hit hard when he needed to. And I mean, he could [*laughs*]. And he drove the band from the drums—he really did. That's where we'd meet [*laughs*] in order to work out where we were going next, with the improvisations. So there were a lot of visual cues and obviously a lot of listening cues. He was just a very thorough musician, instinctive, great groove. I mean, he really swung. People don't realize. Especially when you go to rock concerts now and there's a lot of guys up the front either standing still and counting bars or jumping up and down. But in the Zeppelin days, there were a lot of women up the front dancing [*laughs*]. It was a rock band people could dance to—and wanted to dance to.

# BRING IT ON
# HOME

**PAGE/PLANT/4:19**

As has been the theme through so much of *Led Zeppelin* and *II*, Jimmy wears and bears his influence on his sleeve, and his metal development as well. On "Bring It on Home," the contrast is more crudely pronounced and demarcated than ever.

The murky blues sections at the front and back are a direct tribute (Page's word) to Willie Dixon's "Bring It on Home" as performed by Sonny Boy Williamson II. This is underscored by Plant's shaken vocal and his skilled harmonica playing, recorded at R&D Studios in Vancouver (described as "a hut" with no working headphones) when the band played the PNE Agrodome on May 10, 1969.

Jimmy, using standard tuning, cleaves in what is basically a second song, and not even much of a blues, more of a circular, note-dense riff rocker. Although one would never call Jimmy's hard rock instincts "modern" in any sense, this is still far from the blues, unless one wants to, again, compare Jimmy's funk predilection to a band like the James Gang, who might be called post-blues or American blues boom.

The "tribute" was so close to the original that in 1972, Arc Music, Chess Records' publishing arm, sued for copyright infringement, settling out of court for an undisclosed sum, with later issues crediting Dixon as sole writer.

SEATTLE CENTER COLISEUM
SEPT. 1   8 PM

LED ZEPPELIN

PRESENTED BY
CONCERTS WEST
TICKETS
$3.50   FIDELITY LANE   $4.$5.$6.
SUBURBAN OUTLETS

SIDE

# 1

**Immigrant Song**

**Friends**

**Celebration Day**

**Since I've Been Loving You**

**Out on the Tiles**

SIDE

# 2

**Gallows Pole**

**Tangerine**

**That's the Way**

**Bron-Y-Aur Stomp**

**Hats Off to (Roy) Harper**

Recorded
December 1969 and May–July 1970
Rolling Stone Mobile Studio, Headley Grange, Hampshire, UK
Island Studios and Olympic Studios, London

Release Dates
October 5, 1970 (US, Atlantic SD 7201)
October 23, 1970 (UK, Atlantic 2401002)

Produced by Jimmy Page
Engineers: Andrew Johns and Terry Manning

RIAA Certification: 6x Platinum
Top Billboard Position: No. 1

**1970**

**LED ZEPPELIN III**

# LED ZEPPELIN III

**ROBERT PLANT**
lead vocals,
harmonica

**JIMMY PAGE**
acoustic, electric,
and pedal steel
guitars; banjo;
dulcimer; bass;
backing vocals;
theremin

**JOHN PAUL
JONES**
bass, Hammond
organ, Moog
synthesizer,
mandolin, double
bass, string
arrangement

**JOHN BONHAM**
drums, percussion,
backing vocals

It's hard to overestimate and, paradoxically, sometimes hard to reconcile the shattering impact Led Zeppelin's first album had on so many rockers who would go on to rule the '70s. It might be more understandable if *II* is considered a finetuning of the formula—a formula that maybe appeared mighty in early 1969, but not so much when revisited at year's end.

Fact is, through two albums Led Zeppelin were the best new thing going, evangelically received, yet mortal, uncomfortably attached, as they were, to existing material and the late-'60s British bands that had already covered that ground. Betwixt, there was gorgeous folk, some kerranging hard rock riffs that hit between the eyes like no others (yet), and leading-edge performances from all members. And when all of these elements came together, as in the band's frenzied, improvisational live passages, Led Zeppelin indeed transcended the realm of mere mortals.

Jimmy, Robert, John Paul, and Bonzo next fulfilled the fate of true artists and strode forward, off the treadmill, past the accolades, and out of the safe zone. The first step was to write and decompress at the same time, Robert and Jimmy sequestering themselves for a month in the hilltop Bron-Yr-Aur cottage (misspelled in the song title) in Snowdonia, Wales, with no electricity or running water. Fated was the fact that the band emerged with tranquil acoustic music. The transition to Olympic Studios began in late May with the run-down Headley Grange country manse in East Hampshire allowing further contemplation and song development away from the city.

The brunt of recording emerged from the Olympic sessions prior to and after Headley Grange, with some work from Headley Grange, where they had recorded with a mobile unit, surviving the cut. Additional recording took place in July at Island Records' new facility at Basing Street Studios, Zeppelin being the first to use Studio One (just ahead of Country Joe and the Fish). In a shuddering echo of the hectic *II* process, the band then pared the album down to ten tracks (from seventeen) and had Terry Manning mix it at Ardent Studios in Memphis whilst they embarked on an American tour.

Brave in the extreme, the resulting album was essentially all acoustic-based on side two, with an additional acoustic track on side one (blues with balladic tendencies) alongside three rockers to satisfy the overwhelming fan and industry demand for "Whole Lotta Love Pt. II."

Once the shock wore off, deep listeners quickly began to appreciate the gorgeous pastoral qualities of the light material, which was recorded with much more sympathy than any of the earlier handful of strolls down this cobblestone path. Additionally, "Since I've Been Loving You" vaulted over all the band's previous this-way-that-way bull charges at the blues as an expert example of composition, performance, arrangement, and production, as well as the culmination and last comment the band would

With *III*, Jimmy, Robert, John Paul, and Bonzo fulfilled the fate of true artists and strode forward, past the accolades and out of the safe zone.

ever make on the blues boom. Zeppelin would write sparingly and quite contritely within the blues idiom across the rest of their catalog, as if they knew they'd gone as far as they (or any) band could.

And what of the clutch of rockers on *III*? Well, a spare trio they be, and two of them immediately went over everybody's heads, both "Celebration Day" and "Out on the Tiles" becoming obscure and rarely played but sophisticated for miles beyond anything from *Led Zeppelin* or *II*.

The opening "Immigrant Song" brought fans on the band's ferryboat–crossing into the land of the immortals, Robert going on about the resolute plunder by Viking marauders, fans quickly doing the math and drawing parallels to their touring heroes as they chewed up adversaries across the western lands.

*III* was the work of a band bucking one trend toward harder rock and acknowledging at the other end of the scale a maturing singer-songwriter scene on America's left coast. But set against a universe of their own anchoring, through two effusively received albums and a meteoric touring life, *III* was on balance savaged by critics, sometimes in the worst way possible, as the work of a tired band—simply because the record wasn't relentlessly electric or brutishly black 'n' bluesy.

As a result, the album was a sales disappointment, not helped any by the lack of a single other than the quirky and dark "Immigrant Song." But art will win out in the end. The record has sold steadily over the ensuing decades to the point where it is now six times platinum in the States, although, oddly, still an underperformer in every other territory.

# IMMIGRANT SONG

**PAGE/PLANT/2:26**

The public debut of "Immigrant Song" took place at the Bath Festival, Shepton Mallet, England, June 28, 1970.

With a mysterious sound of tension, manifest as an eerily approaching high-hat sizzle chalked up to echo feedback and masking a faint count from Bonzo, "Immigrant Song" flies off the gyre. Led Zeppelin *III* has begun on a note of frantic surprise—all the more surprising to the listener when she or he discovers that the entire back half of the record will disperse that inaugural tension into the air above Bron-Yr-Aur.

Immediately we are in foreign terrain here, with Robert weaving an olden tale of emotionless Viking conquest, written in a formal style perfect for his timeless tract and the hypnotic and alien musical backing. The parallels to the band and their sense of mission were intentional, at least through geographical reference. Zeppelin were indeed returning from the land of ice and snow, namely Iceland, where they were invited by the government in June 1970 to play as a sort of cultural exchange, only to find the gig nearly scrubbed by a civic strike. The show went on, with the local university sorting out the mess; Zeppelin, in effect, arrived as Englishmen and left as Vikings.

The song had been in progress as the band left Iceland, the guys having worked on it in Germany as well, with its live debut taking place six days after the Reykjavik experience, at the Bath Festival in late June 1970. The event was considered a beachhead for the band, a crack performance in front of a home crowd of about two hundred thousand, where previously, the lion's share of their touring efforts and success had been stateside. Two other songs from the forthcoming album were played that night, namely "That's the Way" (announced by Robert informally as "The Boy Next Door") and the grinding blues "Since I've Been Loving You."

The enduring highlights of "Immigrant Song" from the band's siren are both his ungodly wailing vocal melody, a level of sinister upon already sinister, and his nearly muttered "hammer of the gods" soon picked up to refer to the band's music itself, and further immortalized as the title of Stephen Davis's fine biography of the band. Other creepy Plant parts were removed in the mix to simplify the song, which was further rendered stark by its lack of a guitar solo. Too self-aware to miss the humor in the whole thing, the band was taken slightly aback when they witnessed how seriously fans took the song—heavy metal could have that effect, as the industry was beginning to find out.

Still, besides this reference and the memorable "Valhalla, I'm coming," the song is anchored to the mortal realm, as the restless migrants of the title emigrate and immigrate and emigrate anew.

Musically, the song is a prototype of the heavy metal gallop, and its F minor staccato chug of a riff—essentially the riff is a back-and-forth staccato performance of octave F# notes— along with the Norse subject matter, square the song as a contribution to the proto-metal of the genre's ground-zero year, best represented by Black Sabbath's eponymous debut and *Paranoid*, Deep Purple's *In Rock*, and Uriah Heep's *Very 'Eavy, Very 'Umble*.

John Paul Jones saddles himself with the song's most challenging lick, enormously complicating the song's ersatz chorus with a flurry of notes in an ascending run. Still, Jimmy's high-strung production job was more Zeppelin than Led, with little power put to his riff, and his cross chords taking on an almost Dick Dale surf guitar tone.

An odd pick for a single, save for its brevity and immediacy, "Immigrant Song," a rare US single release, is distinguished by its B-side, "Hey, Hey, What Can I Do," the upbeat full-band acoustic number, credited to the entire band and being the only non-LP B-side they ever issued. In error, the single issue for Japan featured "Out on the Tiles" as B-side and thus quickly became collectible, not that any Zeppelin singles aren't.

An odd pick for a rare Zeppelin US single release, save for its brevity and immediacy, "Immigrant Song" is distinguished by its non-LP B-side, "Hey, Hey, What Can I Do." In error, the single issue for Japan featured "Out on the Tiles" as B-side and thus quickly became collectible (not that any Zeppelin singles aren't). Live, "Immigrant Song," an opener from 1970 until 1972, often took on a fury come jam time that was rarely matched on any of the other creations the band turned inside out onstage, Bonzo going algorithmic until fans lost their minds.

Where's that confounded bridge, indeed.

"Immigrant Song" B-side "Hey, Hey, What Can I Do" featured a west coast vibe, underscoring Robert's love of San Francisco music.

# FRIENDS

**PAGE/PLANT/3:55**

Yea and verily, "Friends" is emphatically *not* the acoustic music of *III*'s elegiac side two, rather, lodged like a cyst between the violence of "Immigrant Song" and the greatest damn Led Zeppelin song of all time, "Celebration Day."

Opening the song is a bit of noise pollution, this time studio chatter, most likely Page, Plant, and engineer Richard Digby Smith. Foreboding and roiling acoustic chords then set the doom in motion, o'er which Robert delivers through a demanding, high vocal a life lesson of love at once at odds with Jimmy's tense soundtrack but also rife with desperation, as if a relapse into depression is imminent if love can't be spread quickly.

"Friends" was one of Robert and Jimmy's Bron-Yr-Aur collaborations, with Jimmy writing it after a massive row with someone and coming up with the music on the balcony of his Pangbourne home. He then wished upon it a Beatles-eque Indian feel, accomplished by the addition of an uncredited John Paul Jones arrangement and simple tribal percussion from Bonham on bongos or congas. The unearthly and compressed tone of Jimmy's Harmony Sovereign H-1260 acoustic was achieved with a tube limiter, either an Altair, an Altec, or an RCA BA-6A, but most likely an Altair.

The open-C6 tuning (C-A-C-G-C-E) is common in Eastern folk music, and the looseness of the strings resulted in the inordinate amount of buzz that Page made no efforts to purge. Both "Bron-Yr-Aur," to emerge three records later on *Physical Graffiti*, and "Poor Tom," non-LP but issued on the posthumous *Coda*, were also recorded at the *III* sessions in this tuning.

But the darkest music on the song is saved for the end where John Paul lays in a Moog synthesizer drone (and, according to Jimmy, "bottleneck string bass") that sounds like a plane losing engine power just before it crashes into the opening chords of "Celebration Day"—Zeppelin using the finest acoustic song in their catalog as an intro to the finest song of their catalog, period. "Friends" was played live only once, on September 29, 1971, in Osaka, Japan.

ATLANTIC
SD 7201
STEREO
LED ZEPPELIN III
1. IMMIGRANT SONG (2:26)
J. Page - R. Plant
ONE
2. FRIENDS (3:55)
J. Page - R. Plant
3. CELEBRATION DAY (3:29)
J. Page - R. Plant - J.P. Jones
4. SINCE I'VE BEEN LOVING YOU (7:25)
J. Page - R. Plant - J.P. Jones
5. OUT ON THE TILES (4:04)
J. Page - R. Plant - J. Bonham
PRODUCED BY JIMMY PAGE
MFD. BY ATLANTIC RECORDING CORP., 75 ROCKEFELLER PLAZA, N.Y.

"Friends" was one of Robert's and Jimmy's Bron-Yr-Aur collaborations, with Jimmy offering an unearthly compressed tone on acoustic guitar. The Forum, Los Angeles, September 4, 1970.

# CELEBRATION DAY

**PAGE/PLANT/JONES/3:29**

The intellectual quality and rhythmic counterpoint of the origami-like "Celebration Day" is such that it's a marvel John Paul Jones didn't write it—or rather didn't write it *completely.* Page added response riffing to Jones's complexity, making "Celebration Day" a testimony to the whole as greater than the sum of its parts.

"Celebration Day" originated in the raucous Headley Grange sessions, utilizing the Rolling Stones' mobile recording unit. It was supposed to open with a John Bonham drum intro, which was accidentally recorded over by the engineer. Good thing, because that naked riff (conceived by Jones on an old Danelectro baritone guitar) placed over a fading Moog drone is ideal for when everybody comes crashing in, in what Page called a "salvage" job.

There's further rhythmic hippie math in Robert's complicated phrasing, not to mention one of his most cryptic lyrics of the catalog, something to do with impressions of New York City, underscored by the fact that he would occasionally introduce the song as "the New York song." Fans have conjectured that the lyric is about the Statue of Liberty, (thus tying

"Celebration Day" is one of three songs holding up the hard rock part of *III*, and the most creative construct on an album that is purposely spare. Robert's vamping and Jimmy's soloing help carry its sense of optimism. Empire Pool, Wembley, London, November 1971.

in nicely with "Immigrant Song"), and exploration of race issues related to immigration, and even a historical narration of race relations, namely the escape from slavery. Others have guessed it's about groupies in general, a particular groupie in particular, heroin, a pact with Satan, and a mockery of some poor sap on a bad acid trip. Whatever the case, "Celebration Day" is a shining example of a lyric that keeps on giving long past its intended meaning.

At the musical end, there are a couple of completely different guitar tracks, plus soloing; Jimmy has said one guitar was tuned standard, and the other was a slide tuned to open A. Due mostly to Jimmy's creativity, "Celebration Day" is the first of the band's songs clever enough to sit shoulder to shoulder with all those fine *Physical Graffiti* numbers, and it is a candidate for the author's favorite Led Zeppelin song of all time. The riff is a lesson in insanity, Jimmy conjuring an old-school country music vibe filtered through acid rock. Without much distortion, and without a single dominant riff, but rather two moderately recorded riffs—not even riffs, more like licks—playing at once, the song is not a particularly heavy number, certainly not as heavy as "Out on the Tiles" and about in the same curious metal midrange zone as "Immigrant Song."

But of course, "Celebration Day" is one of three songs holding up the hard rock side of *III*, and the most creative construct on an album that is purposely spare. There's a great motion to the thing, with Bonham's no-nonsense drum and gorgeously collapsing fills locked tightly with Jones' conservative, throbbing eight-string bass line anchored to the "ands" rather than the 1, 2, 3, and 4.

Set against the sober emotions of the verse (not particularly spooky or particularly jubilant) is a chorus that literally says, *I'm so happy* and promises dancing, singing, and celebration, quickly putting the listener in that West Coast vibe of "Immigrant Song" B-side "Hey, Hey, What Can I Do," as well as "Tangerine" and the chorus to "Out on the Tiles." That sense of optimism is carried over to the verse for the closing jam through Robert's vamping and Jimmy's cheerful soloing. It's Zeppelin magic of an almost aristocratic nature.

Again, for those wishing more from Led Zeppelin, more imagination of arrangement, more note-density out of Jimmy, less blues, and oblique yet evocative lyrics out of Robert, well, "Celebration Day" is the first intellectually hefty Zeppelin song of many to come.

"Since I've Been Loving You" was one of the first things recorded for *III*. It also helped the band win over blues skeptics.

# SINCE I'VE BEEN LOVING YOU

**PAGE/PLANT/JONES/7:25**

Really, it was with "Since I've Been Loving You" that Led Zeppelin became capable of winning over any blues skeptic, more specifically that particular subset of blues skeptics who would not accept hotshot white guys from England with long hair as part of the tribe. The torrid song is a shining example from start to finish, and one might argue that, in particular, Robert (but also Jimmy and even an increasingly frantic John Bonham as the song grinds on) is spurred by the complicated chord choices surreptitiously framing this blues lyric and blues beat.

Both the lyric, essentially about the workaday grind giving an interloper the opportunity to intrude upon the protagonist's relationship, and the stealth-like blues pacing bear similarity to Moby Grape's "Never," from *Wow/Grape Jam*, issued in early 1968. The intro and other elements also bear similarity to the Yardbirds' "New York City Blues." But true to the modus operandi demonstrated in earlier examples, Jimmy inundates the idea with rich melodic sophistication, taking the listener to a whole new place, a locale that Robert admits challenged his abilities to the fullest.

John Paul Jones plays bass pedals and a conventional Hammond C3 simultaneously, demonstrating command of light and shade through use of the swell pedal on the choruses. This setup allowed the band to play the song live at nearly every concert they ever did. One amusing note, this song, recorded pretty much live as ensemble, features Bonham stomping his Ludwig Speed King Model 201 bass drum pedal, dubbed the "Squeak King" because of the chirp that can be clearly heard, although only once it has been pointed out, as Page knows all too well, chuckling about not being able to listen to the song without rolling his eyes at the unintended effect.

"Since I've Been Loving You" was one of the first things recorded for the album, but a real monster to get right. In fact, it had been considered for use on the previous album (bumped for "Whole Lotta Love") and played live prior to recording.

Recording of the song kicked off in early June 1970 and took place at Olympic and Island. It is further distinguished by the fact that Jimmy's epic, top-shelf bluesy guitar solo (not one of his favorites) was recorded in Memphis with Terry Manning during sessions that were supposed to be all about mixing.

# OUT ON THE
## TILES

**PAGE/PLANT/BONHAM/4:04**

Again, underscoring the idea that the band was advancing quickly in the grumbling crunch-rock department, "Out on the Tiles" is a near progressive rock improvement on past Zep rockers, complex of rhythm, pockmarked with pregnant pauses in which Bonham gets in his licks, all while maintaining an evolved shuffle. And against all of that, there's a sense of 4/4 anchoring and an undeniable pop hook to the chorus.

Lyrically, Robert almost builds a concept album when this song is added to the likes of "Friends" and "Celebration Day," the singer speaking of the importance of personal attachment, of people, of the optimism that can flow by staying engaged and sociable. The title itself, the fourth in the first five tracks so far not referenced in the lyrics, derives from John Bonham's use of an idiom for heading out to the pubs. Typical of the band's desire to build extra meaning into what they do, the lyrics are more about a man celebrating his woman, possibly with her at his side, walking long distances with pleasant thoughts of her.

Inspired by Bonham's rhyming idiom, Page built a riff around the idea, hence Bonzo getting in on the credits. Not knowing this, one could imagine, given the challenging rhythmic charge of the song, that this is the type of track a drummer would instigate, either with a novel rhythm like this song presents and a handful of rudimentary chords to boot. But there's no way that Bonzo could have suggested a riff this lengthy; "Out on the Tiles" rises to the novel construction of "Celebration Day" and matches the same meandering path to resolution as "Black Dog."

Page's descending chords and Bonzo's wide-angled drums are recorded somewhat turgidly, or to put it more politely, carnally, and aggressively, an effect achieved by remote miking, a technique Page had been almost mathematically charting since the debut album. Much has been said about

OPPOSITE: Lyrically, with "Out on the Tiles," "Friends," and "Celebration Day," Robert nearly offers a mini concept album about personal attachments. Madison Square Garden, New York City, September 3, 1971.

"Out on the Tiles" is a near progressive rock improvement on past Zep rockers, complex of rhythm, with Bonham providing the titular inspiration and drawing most of the sonic attention.

the detectable "Stop" heard at about the 1:26 mark, although consensus is that it's Jimmy cueing the arduous time changes all over the song. Things get a little more instinctive, though, for the rumbling 4/4 jam that suddenly takes over for fully the final minute and a half, in which Robert fires off the *ooh yeah*'s for which he's known (but no *baby, baby*'s) and Bonham thunders away, drawing most of the attention (especially considering there's no guitar solo).

"Out on the Tiles" was played "properly" live on the band's US dates in September 1970, but then became a tease track, cranking up and then abruptly turning into "Black Dog" or Bonham's drum solo, in a move away from "Moby Dick," which had half the brains applied to its making and baking as did this song of magnetic personality and good-time hard rock vibes.

# UNPLUGGED, INSPIRED, RARELY IMITATED

**F**ans and critics alike were shocked by the acoustic nature of Led Zeppelin's third album, especially as they flipped it over and wended their way through side two.

But as John Paul Jones told me with a shrug, "I don't know, we were into Joni Mitchell a lot and listened to a lot of Fairport Convention as well. There was a lot of music around that was softer. Remember Ian Matthews's *Southern Comfort*? And there was an American group, Poco. We listened to a lot of that and thought we had done a couple of heavy albums. It's funny, though, a lot of heavy Zeppelin songs were written on the acoustic guitar. Plus there was a lot of acoustic stuff on the first album, which people forget. You know, after the second album, they always go, 'Oh, the third album's acoustic. What are you doing?' And we were like, 'What about "Babe I'm Gonna Leave You?"' I mean, there are acoustic numbers, but they had heavier parts. And I had started playing mandolin by then as well, so like 'Going to California' and 'That's the Way;' those were all my mandolin parts. It just seemed a nice thing to do. And by then we realized that, again, there were no rules. We didn't have to do it this way or that way. We just made our own judgment and said, 'Well, this is nice, this is good, let's use it.'"

Of course, there are the likes of "Celebration Day," "Out on the Tiles," and "Immigrant Song," too, the latter of which contains John's notorious bass part, much to the disdain of cover bands everywhere.

"Yes, well, the first part is fairly easy [*sings it*], but then I decided to do these runs, which are quite fast. But in fact, it's nowhere near as fast. . . . I heard some bootlegs once. I'm not sure, did we used to start the show with it? But it was enormously fast, almost twice as fast! How we played that, I don't know. And we still made them swing. I remember, one funny thing, in the old days, black music was always taken at a much slower tempo, and it had that groove while white groups used to speed up too much. Except for rock 'n' roll—black rock 'n' roll, like Little Richard, was always really fast. And I remember Little Richard quoted as saying that we used to speed them up so the white bands could never play them and swing at the same time [*laughs*]. That was quite funny. But Zeppelin could play fast and swing at the same time."

Indeed, they could, and as engineer Andy Johns agrees, Zeppelin were an impressive lot, acoustic or electric. "By the time we were doing their third album, which I did all of, the musicality of that band was incredible," Johns said. "Because Jimmy and John were extremely well-trained, and Bonham was just a natural. And so was Robert—a natural. They would bang out two, three tracks a night sometimes, and it'd go by quite quickly. Because of the standard of musicianship. As soon as I got a decent sound, off we went. And that record, I think turned out

okay. There are some very nice things on it. 'Gallows Pole' was wonderful, and 'Since I've Been Loving You' is still a favorite of mine. One was distinctly aware that you were dealing with real class. They were a step above the others, and nobody could really imitate them. People have tried ever since, and they never really quite get it.

"Jimmy had made his mind up that they were going to blow everyone off the stage," continues Johns. "That's what my brother [legendary producer Glyn Johns] told me. This is when Jimmy still had the Yardbirds thing going. Glyn said, 'I was with Jimmy the other day, and Jimmy said, "I've got this new lineup now, and we're going to blow everyone offstage."' So that was an intentional thing, to be as dramatic and as riff-conscious as possible. And Jimmy was a fabulous writer, and had a lot of great ideas in the studio, and was just wonderful to work with."

Adds noted UK Zeppelin expert Dave Lewis, "The prime example of allowing space and the use of loud and soft on the first Zeppelin album would be 'Babe I'm Gonna Leave You.' You can have this crescendo of composition going over six minutes into a loud and soft scenario. And again, with Zeppelin, there were always acoustic guitars from the beginning. If anyone should have been shocked by Zeppelin *III*, well, they should have gone back to Zep *I* and 'Babe I'm Gonna Leave You' and 'Black Mountain Side.' So again, with the metal genre—and I think Zeppelin was unfairly pushed into that, and I'm not trying to be a snob about it—but they were pushed into that limited genre, which I think in some cases metal has been. Not always. I'm saying there was always much more to Zeppelin than a metal thing. Jimmy had a vast canvas he wanted to cover, and part of it might have been riff-orientated rock, which is what it was, but that was never going to be the end of it. It wasn't just going to be about Marshall amplifiers turned up to eleven. Zeppelin was always much more than that."

**OPPOSITE: If fans were freaked by the acoustic nature of *III*, John Paul Jones didn't get the fuss. "I don't know," he told the author, "we were into Joni Mitchell a lot and listened to a lot of Fairport Convention as well." Here, Jones appears to be placing a flower in the nut of his bass backstage at the Forum in Los Angeles, September 4, 1970.**

# GALLOWS POLE

**TRAD. ARR. PAGE/PLANT/4:58**

Zep's layered take on the traditional "The Maid Freed from the Gallows Pole" or "Gallis Pole" is a raucous kitchen party anthem, a spirited introduction to a serious song. Page said he was inspired by fiddling around with Jones's mandolin, but it was John Paul who played the mando part on the recording. Civic Auditorium, Honolulu, Hawaii, September 1971.

"Gallows Pole" was recorded in the same early-July sessions as "St. Tristan's Sword" and cover medley "Key to the Highway/Trouble in Mind." "Gallows Pole" itself is a cover, but of a traditional song with a rich and circuitous centuries-long history. A popular blues version was Lead Belly's "Gallis Pole" from the 1930s, but the closest antecedent that Page admired was a frantic art-folk version by Fred Gerlach from his 1962 album, *Twelve-String Guitar.*

But the Zeppelin version was nothing like either of those, fully transforming the song, the most notable upsells being Bonham's frantic dervish-style drum part and the fact that the band make it as near to a Led Zeppelin rock number as they can without power chords, thanks to electric bass, Robert in full rock shriek, and layered tracks, including mandolin, banjo, electric guitar solo, and backing vocals. Page plays six- and twelve-string acoustics and banjo, one of the first times he ever picked one up. He has said that the germination of the song, one of his favorites on *III*, came from fiddling about with Jones's mandolin, but it is Jones who plays the mando part on the song. The result is a raucous kitchen party anthem, a spirited introduction to a serious song, with Jimmy's solo subtly filling the role that the fiddle would play in a more traditional arrangement.

Lyrically, the song is a rich and wry tale. The hard-luck male protagonist (in some tellings it is a female) bats two out of three in attempts to save his neck. The friends bring no bribe, but his brother brings a little silver and gold. His sister even shows up and prostitutes herself to the hangman. But it's all to no avail as the executioner gleefully carries out his duty. Trust Page to create the epic version of this classic and trust Robert to match him stride for stride, while making explicit the execution, sometimes left ambiguous in earlier versions and folklores.

A white-label advance of "Gallows Pole," stereo on one side, mono on the other, offers a version eleven seconds longer than the LP take. This would seem inconsequential, but indeed those eleven seconds find Page turning in clever and arcane licks, indicative of what the band would do live across various tracks, turning relatively sober songs manic and memories of Zeppelin all the more magical.

# TANGERINE

**PAGE/3:12**

Jimmy wrote this gorgeous folk song back in the Yardbirds days after an emotional breakup (possibly with Jackie DeShannon) and revised the lyrics for the verbally spare version he was to do with Zeppelin, his handiwork marking the last time he would contribute lyrically unless in collaboration with Plant, who interprets this track as "a song of love in its most innocent stages."

The Yardbirds song, "Knowing That I'm Losing You," had been cooked up in demo form only, recorded April 4, 1968, at Columbia in New York, with the Yardbirds on their last legs. That demo is nearly identical to "Tangerine" in the verse section, but with a different melody come chorus time. Several of the lyrical lines are upcycled as well, and Jimmy reprises the solo pretty much note for note.

Like "Gallows Pole," the song (in both the Yardbirds version and the Zeppelin version) is only provisionally acoustic, Jimmy playing twelve-string and allowing electric bass, a full drum kit, and pedal steel. Even the pedal steel (Page has indicated he got the idea from Chuck Berry) was part of the original demo, recorded as part of a bank of contractual obligation songs at what would be the Yardbirds' last session.

"Tangerine" was the product of the Headley Grange sessions, with Andy Johns engineering at the East Hampshire manse and mixing the track at Olympic. The song begins with an amusing false start, which Page grew to regret. In any event, the effect is an informal coffeehouse vibe before the first Renaissance-vibe verse begins, followed by the song's romantic chorus in which Robert is supported by an irresistible musical hook and harmonic backing vocals from Jones, Bonham, and a second track of himself.

Besides the verse and the chorus, this short ballad contains a wholly different break supporting Jimmy's effect-drenched and possibly double-tracked solo, as well as a distinct outro that underscores the thought process that was put into the construction of these *III* tracks that are often considered "lightweight."

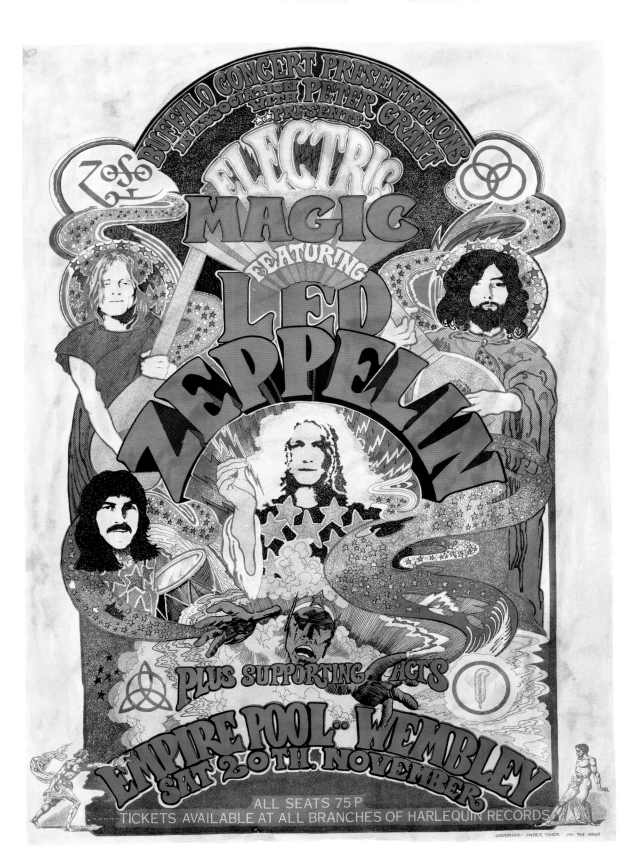

# THAT'S THE WAY

**PAGE/PLANT/5:38**

"That's the Way," the fluttery heart of *III*, might be Zeppelin's folkiest track, featuring no drums, Jones on mandolin, and Plant mostly in a delicate frame of mind and adding heavenly harmonies. Page remains fairly busy throughout the song, stringing ethereal pedal steel o'er cascading acoustic guitar tuned to G flat.

The joy of this track is elevated in the closing section, where Page adds dulcimer as a tasteful bit of tambourine from Bonham accompanies the lush acoustic strumming joined by an electric bass that almost seems an in-joke pointing out the necessity of having a loud bit in every Zeppelin softie.

Page says that the song was written at Bron-Yr-Aur after a long and tiring walk with Robert through a ravine. They had a tape recorder handy, Jimmy started playing, and Robert began adding lines off the top of his head. (Robert let slip from the stage in 1994 that Jimmy's daughter Scarlet, now a famed photographer, was conceived a half hour after they wrote the song.)

The final Plant lyric is cryptic and dense, an admirable effect achieved through simple words arranged almost disconnectedly. Robert had fans reading between the lines for meanings of varying weight and volume that touched upon an intense but ultimately forbidden love, as well as the environment and the disdain of hippie culture by authorities. The specific section about the "darker side of town" is said to be a lament about the way the band were treated when they toured in the American South, being kicked out of restaurants, threatened because of their long hair, and called drug addicts by the police. Yet another popular reading has it that the song is about two young boys who are friends, one white and one black, and how society conspires to keep their lives separate.

Page claims the song was written at Bron-Yr-Aur after a tiring walk with Robert through a ravine. This is Bron-Yr-Aur as photographed in 2014

"That's the Way" is the fluttery heart of *III*, featuring no drums, Jones on mandolin, and Plant mostly in a delicate frame of mind.

Bonzo turned the happy folk of "Bron-Y-Aur Stomp" into, well, a stomper with his bass thump and high hat work. As for the place of the song's title, Jimmy has said that the band's sojourn to Bron-Yr-Aur was the first time he got to know Robert. Here, Bonham and Page check the local music press in Hiroshima, Japan, while touring in support of *III* in September 1971.

# BRON-Y-AUR STOMP

### PAGE/PLANT/JONES/4:20

Party animal John Bonham turns this happy folkie into a kitchen party *ceilidh* classic with his simple but effecting bass thump on one and three and high hat on two and four, while Robert sings the praises of his dog Strider, one of the nicknames for Aragorn from *The Lord of the Rings*. There's also a reference to the 1933 Clyde Foley and Arthur Willis song "Old Shep," but the gist of the lyric celebrates a sensual sharing of nature as human and dog walk a country lane. There's some poetic license in calling the dog a "blue-eyed merle," as merle is a pattern in a dog's coat, sometimes with blue patches, sometimes red or brown, although the merle gene can sometimes cause blue eyes.

The title, alternate spelling notwithstanding, celebrates the idyllic country locale of the writing sessions, Bron-Yr-Aur, Welsh for "breast of gold" or "golden breast," a geographic descriptive depicting the pastoral hillside of the place. Jimmy has said that the band's sojourn there represented the first time he really got to know Robert after the hectic roadwork the band had been on virtually nonstop since forming.

For the final picked arrangement, John Bonham added spoons and castanets. There are also handclaps and harmonies—very different from the earlier, louder "Jennings Farm Blues" variant. Jones plays a five-string fretless acoustic bass, while Jimmy tuned to open D with a capo at the third fret, using his 1971 Martin D-28.

"Bron-Y-Aur Stomp" was mostly the product of the Headley Grange sessions utilizing the mobile recording unit, with additional work completed at Island and Ardent. Played live on and off as part of the band's acoustic set, sometimes with Jones on standup bass, the song ended its life as part of a medley with "Black Country Woman."

Italian promo pressing of "Bron-Y-Aur Stomp." *Voyageur Press collection*

# HATS OFF TO (ROY) HARPER

**TRAD. ARR. CHARLES OBSCURE/3:41**

This somewhat psychedelic swamp blues closer features Robert's vigorous voice in tunnel effect, achieved through a vibrato amp that he had first used for harmonica, while Page, credited with the pseudonym Charlie Obscure, plays buzzing bottleneck acoustic slide just as aggressively as Robert sings. Jones and Bonham do not appear on the track, but tambourine and backing vocals were provided by a bunch of the band's roadies, according to Plant.

The title was in dedication to Northern folkie Roy Harper, who the band met and befriended at the Bath Festival (Harper was not on the bill), with Zeppelin later using him as support act on occasion. Page admired Harper's artistic integrity and would later try to sign him to the band-run label Swan Song, a deal that fell through due to Harper's affiliation with Harvest. Page would work with Harper here and there over the years before collaborating fully on 1985's *Whatever Happened to Jugula?* Incidentally, the Bath set list, full of old blues and rock 'n' fragments, supports Page's assertions that the band was trying out at several old blues and country blues numbers to work up "Harper-style."

Page's slide work on "Hats Off," credited to "Charlie Obscure," was a tip of the hat to Bukka White's 1937 classic "Shake 'Em on Down."

Compositionally, the band was back to sending up old blues tunes in their own way, this time Bukka White's 1937 classic "Shake 'Em on Down" getting a tip of the hat (it would be revisited on "Custard Pie").

Of note, Savoy Brown covered "Shake 'Em on Down" (and loudly) on their 1967 debut *Shake Down*, with that band also crediting the song as traditional with their own arrangement. "Hats Off to (Roy) Harper," never to be performed live, is much closer to the original than Savoy Brown's, although as expected more experimental and almost nightmarish, given the deep swampiness achieved by Page and Plant.

Zeppelin met folkie Roy Harper at the Bath Festival and on occasion later used him as a support act. Page would later try to sign Harper to the band's Swan Song label.

### SIDE
# 1

**Black Dog**

**Rock and Roll**

**The Battle of Evermore**

**Stairway to Heaven**

### SIDE
# 2

**Misty Mountain Hop**

**Four Sticks**

**Going to California**

**When the Levee Breaks**

Recorded
November 1970–January 1971
Rolling Stones Mobile Studio, Headley Grange,
Hampshire, UK
Island Studios, London
Sunset Sound, Los Angeles (credited as
"Recorded at" but used for mixing only)

Release Dates
November 8, 1971 (US, SD 7208)
November 19, 1971 (UK, 2401012)

Produced by Jimmy Page
Engineer: Andy Johns

RIAA Certification: 23x Platinum
Top Billboard Position: No. 2

1971 UNTITLED

# UN**TITLED**

**ROBERT PLANT**
lead and backing
vocals, tambourine,
harmonica

**JIMMY PAGE**
guitars, mandolin

**JOHN PAUL
JONES**
bass, electric piano,
Mellotron, mandolin,
recorders, acoustic
guitar

**JOHN BONHAM**
drums

**SANDY DENNY**
vocals on "The Battle
of Evermore"

**IAN STEWART**
piano on "Rock
and Roll"

Led Zeppelin's untitled fourth album, commonly referred to as *IV* (and less often, *Zoso* or *Runes*), emerged after a time of relative career quiet, exploding like a supernova and representing the ultimate manifestation of light and shade as the band moved from the pastoral qualities of *III* into the hustle and bustle of *IV*.

After the lukewarm reception to *III*, Jimmy got it into his head that as a sort of protest, there would be no text printed over the art of the next album—no title, no song listings, not even anything on the spine. The credits on the inner sleeve were sparse as well—no performance credits, just one side featuring the mystical lyrics to a little something called "Stairway to Heaven"; on the other side, a few bones thrown to the listener, and the band members represented by symbols.

The point of all this . . . well, there wasn't much of one, but ironically, even though intended as a dismissive hand held up to the press, it gave the press something additional and mildly interesting to talk about. But another component of Plant's strategy was to let the music do the talking, and that it did. *IV* offered a canny and balanced celebration of all the music fans loved from their audacious heroes. It was *II* with more imagination and *Led Zeppelin* with *much* more imagination. Or if not exactly imagination (not even really advanced craftsmanship, given the Headley Grange grit) more like top-shelf examples of songwriting within the genre buckets Zeppelin had lined up with which to demonstrate their Moroccan-bound credo as bringers of light against shade.

And so we got folk music as committed and drum-less as anything on *III* ("The Battle of Evermore" and "Going to California"). Did radio programmers miss the hard blues songs to play deep into the morning hours? Well, there's "When the Levee Breaks" and "Four Sticks." Turn that up a notch—with Jimmy, in similarly professorial mode, proposing a heavy metal version of the blues—and you've got "Black Dog" and "Rock and Roll." That leaves "Misty Mountain Hop" as possibly the record's most creative, least derivative song, and "Stairway to Heaven" as the track that wraps up everything you loved about Led Zeppelin with a big red bow (save for the blues): namely the folk, the rock, the cryptic lyrics, the epic journey.

All of this, of course, would go over famously, *IV* becoming one of the top five greatest selling albums of all time, blowing past diamond status with twenty-three million happy customers and counting in the United States alone. Interestingly, Canada would far and away stack up as the second top market

at two million copies, and that with one-tenth the population of the United States. Everywhere else the album did fetching business, too, although the numbers were at least mortal and not so stratospheric. The lesson in the performance of this crowd-pleasing record was, again, in broad strokes, that Led Zeppelin was a British band in rapt mutual embrace with the Americas, while perpetuating the subplot of a spurning back home—said tension producing press inches, said press inches producing mythic status.

One strategy with the fourth album was to let the music do the talking—which it did. *IV* offered a canny and balanced celebration of all that music fans loved from their audacious heroes.

# BLACK DOG

**PAGE/PLANT/JONES/4:55**

Jones's circuitous "Black Dog" riff—doubled an octave higher by Jimmy—is a corker. The band soundchecks at Oude Rai in Amsterdam on May 27, 1972.

With a scratchy bit of "Is my guitar on?" and a *Hey, hey mama*, Led Zeppelin are off to one of the most iconic openers of all time, finding the band in progressive metal mode once again, building on the brainiac power of "Celebration Day" and "Out on the Tiles" while connecting the dots to the blues through their own super-duper overhaul of Fleetwood Mac's "Oh Well" (the legendary blues band having also recorded at Headley Grange).

Jones's circuitous "Black Dog" riff—in A and E, and doubled an octave higher by Jimmy—is a corker, but it's tamed by a deceptively simple 4/4 beat out of

Bonham, who tried various fancier approaches until, realizing that the rhythmic counterpoint was more interesting, merely got out of the way and let it swagger independently. The effect is a song said to be constructed to scare off cover bands, which didn't work in the end, because every musician likes a challenge. And for the record, a challenge it is, with Bonham's screwy cymbal crash and simultaneous bass drum whack on the 2 confounding those looking for the 1.

Jimmy's guitar sound is downright rude, achieved through a voodoo combination of Gibson Les Paul, mic amp, paired Universal Audio 1176 compressor mics, and triple tracking (left, right, and middle), arriving at a distortion level that set the standard for much of the rest of this noisy record. Jimmy's solo, apparently four tracks of guitar in total, sounds quite raw and basic, but up to the challenge of the rhythmic backing, Jimmy throwing pages of hippie math at the thing—funky, buoyant, humorous, simply rocking up a storm with the best of intentions. And at 3:05, he adds a harmony to stretch the octave of Jones and his bass part.

Lyrically, this ain't Robert up to much, using as inspiration an old black Labrador retriever who hung around Headley Grange, visiting the dog next door for as much action as he could get. Nonetheless, Plant, laying down his fearless call-and-response vocal in just two takes, cooks up a sexually intense torrent of suggestiveness that matches the song's proto-metal thrust and parry.

"Black Dog" saw Atlantic thwart Peter Grant's "no singles" policy, issuing the song everywhere, but back home, allowing Grant to save some semblance of face. Backed with "Misty Mountain Hop" in the United States and issued three weeks after the album's unveiling, "Black Dog" reached No. 15 on the Billboard charts, supporting the case that there was an appetite for considerably abrasive rock in America, soon to be served by the likes of Blue Öyster Cult, Aerosmith, Kiss, Ted Nugent, and Canadian rockers Rush, who would conjure a little "Black Dog" magic on their own five-minute album opener, "Finding My Way."

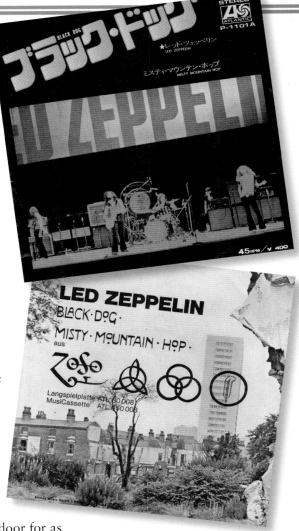

Japanese and German "Black Dog" picture sleeves.

# ROCK AND ROLL

**PAGE/PLANT/JONES/BONHAM/3:40**

Amusingly, on "Rock and Roll" as with "Black Dog," John Bonham lays down some trick drumming to weed out the posers, here at the very beginning, with his weirdly timed snare and high-hat combination, and at the end with his wind-up mini solo, a maelstrom of fill involving bass drum. The rest of the time, he's a pounding punk rocker abusing an open high hat while his heavy right foot stomps an exquisitely recorded bass drum, although, listen closely, there's a lot more bass drum than is readily apparent.

"Rock and Roll," like a half dozen Zeppelin songs before it, marries a new heavy metal sound—lots of distortion and a hint of riff—to an old blues signature, this time, a standard twelve-bar progression in A. The song practically fell out of a jam as the band was working on the quite divergent "Four Sticks." Bonham, frustrated with trying to nail the complex dirge quality of "Four Sticks," threw a percussive tantrum at Little Richard's "Keep a-Knockin'"; Page started riffing, retelling the blues for the blue jean army of the American Midwest, while Plant joined in with placeholders. It's been conjectured that Fleetwood Mac, hanging around Headley at the time, might have influenced the frenzied arrangement of "Rock and Roll" through their own hard-rocking live version of "Keep a-Knockin'"; seems possible, given the possible concurrent influence of "Oh Well" on "Black Dog."

Provisionally titled "It's Been a Long Time," the song was essentially there after a half hour's work and, given its spontaneous eruption, could only be credited to the entire band. A basic Jerry Lee Lewis piano track added by Stones adjunct Ian Stewart, who was given that band's mobile studio (a flash, camo-colored GMC) to manage whilst in service to the band at Headley

Grange, helps maintain the jamming quality of this ultimate Zeppelin rave-up.

Page's nasty guitar sound comes from a direct patch into the mixing console, allowing for no ambience and lots of cut. The aggression out of Bonham, combined with Page's nods to note density between the predictable framing rock 'n' roll chords, along with one of rock's greatest vocalists committed to pushing air (and let's face it, Robert's commitment could wane live, evidenced by most boots of this challenging song), made for a tour de force despite the song's simple structure. Also, what propels the track is Jones's punk rock eighth notes over Bonham's insanely energetic drumming. O'er top, Page mostly drapes big hanging chords, allowing us to hear the rhythm section go completely off their heads.

Lyrically, the idea is also simple, although with an interesting back story: Robert was responding to the digs that the band was too mellow on *III*, conceding, tongue-in-cheek, that it had indeed been a long time since they rock 'n' rolled.

Indeed, the one-two of "Black Dog" and "Rock and Roll," coupled with the insane market penetration of the full-length album, would do much in retrospect to file Led Zeppelin under heavy metal. In truth, hearing a band crank it like this in 1971 was actually quite a shock. Even though they would never do heavy metal often—or particularly well.

As testimony to its near peerless status in the band's canon, a rendition of "Rock and Roll" from Madison Square Garden recorded in 1973 opened the first side of the otherwise dreary *The Song Remains the Same* live album from 1976, the band's ill-advised only live spread during their '70s reign. Indeed, "Rock and Roll," issued as a single in the US in February 1972, became the band's faithful show opener in 1972, holding that pole position until 1975. In the twilight years, it became a guaranteed crowd-pleasing encore.

Page's nasty guitar sound on "Rock and Roll" comes from a direct patch into the mixing console of the Rolling Stones Mobile Studio being used at Headley Grange, resulting in no ambience and lots of cut.

# THE BATTLE OF EVERMORE

**PAGE/PLANT/5:38**

The shimmering acoustics that engulf "The Battle of Evermore" came quickly and easily, even with Jones and Page swapping their usual guitar and mandolin assignments.

The beautiful torrent of shimmering acoustics that is "The Battle of Evermore" came quickly and easily at Headley Grange, Jimmy late one evening picking up John Paul Jones's mandolin and improvising the melody on the spot using the rudimentary Earl Scruggs– and Pete Seeger–influenced fingerpicking technique he had picked up as a studio musician. Engineer Andy Johns was handy with a microphone and a Binson echo machine (also used on the drums on "When the Levee Breaks") to capture the right ambience.

Robert, on the other hand, viewing his many mouthfuls of mystical words as a "playlet" (a short dramatic piece), felt he needed another voice involved. Enter Sandy Denny, ex–Fairport Convention and Fotheringay member, and now a solo artist and friend of the band, who, singing directly with Robert, turns in the grandest cameo by anybody on a Zeppelin album.

Denny drifts out in a dreamy sort of call and response, providing a sort of slippery color commentary to a story from Robert whose lines are typically opaque with description, each not necessarily connected to the next. Robert was inspired by a book of Scottish history detailing the Anglo-Scottish wars of the fifteenth and sixteenth centuries, although he makes his tale universal by weaving a yarn about the eternal battle between night and day and all that such a story might symbolize. Interpreters have noted references and imagery from *The Lord of the Rings*, as well, including mention of the Ringwraiths and the Dark Lord, a term much less common then than it is today.

Denny, for her efforts, even gets her own symbol on the inner sleeve of the album, albeit smaller than the famous four (three inverted triangles joined at the center). And on a sleeve with scant credits, her name is prominent indeed, due to the necessity of thanking Island Records for allowing her visitation of Led Zeppelin's world.

It is interesting that John Paul Jones and Jimmy Page both demonstrate their diversity, with Jimmy playing mandolin and Jones playing acoustic guitar (Robert plays a bit, too, according to Page), creating a near constant wall of sound reinforced by the interlocking and overlapping vocals and aided by Page doubling his mandolin tracks and utilizing tape echo.

Denny passed away from a brain hemorrhage in 1978 and Zeppelin performed the song only in the spring and summer of 1977—very briskly and aggressively, with Jones struggling through Denny's part, occasionally joined by Bonham. Plant later performed "Evermore" as guest of Fairport Convention and with Alison Krauss on the duo's successful *Raising Sand* concert run (although not on the album). Page/Plant also reprised it as part of their set, bringing on British recording artist Najma Akhtar to perform the role of Denny's "town crier" or against Robert's blustery tale of battle.

Sandy Denny, ex–Fairport Convention and Fotheringay member, turns in the grandest cameo by anybody on a Zeppelin album.

# STAIRWAY TO
## HEAVEN

**PAGE/PLANT/7:55**

"Stairway to Heaven" is neither Zeppelin's most complicated song nor most original, but it's multimovement enough and bluesless enough that the emotion with which the band infuses it results in a tour de force that regularly tops polls and boozy late-night discussions as the greatest rock song of all time.

Whether you dig "Stairway to Heaven" or not, it's often the first song that comes to mind when music fans are asked to consider the greatest song-length achievement in the rock idiom, personal pick or otherwise. And, if it's any indication, the song represents the biggest-selling piece of sheet music of all time, with over a million sold to date.

But it would be remiss not to mention the controversy over the song's resemblance to "Taurus" by Spirit, or at least its descending guitar figure, one recurring part of many in "Taurus" (despite that song's two-minute brevity). Zeppelin played with Spirit, Spirit played "Taurus" live, and the Zeppelin guys expressed their admiration for Spirit, even covering the band's hard-rocking "Fresh Garbage," one of the greatest Zeppelin covers, second perhaps only to their take on Garnet Mimms's "As Long as I Have You."

OPPOSITE: Jimmy's double-neck Gibson EDS-1275—twelve strings on top, six on bottom—helped make "Stairway" possible as a live performance. Here, he's seen playing the iconic instrument at Wembley Pool in London, in November 1971, the month of *IV*'s release.

RIGHT: Robert leads the charge through the song's much vaunted zenith.

I refer to "Stairway" as having many parts to underscore the concept that the supposedly appropriated part is a fairly basic spot, along with the fact that Jimmy ends the acoustic lick at a different place than Spirit guitarist Randy California. In fact, the chord sequence in question is centuries old, *and* "Taurus" is a short instrumental distinguished by harpsichord while "Stairway" is an eight-minute song with vocals punctuated by two hard rock sections. Still, one can't be surprised that a lawsuit was brought, given the commercial enormity of "Stairway," not to mention the fact that the four measures of acoustic guitar in question and the melody they create are the song's bedrock. Regardless, in the summer of 2016, Zeppelin prevailed in the case.

The beauty of "Stairway to Heaven" is in its purposeful arrangement, introduced with Jones playing four or five tracks on wooden recorders as Jimmy's mournful and simple acoustic picking (in A minor, on his trusty Harmony, his main writing guitar through three albums and the only acoustic he used throughout *III*) frames the song quietly at first. Over it, Robert offers a solemn vocal. At the 2:12 mark, a deft increase of activity is registered when a well-behaved electric is added. Jones is not playing bass, but rather a very low-def bass part with his left hand on a Hohner ElectraPiano direct into the console, with Andy Johns adding a lot of bottom end to emphasize the effect.

It's not until 4:19 that John Bonham enters. Yet still, all we hear is a slightly more electric arrangement of the original premise, Jimmy underscoring the shift with added attack to his still laid-back electric picking. At 5:35 there's a regal break before we enter a sober rocking section. Page solos gorgeously on the '59 "Dragon" Telecaster he got from Jeff Beck, plugged into a Supro amp. Jimmy has also mentioned using his Vox Phantom and Fender Electric XII twelve-string on the song.

The final solo was the result of having to take three runs at it, more than usual, with engineer Andy Johns accusing Page of making him paranoid and vice versa. Richard Digby Smith, one of a handful of assistants in the studio, recalls watching all three takes, which were blasted loudly through big orange

"Stairway to Heaven" represents the biggest-selling piece of sheet music of all time.

Tannoy speakers, Page leaned up against one of them with his ear right, smoking a cigarette at the same time. Underneath, Bonzo impatiently massages in some muscular fills.

Even the song's much-vaunted zenith, its heavy descending chord section at 6:44 (similarities to "Babe I'm Gonna Leave You") is light on distortion, softly played by all, save for Robert who leads the charge as he moves into his upper register. His a cappella closing pronouncement is one of the most famous vocal lines in rock, a veritable statement of immortality shared in the listener's fired imagination. Technically, the song never resolves, leaving a sense of dissonance.

Lyrically, Robert began with a tale about a woman oblivious to her own greed, then quickly rolled into more mythical but also more hopeful terrain, all couched in imagery inspired by his reading of Lewis Spence, notably *Magic Arts in Celtic Britain*, but also offering wisps of imagery that might be attributed to *The Lord of the Rings*, notably the gold and the rings of smoke. Plant has mused that the abstract quality of the lyric is the reason for its popularity, saying that he still pulls new interpretations from it each time he hears it.

Begun at Bron-Yr-Aur, the song made its way through Island's large Basing Street studio to Headley Grange for additional vocals (Jimmy testified in 2016 that the acoustic intro to the song was written there as well) and back to Island for Page's solo. For Page's acoustic guitar tracks, he was near completely enclosed in a baffled box.

From the chimera of "Evermore" to the chainsaw slash of "Black Dog" and "Rock and Roll" to the bold bleed of side two, everything on *IV* is recorded with panache—save "Stairway," which sounds flat or at least conservative in comparison. But then that's what lets the song's strength shine, that strength being its insistent, measured, and serious melody. A bit too serious, it seems, for Robert, who grew to find the song pompous. In fact, he nearly refused to sing it at the fortieth anniversary of Atlantic Records in 1988. Page, on the other hand, would go on to perform "Stairway" as an instrumental, revering the track so much that he never let anyone but Robert sing it with him.

Lyrically, Robert was inspired by imagery from Lewis Spence's *Magic Arts in Celtic Britain*.

# THE HOUSE AND ITS STAIRWAY

One song looms larger than all others among the word-beaters spread all over Led Zeppelin's fourth album, and that sweeping epic is, of course, "Stairway to Heaven." Of humble genesis, the track eventually needed a more professional environment in which to realize its final five-star form.

"By the time the fourth record came along," explains Andy Johns, "it was my idea to use the [Rolling] Stones mobile, which I'd been working in with the Stones and one or two other acts. And we would go to Mick Jagger's house, Stargroves . . . which was somewhat Spartan, not a lot of furniture, but a great recording space. And Jimmy said, 'Well, how much would that cost?' And I said, 'Well, the trucks are one thousand pounds a week,' which was quite a bit of money back then. 'And then Mick's house's one thousand pounds week.' And he says, 'I'm not paying Mick Jagger one thousand pounds a week for some bloody place. I'm going to find somewhere else.' So he did. He found this sort of down-at-the-heels, old farmer's mansion-type place, Headley Grange, and I'm glad that he did."

"Headley Grange was a big cold, damp house," adds John Paul Jones. "You had very large rooms which were very echoey. You had a big stairwell, which was even more echoey. The sound on 'When the Levee Breaks' happened because Bonzo was so loud in the room we were playing in—because it had these hardwood floors—that we pushed his set out into the hall [*laughs*], into the stairwell, because the sound was smashing around all over the place. And we just stuck a couple of mics up and got this huge drum sound. So things like that came by accident. And you'd have amplifiers in the cupboards and amplifiers outside in the garden, but it was quite good fun."

"I remember 'Stairway to Heaven' was done kind of around the fire, a big fireplace, sitting around drinking cider," Jones continues. "Page had a few things worked out on the guitar. He had these different sections and he was just playing them through and I remember picking up . . . I had brought all my recorders and my bits and pieces and I picked up the bass recorder and started playing that run-down with the guitar. Then Robert started jotting a few lyrics down. It was a very organic process, as most of our music was. Somebody would start something and somebody would follow, and it would turn into something else and you would sit down and work out what sections you've got and you'd put them together. It was all very easy, very relaxed."

As for the lyrics, laughs Jones, "They seem to be right in context. I mean, nobody's quite sure what 'Stairway to Heaven' means, but it seems to fit [*laughs*]. And it probably added to the overall mysticism, the mystique that surrounded the band."

"After we had worked [at Headley Grange] for a while," continues Johns, "I took them to Island Studios, which was a very, very nice place, and I asked Jimmy, 'You know, we need to have some kind of song that is a building song, that is dramatic and has a lot of dynamics.' 'Oh, I think I've got something you might like.' And then the next Monday, whatever it was, and he comes in, and that was 'Stairway to Heaven.' Which was tracked in an unusual fashion, with drums, acoustic guitar, and John Paul Jones was playing this upright Hohner electric piano, so there was no bass.

"So I did a bunch of bottom end, so that the left hand on the electric piano would supply some kind of support for everything. And then Jones put the bass on, and I could see this was going to be quite something. And then I think Jimmy put the electric rhythm on, and then it was time for the twelve-strings. And you know, normally, Jimmy would play his twelve-strings through a Vox, and I said, 'No, no, no, let's do it direct. Because we'll get more of a pure bell-like quality.' 'Oh, all right then.' So we did that and we doubled it up, and it started to really come alive. There was a little bit of a hassle with the solo, but these days, if somebody takes half an hour for a solo, you're lucky. Back then, it was supposed to be done in two or three takes [*laughs*].

"Nothing was ever hard to get," continues Johns. "They would just come in and play, because they were all so good. There was never a struggle to get a decent groove. Like with the Stones, sometimes you would sit there for days and days and days and days, just trying to get a basic track. But they were all so very good, and Pagey had his hands on the reins, and John Paul would come up with some very nice special ideas, and off they would go, bang, and it's pretty much done. And Robert would sing, and it wouldn't be any torture at all. He would get a vocal in a couple, three takes. In fact, I remember on 'Stairway to Heaven,' we'd just about finished everything else, and John Paul had done the recorders on the beginning and the end. Robert is sitting at the back of the control room, and I said, 'Robert, it's your turn to sing.' 'Oh really? Well, I'm not finished with the lyrics. Can you play it again?' And he's scribbling away on this pad. 'Okay, I'm ready now.' And I think it was just two takes with one punch somewhere or another, done."

Gatefold to the fourth album.

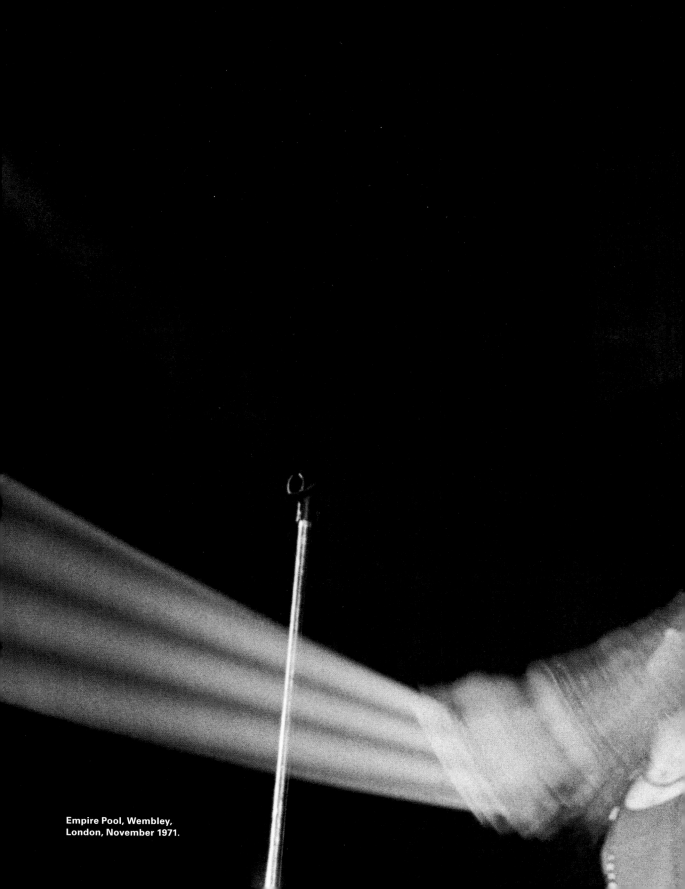

Empire Pool, Wembley,
London, November 1971.

# MISTY MOUNTAIN HOP

**PAGE/PLANT/JONES/4:39**

"Misty Mountain Hop" is another deft example of a Zeppelin track where all four members of the band shine. John Bonham turns in a tasty 4/4 groove by subtly shuffling his high-hat work and punctuating his engine room bluster with a series of memorable, thoughtful fills. Jimmy turns in a rare harmony guitar solo and then, when not harmonizing with himself, infuses solo with the idea of riff, creating singable solo sections. Robert expertly oscillates between laconic monotone and some of his most powerful high-register interjections.

Finally, John Paul Jones helps Bonzo drive the song with what Deep Purple and Rainbow bassist Roger Glover once called "teenaged eighth notes," additionally layering in a crucial Hohner ElectraPiano part. Amusingly, near the end of the song, Jones tries his hand at Jimmy's signature harmony solo part, but is harmonizing with nothing. Jones's performance here on the same instrument he used on "Stairway to Heaven" is more prominent and aggressive because "Stairway" had him plugged directly to the console; here, they captured the Hohner by miking its amp and speaker.

In fact, the central premise of the song is a harmony riff between Jimmy and John Paul, and there is an interesting rend in the fabric at approximately 2:10, where they fall out of sync but later decide that the take was too good not to be the final. Indicating that he is responsible for the verse riff, coming up with it while everybody else was sleeping, Page gives credit for the chorus to Jones. Much of this took place at Headley Grange, where it was rehearsed into shape and recorded, with mixdown taking place at Olympic.

"Misty Mountain Hop" is a beneficiary of the ambient bass and snare sound most commonly attached to discussions of "When the Levee Breaks," only adding to its heaviness. Conversely, some consider the song to represent Led Zeppelin in pop mode, which confounds in similar fashion to debate about "Living Loving Maid" somehow courting pop. In fact, "Misty Mountain Hop" is quite the rocker, thanks to its driving single-note bass line, the electric quality of the sturdy A-G-E riff, and, yes, the boomy

brashness of the drum recording—it's a wall of sound despite its strong melodic sense and prominent keys. To boot, the song should remind no one of the blues, nor is it folk.

Although the title is yet another Tolkien reference, as in *The Hobbit*'s Misty Mountains, the central premise celebrates the legalize pot rally in Hyde Park on July 7, 1968, with Robert slyly evoking the addled thought processes of a pot buzz, a reference supported by the laid-back halftime break. More generally, Robert has said the song is simply about hippies being hassled by the man in any park. Whatever the case, the narrator's mood floats like a balloon despite the gentle nudge of the authorities, culminating in a wistful and possibly rash plan to escape the city for misty mountains sure to be as smoky as they are rain-kissed.

"Misty Mountain Hop" is a prime example of each of the four members running on all cylinders. City Hall, Newcastle, England, December 1, 1972.

# FOUR STICKS

**PAGE/PLANT/4:49**

Yet another blustery heavy rocker, "Four Sticks" further helped distinguish the fourth record from the acoustic lilt of *III*. Despite the heaviness on this track, Zeppelin managed an Indian or raga vibe with the song's hypnotic circular riffs (similar in this regard to the record's previous track). Robert sings the blues over the top, an intriguing juxtaposition to the odd-time riff—a mix of 5/8 and 6/8—and John Bonham's tribal beat, achieved using four sticks (hence the title) and, according to Jimmy, two takes. And what can one accomplish with four sticks? Well, in many ways less than with two, but you can get them clacking together, which accounts for an additional texture to his performance's Indian percussion vibe.

On the literary front, Robert's lyrics, however sparse, are nonetheless rife with apocalyptic images that stop the listener in their tracks. Half of the sentiments are pure blues, as is the delivery. The result is a tension that began to take shape way back on "The Battle of Evermore" and is there through the end of the record, when a levee breaks.

"Four Sticks," a product of the Island Studios sessions, is famously the song the band was trying in vain to sort out when they took a break and spontaneously came up with "Rock and Roll." The track is also distinguished by the psychedelic effects added to Robert's voice and the extreme compression on the drums, which made for a difficult mixing job for Andy Johns.

Jimmy has said the song was supposed to be "abstract," and indeed there are challenging disconnects between the two main movements. After the rock and roil of the first movement comes the ethereal second movement, Jimmy playing both acoustic and electric John Paul Jones adds a prog rock dimension with some pastoral playing on his recently acquired EMS VCS 3 synth. With his bass part, Jones simultaneously holds the bottom end in place while adding his high central melody lick. Later still, Robert takes us out with Indian chanting to underscore the theme.

Intriguingly, "Four Sticks," along with "Friends," was worked up with an ensemble cast of local session musicians on a trip to India the following year at EMI Recording Studios on Pherozeshah Mehta Road in Mumbai (although the penultimate recording, taken back and shelved by Jimmy, was managed on a Stellavox quadrophonic field recorder the band had lugged with them). The

Robert's blues wailing is an intriguing juxtaposition to the odd-time riff—a mix of 5/8 and 6/8—and Bonham's tribal beat.

Mumbai version of "Four Sticks" includes sarangi, sitar, violin, shehnai, flute, tambura, and assorted other percussion. It was recorded as an instrumental, while "Friends" features both Jimmy playing acoustic guitar and Robert singing. "Friends" also exists as a thirty-one-minute jam, on which Jimmy can be heard coaching the musicians through the chord changes.

Page has said that the sessions fell apart due to everybody involved, including himself, getting progressively drunker as they tried to deal with this fairly elaborate music. Some confusion exists as to when the session took place, but most accounts place it as the first of the band's two 1972 visits, in March, following a tour leg that had taken them to Australia and New Zealand. The tracks were issued officially on the deluxe reissue of *Coda*, however, with liner notes placing the session on October 19, 1972.

# GOING TO CALIFORNIA

**PAGE/PLANT/3:36**

When Zeppelin went full folk on *IV*, they matched the plush recline of the most elegant moments from *III*. "Going to California" is flooded with expertly recorded acoustics from Jimmy (in DADGBD, or double drop-D tuning) along with Jones on mandolin and Robert on intimate vocals.

The song emerged from one of many late-night jam sessions at Headley Grange and would become a live favorite and anchor the band's acoustic set.

Interestingly, as with "Misty Mountain Hop," the song paints a picture of hippie ideals gone awry. While the former track does so amusingly, this one is as apocalyptic in its imagery as "Four Sticks." The song begins as hippie heavenly as could be imagined, but then descends into paranoiac shrieking and attendant visual horror. Still, Robert called it "a song about the would-be hope for the ultimate." Once again, there's this line of thinking that Robert is best remembered for his most anodyne lyrics, while weightier lines cut through the night without much reflection from Zeppelin's listening collective.

Indeed, a lot is going on here lyrically. The song, provisionally titled "Guide to California," was partially inspired by the Joni Mitchell song "California"—live, Robert was known to follow the description of a female musician in the song with a simple, "Joni." Additionally, the identification of this minstrel as a queen without a king is said to be a reference to Mitchell's 1968 song "I Had a King." The earthquake imagery is also inspired by California—in fact, when Page, Peter Grant, and Andy Johns flew to LA in February to mix the track at Sunset Sound, a minor earthquake struck the Sylmar/San Fernando area north of LA as they were descending the escalator in the airport terminal.

On the surface, the song celebrates the band's general admiration of California, with the narrator believing it to be a redemptive place of fresh starts, hopefully with a perfect hippie pixie awaiting to embrace him. Thorny omens throughout, however, hint that all is not what it seems and that the plan may not be so easily, and naïvely, fulfilled.

OPPOSITE: "Going to California" emerged from one of many late-night jam sessions at Headley Grange to become a live favorite and anchor the band's acoustic set.

ABOVE: "Going to California" was said to be partially inspired by singer-songwriter Joni Mitchell and her song "California."

# WHEN THE LEVEE BREAKS

## PAGE/PLANT/JONES/BONHAM/MEMPHIS MINNIE/7:08

OPPOSITE: "When the Levee Breaks" is *IV*'s foremost production clinic, with Jimmy adding all manner of phasing and flanging guitar effects, backward echo, and more. Due to its complicated production, it was rarely played live.

BELOW: Lyrically, "Levee" is a rather traditional retelling of the 1929 Kansas Joe McCoy and Memphis Minnie song, a copy of which Robert had in his record collection.

"When the Levee Breaks" is arguably the record's third blues song after the album's two explosive openers. As with those songs, and characteristic of a recurring credo through *I* and *II*, Led Zeppelin supercharge the idiom, here with the help of Page's semi-riffing (on a Fender electric twelve-string), but more so through Bonham's expansive and hard-hitting drum performance and the innovative recording thereof (Robert has claimed they were trying to capture the drum sound on the early Elvis Presley records!). There's also a melodic hippie rock adjunct or breakdown to what is otherwise a fairly traditional retelling (at least melodically and lyrically) of this swampy 1929 Kansas Joe and Memphis Minnie song, a copy of which Robert had in his record collection.

Lyrically, Memphis Minnie was recalling the African-American plight in the flood of 1927, when black workers near Greenville, Mississippi, were forced at gunpoint to stack sandbags against the relentless waters, which at the same time were taking away their livelihood by flooding the nearby fields.

Jimmy has called this the album's foremost production clinic, on which he added all manner of phasing and flanging guitar effects, as well as his celebrated, if subtle, backward echo technique to Robert's harmonica part, played at Island through a miked Fender Princeton amp with tremolo. Jimmy's appropriately buzzy slide parts on the nonblues adjunct were played on his Danelectro in

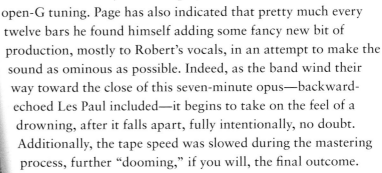

open-G tuning. Page has also indicated that pretty much every twelve bars he found himself adding some fancy new bit of production, mostly to Robert's vocals, in an attempt to make the sound as ominous as possible. Indeed, as the band wind their way toward the close of this seven-minute opus—backward-echoed Les Paul included—it begins to take on the feel of a drowning, after it falls apart, fully intentionally, no doubt. Additionally, the tape speed was slowed during the mastering process, further "dooming," if you will, the final outcome.

Due to the track's complicated assembly process, it was not subject to a mixing overhaul, as was the rest of the album, nor was it played much live.

### SIDE
# 1

**The Song Remains the Same**

**The Rain Song**

**Over the Hills and Far Away**

**The Crunge**

### SIDE
# 2

**Dancing Days**

**D'yer Mak'er**

**No Quarter**

**The Ocean**

Recorded
December 1971–August 1972
Rolling Stones Mobile Studio, Stargroves, Berkshire,
UK (omitted in official credits)
Electric Ladyland Studios, New York
Olympic Studios, London

Release Date
March 28, 1973 (US, SD 7255; UK, K 50014)

Produced by Jimmy Page
Engineered by Eddie Kramer, George Chkiantz, and Keith
Harwood

RIAA Certification: 11x Platinum
Top Billboard Position: No. 1

# 1973

# HOUSES OF THE HOLY

# HOUSES OF
## THE HOLY

**ROBERT PLANT**
vocals, backing
vocals

**JIMMY PAGE**
guitars

**JOHN PAUL
JONES**
bass, Mellotron,
synthesizer, organ,
piano, grand piano,
synthesizer piano,
synthesized bass,
backing vocals

**JOHN BONHAM**
drums, backing
vocals

With *Houses of the Holy*, Led Zeppelin found themselves confronting a very different set of circumstances regarding their place in the music industry. Call it a mature phase, call it malaise, call it distraction, call it having to compete in a crowding field—whatever it was, Led Zeppelin were about to get knocked down a peg.

The reasons are many. Let's start with the standard they set for themselves: a panicked clutch of storming, exciting records accompanied by equally ecstatic touring and tour receipts, all within a little over three years. But then came family time, less touring, a longer gap before record number five, a continuing adversarial relationship with the press, and then, at the end of this not-so-fallow period, *Houses of the Holy*.

There's no point in talking disparagingly of a record that is eleven-times platinum in the United States, or about a band that deftly transitioned from the era of low-tech, modest touring to the mass hysteria of arena and stadium rock. *Houses of the Holy* was a huge success by any standard other than Led Goddamn Zeppelin's, and the band would play out its fate for a number of years as one of perhaps five Valhalla-level bands on the planet until—they were no more.

Nor am I about to overplay the idea of a crowding field, of bands that were leapfrogging Led Zeppelin creatively. In my addled mind, Jimmy, Robert, John Paul, and Bonzo continued to trounce the competition for another full two years, and only come to sound like also-rans on any level beginning with *Presence*. Yes, begin the deluge of hate mail, but we'll address that thought in a later chapter, and maybe, just maybe, you'll see my side of it.

But back to the matter at hand. I'll defend *Houses of the Holy* as every bit an' stitch as fine a record as any Led Zeppelin album that came before it, even if that goes against what the rock critics—in general and across the spectrum—said at the time, and I suppose still maintain as a median view even today (a position they hold based largely on those dusty old reviews).

But one could see where they were coming from. The industry was seeing more records all the time against which to compare any Led Zeppelin offering, and they were getting excited about some of these newer bands. And then they were presented with "another Led Zeppelin record," which, for starters, wasn't particularly high fidelity, and then coughed up songs such as "The Crunge" and

"D'yer Mak'er." Not too sure if "The Ocean," a clumsy and behind-the-curve heavy metal stomper, was a particularly deft and creative high point either. Hippie hangover ballad "The Rain Song" was not particularly well received either.

But opener "The Song Remains the Same" is a sparkly, daring progressive metal tour de force. "No Quarter" is a dark-lorded reprise of "Dazed and Confused," and "Dancing Days" foreshadows the pan-world majesty of *Physical Graffiti*. All that's left is "Over the Hills and Far Away," on which Jimmy proves that he has more to add to his bulging hope chest of fine folk and acoustic songs, and reminds the band's established but maybe less and less adoring fans of the attention to dynamics he's always maintained in his heavy balloon of a band.

Any denigration of this record tends to focus on the arguably tossed-off quality of "The Crunge" and "D'yer Mak'er." Pretty unfair, although I think it *is* fair to begin to question the quality of the sonics presented by Led Zeppelin in 1973. In any event, fact of the matter is that pretty much the entirety of *Houses of the Holy* lives on in classic rock radio, save for "The Crunge"—that's seven long-ball, deep-horizon hits out of eight tracks. And despite the mixed reviews at the time, the inherent charm of these wildly divergent songs logically must have been obvious at the time, the proof in the pudding being the band's insane touring and sales success throughout the decade's mid-riff, before *Physical Graffiti* would summarily halt any talk of a Zeppelin in decline.

*Houses of the Holy came on the heels of more family time, a longer gap between albums, a continuing adversarial relationship with the press, and less touring. Here, the band prepares to head back on tour in 1973 with their infamous airliner, The Starship.*

# THE SONG REMAINS THE SAME

**PAGE/PLANT/5:29***

One might propose "The Song Remains the Same" as a metaphor for the *Houses of the Holy* at large, given its internal fresh variety and even its somewhat tossed-off, devil-may-care attitude. The song is art in soaring flight, a springboard for Jimmy to let fly with some of his most inventive riffing and relentless soloing, followed by an odd, yet charming marijuana haze of a breakdown in which Robert mumbles some additional love-generation-gone-wrong musings to match some of his curious turns all over *IV.*

When one considers the title from a different angle, however, there's the notion that music is music the world 'round, and it's likely doing the same unfathomable thing to people at all four corners. As Robert explained once from the stage, "During these travels we found that the people that we met, even from the Caribbean, well, the mellowness is always there if you look for it. If you give it, you get it back."

As Lester Bangs pointed out in his long review in *Creem*, this was not exactly an opportune time to start providing lyrics with Led Zeppelin albums, with many of these songs, and especially the aggressively nonsensical "The Song Remains the Same," falling short in the literary department compared, especially, to underrated songs on *IV.*

Although, granted, the lyrics were kind of an afterthought on this one, with "The Song Remains the Same" beginning life as an instrumental called "The Overture." Indeed, Robert later singled out this as one where he sorta dropped the ball. But its slipshod vibe, with its disconnected verse and white-knuckled accompaniment by Plant on the fast bits (second working title, "The Campaign"), serve almost as a lively, mischievous sprite of an introduction to the rest of the record, an energetic backslapped greeting before the guys ask you to take a seat and listen, just listen. Indeed, Page explained that the song was originally intended to serve as an instrumental opening to "The Rain Song" and that Robert liked the music so much he thought he'd better tack on some words.

OPPOSITE: "The Song Remains the Same" began life as an instrumental called "The Overture." Madison Square Garden, July 29, 1973.

For all its remarkable briskness, John Bonham plays the song quite straight, while Jones excels with a sophisticated bass line. The track came together quickly, within a day, with Jimmy utilizing a Fender twelve-string as well as his Les Paul. Robert's vocals had been "sped up," hence the thin, hysterical sound of his voice (also mixed quite back) during the thundering-along bits. Early writing took place at a rehearsal facility in Dorset, with the bulk of the recording occurring in May 1972 at Mick Jagger's Stargroves home utilizing the Rolling Stones mobile.

"The Song Remains the Same" would be a regular live standard throughout the rest of Zeppelin's run, even showing up before the album, on the band's tour of Japan in 1972, still without its final title and sometimes just called "Zep." Of course, the track's profile was raised when its title was reconstituted for the band's only live album in the 1970s and its attendant conceptual/concert film.

*Note: Timings are quoted from 2014 CD reissue, given that the original UK vinyl featured substantial errors.*

The Forum, Los Angeles, June 3, 1973.

# THE SONG *STILL* REMAINS THE SAME

Although the words are sparse and few, the premise to the showcase opener on *Houses of the Holy* is the perception that people and the music they make and the humanity expressed through that music are the same the world over. Later songs like "Kashmir" and "Achilles Last Stand" would reinforce this idea, even if they focused on exotic inspirations in a more general sense.

As Robert said years later, in a press call for one of his solo albums, his views concerning where music comes from, as expressed in "The Song Remains the Same," only deepened post-Zeppelin.

"Well, what I do is, I sort of pillage," Plant laughed. "Not in the sort of hotel rooms with unidentified members of the public so much, really, but just musically—I move through the spheres. But I do; I am drawn to the same scales, musical scales, that exist in Africa and in Arabic music, that slightly end up in the Mississippi Delta, the music of West Africa, particularly. There's something quite mournful about a lot of the modal scales that draw me in. It has an effect on me; it encourages me to write. So I don't think I'll be, you know, hopping on a plane to Beijing and recording with some guys out there. This is what music in Britain is all about. I think there's a lot of people around who are doing a lot of different stuff—these combinations of style and music are not unusual over here, so much."

And just as Robert has learned from his world travels, even his first love, a western music—the blues—came from afar.

"The thing is, you know, the Dutch and the British and the Americans were transporting Africans across to the new world, as much as they possibly could, and they brought with them the music. For example, the Africans that had been taken from Sierra Leone on the West Coast of Africa were shipped to the Georgia Sea Islands, where they could grow rice, because that was their inherent job as farmers. But they brought with them their own music, which is called Gullah music. And really, it's slightly different to the blues. And they were there also during the American Civil War, and they were left to their own devices for a long time, so they kind of kept their own traditions and their own language, patois, and that sort of thing.

"And I mean, when I was playing in Mali and in southern Morocco, I heard so much stuff. I was talking to a guy who's quite a famous musician in Mali, and very popular in Canada and the United States, from a group called Tinariwen, who said when he was working on the docks in Algiers, he thought that Western music was basically the Bee Gees. He didn't really know that there was anything else going on, because that's all he heard on the kind of radio networks that were playing Western music. But then when he heard John Lee Hooker, he went, 'Oh, but wait a

Plant: "Basically, that's what you get when you hear my songs, is what I feel. And this is down to the people that I've met, and the instances and the situations that have passed through me." Apparently, those situations sometimes involved reptiles. West Hollywood's notorious Continental "Riot House," July 1973, with Zep tour members BP Fallon (center) and Vanessa Gilbert.

minute; that's what we do.' So the awareness is quite something. And switching it over, that kind of whole mirror of music across the Atlantic is quite something. Just like Irish music and Scottish music and French music has made its way into North America and ended up in the hills and in the Blue Ridge Mountains and the Smoky Mountains in Tennessee, and with you guys in Canada. It's quite something, really. It's beautiful to have all these different cultures. Obviously, they're gonna end up in North America, because that's where the whole drive of the populace went to."

Which circles back to the theme of this remarkable song on *Houses of the Holy* . . . "I guess what I did was, I spent a lot of time traveling around using music as a sort of compass. And it's taken me to these various places, with various people. And I write a celebration and a reflection of the journey along the way. Basically, that's what you get when you hear my songs, is what I feel. And this is down to the people that I've met, and the instances and the situations that have passed through me."

# THE RAIN SONG

**PAGE/PLANT/7:39**

Perhaps crossing "Tangerine" with "Stairway to Heaven," "The Rain Song" represents Plant in egregiously romantic mode over a skilled musical ensemble expertly paced and presciently placed in the power ballad category with its long, slow build to a full-band blast (even if the volume is carried mostly by Bonham's kit). As the story goes, George Harrison had told Bonzo the problem with Zeppelin was that they never wrote any ballads. Jimmy responded by mischievously quoting The Dark Horse's "Something" in the song's first couple of chords.

Plant's lyric attached love's life cycle to that of weather and the seasons, a strong theme maintained throughout, underscoring his deliberateness. Jimmy recognized this, musing that the album, as a whole, echoed this theme, namely reflections of seasons, weather, and country. The musical track marked an uptick in fidelity from the album opener, producer Page striking deft balance between gorgeous acoustic (fret noise intact), Bonham's smart and groovy drumming, and Jones's prominent orchestral Mellotron Mark II and Steinway grand piano.

"The Rain Song," it was stated on the gatefold of the original UK vinyl, was 6:32 in length—the worst of a handful of such errors, given the track's actual 7:39 length, comparable to "Stairway to Heaven" though not as involved, given its the adherence to a couple of themes, though it includes a tasty treat of a conclusion with Jimmy's deliciously wandering acoustic wind-up building a nice bridge to the opening of the next track.

This was one of the songs that Jimmy worked on independently at his new Plumpton, England, home studio setup, built in part from the remains of the famed Pye Mobile Studio used to record the Who's *Live at Leeds* and Zeppelin's own Royal Albert Hall performance. Page plays a Danelectro on this track that was provisionally titled "Slush" due to its soft-rock textures. Bonham enters the fray with brushes, but goes on to employ both brushes and sticks.

Live, the band played the song in the sequence of the record, given its intentional relation to "The Song Remains the Same," but also because Jimmy used his double-neck Gibson EDS-1275 on both songs—the twelve-string top for the opener, the six-string lower neck for the latter. The twelve-string was tuned standard, but the six-string used an alternate tuning different from the alternate tuning used on the studio version.

OPPOSITE: "The Rain Song" followed "The Song Remains the Same" on the setlist, Jimmy employing the Gibson EDS-1275 for both: the twelve-string top for the opener, the six-string lower neck for the latter.

# OVER THE HILLS AND FAR AWAY

**PAGE/PLANT/4:50**

Like a "Ramble On" reprise, "Over the Hills and Far Away" plays to character but finds the band growing with grace, Jimmy turning in his most interesting acoustic piece yet, Robert elegant with romance, and the band finding a tasteful alloy of acoustic and electric come the heavy bits, which arrive after a dramatic yet measured build.

And with "The Rain Song" not feeling particularly acoustic, and the rest of the album somewhat raw, "Over the Hills and Far Away" represents the pinnacle of high fidelity on an album with a pretty low bar. Save for a bit of bass pedal squeak (also heard on "The Crunge" and "Dancing Days"), Bonzo's drum track is flawless, with a smart bass drum/high-hat pattern punctuating and elevating a basic rock pattern.

But what is most signature about the song is Jimmy's plush acoustic passage that opens the piece, beginning on six-string and then doubling with a twelve-string while Robert sings close and intimate. Instigated back at Bron-Yr-Aur in 1970 as "Many, Many Times" and borrowing from the Yardbirds' "White Summer," the song began appearing live as early as June 1972, albeit with Jimmy simply playing the whole thing on electric. On the studio version, in fact, Jimmy's acoustic runs right through the whole thing.

The title "Over the Hills and Far Away" was the name of an eighteenth-century English song that showed up in John Gay's *The Beggar's Opera*, as well as the title of a long Tolkien poem from 1915. Plant, of course, lightly sprinkled *Lord of the Rings* references here and there, but any commonalities with the present track are tenuous at best, even if the flowery language and timelessness of this lyric might suggest a link, perhaps to Samwise "Sam" Gamgee's oratory on his travels.

Of note is the sophisticated close where Jimmy is left to ring out with echo-drenched guitar accompanied lightly by Jones and his clavinet. As his lonely, melancholy picking fades into the distance, a pedal steel–like swell emerges, created by Jones on synth, for a second run at the ending.

"Over the Hills and Far Away," issued as the album's debut single and backed with "Dancing Days," managed a No. 51 on the US Billboard

OPPOSITE: Bonzo's drum track on "Over the Hills and Far Away" is flawless, with a smart bass drum/high-hat pattern punctuating and elevating a basic rock pattern.

chart, embedding itself into classic rock radio consciousness, along with, interestingly, pretty much every other song from the album, all regular plays but none massive hits.

As for Robert's aphorism-like wisdoms throughout, mostly about living a full and inquisitive life, the most memorable image is that he lives for his dreams and "a pocket full of gold." It is of little consequence whether he meant that he lived in part for money or that he required only a modest bit of pocket change—once he hit the stage, he made it clear that what was most important was "Acapulco gold"!

# THE CRUNGE

**BONHAM/JONES/PAGE/PLANT/3:17**

Zep got stuck in progressive rock knots for this experimental song with a sort of James Brown funk—most notably through the high-strung Jimmy Nolen–inspired guitar work. The song began as a jam based one of Bonham's most complex beats, with Jones adding the more conservative funk bass line to Bonzo's contorted herky-jerky dance, a sort of floating 9/8 beat, but with Zeppelin's famous crumpling of the math. In fact, even before Bonzo's first synchronized high-hat and bass drum whack, the casual nature of the song is reinforced by left-in studio chatter between Jimmy and engineer George Chkiantz. Playing a Fender Stratocaster, Page, like Jones, opts for straight yet uptight funk (something he'd been toying with since 1970). The guitarist has noted a slight whammy bar press at the end of each phrase, although, as he concedes, it's quite hard to detect. In any event, Page and Jones anchor a rhythm Bonham wants to upset—and Plant wants to completely ignore.

Plant mathematically growls and patters his patois, rapping an almost stream-of-conscious conversation about a buddy and then a good girl. Robert says the original plan was for him and Bonham to just go in and have an off-the-cuff conversation in their rough hometown Black Country dialect. In any event, Robert's mental musings—sans Bonzo—end with the famed *I'm just trying to find the bridge* closing sequence, whereby Plant pays tribute to Brown's common in-vocal rap about the bridge on what seems almost any given song. The added joke is that this occurs at the end, with an exasperated Plant asking, *Where's that confounded bridge?* after the music is over without anything remotely like a bridge having taken place.

There's also a nod to Otis Redding with Plant saying, *Call me Mr. Pitiful* and *respect* within a half dozen words of each other ("Respect" being the name of the Aretha Franklin classic written by and also performed by Redding). As for the title, "The Crunge" refers to a cooked-up dance one might perform to the song, with Page even musing about including instructional dance steps as part of the album's artwork.

Jones doesn't entirely sit out the creative construction, adding a simple keyboard part that is nonetheless sophisticated of arranged placement, with a little Steve Wonder vibe to it. Jones considers this one of his favorite Zeppelin tracks.

As mentioned, "The Crunge" was not a well-received selection from the record, partly because of what it is, partly because of the inclusion of a second arguably light moment, "D'yer Mak'er," and the idea that this was just too much of Zeppelin outside the box. As well, as much as people don't want to admit it, there may have been some fan and even radio industry bias against the song as sounding too black.

In fact, the song was picked as the B-side to the "D'yer Mak'er" US single release of September 17, 1973, five months after album issue. Jimmy did admit that these two tracks were perhaps "self-indulgent," but he also called them "a giggle" and "send-ups." Robert also acknowledged the songs as "flippant," but made no apologies, stating that he preferred *Houses of the Holy* to its predecessor, and that these lighthearted compositions established a basis for later efforts like "Candy Store Rock" and "Hot Dog."

"The Crunge" was played sparingly live and then mostly in medley form, with its most complete performance occurring on the 1975 US tour, when it was attempted (not always with success or certainly the smoothness of the studio version) as part of the transition between "Whole Lotta Love" and "Black Dog."

OPPOSITE: *Where's that confounded bridge?* "The Crunge" was a name ginned up for an imagined dance one might perform to the song. Page even considered including instructional dance steps as part of the album artwork. Live, it was used sparingly.

# DANCING DAYS

**PAGE/PLANT/3:43**

"Dancing Days" was the first of Led Zeppelin's great Eastern-influenced songs, this one inspired by a tune the band heard on their exploratory trip to Mumbai, but also by their visit to Japan and by the Indian music heard in Birmingham, England. Sure, the band had experimented with these mysterious melodic juxtapositions before, but now they were employing them in the context of an eyes-forward rock song every bit the equal of many on the band's forthcoming creative tour de force, *Physical Graffiti*.

Not only was the track the first from the new record played on the radio, debuting on BBC Radio five days before the album's launch, it was played live repeatedly beginning in the summer of 1972, more or less in a form matching the final version (save the lack of Jones's gorgeous keyboard part, his only use of a Farfisa VIP-255 on a Zeppelin track). "Dancing Days" was also picked as the B-side to the band's widely issued "Over the Hills and Far Away" single, the song having been so well regarded that immediately upon recording it at Stargroves, the band went outside and did a little victory dance, according to engineer Eddie Kramer.

Musically, this is Jimmy at his experimental best, creating a snaky and ethereal foreshadowing of grunge, while Bonham holds the fort with a forceful, simple beat—subtle shuffle to his high-hat work, spare bass drum, gorgeously accented the beats at song's close. Jimmy recalls recording his slide parts in the Olympic Studio One control room with his cord running to an amp situated in the studio and cranked to create a swell of room ambience. An additional number of touch-ups and double-tracking and it was done, quicker than usual. Filling out the sound, Jones adds the aforementioned innovative keyboard work much like he did on "The Crunge," while Robert turns in a laconic, monotone vocal, capturing the lazy haze of midsummer and a hippie-fried affair that may go nowhere, harassed by the heat.

On that note, the band had hoped the album would have come out in August 1972, at the conclusion of nine on-and-off months of recording, in time for "Dancing Days" to be the song of the summer. However, more work (mostly mixing and sorting out the cover, the main cause of the delays) up to the end of the year pushed the anticipated release date into 1973. A final delay of nearly seven months into March 1973 set up "Dancing Days" to be an anthem for the *following* summer, essentially a year after the band was done—and with nearly enough material for a double.

Markedly *not* summer music is the twenty-four minutes of eerie soundtrack material Jimmy would work on at his Boleskine House home, previously owned by Aleister Crowley, in November 1973 for Kenneth Anger's *Lucifer Rising* project. Jimmy's music—featuring synths, theremin, guitar, chanting, percussion, and chilling storm effects—would not be used in the final short piece, but the material has been issued in various forms over the years and is testimony to the exotic sounds of which Jimmy was capable, as evidenced on "Dancing Days," which is musically dark enough to add a sense of unease to Plant's idyllic lyric, a foretelling that the hippie era will end just as every summer does.

OPPOSITE: The first track from the new album to make the radio, "Dancing Days" featured a gorgeous keyboard part from Jones. Here, Jonesy entertains the Zep entourage aboard *The Starship* with the Boeing airliner's Thomas electric organ, July 30, 1973.

BELOW: In Yugoslavia, "Dancing Days" was offered as the B-side to "Over the Hills and Far Away."

DANCING
DAYS

LED ZEPPELIN

# D'YER MAK'ER

**BONHAM/JONES/PAGE/PLANT/4:22**

Often spoken of in strictly reggae terms, "D'yer Mak'er" began life fairly early in the album's recording process as more of a romantic '50s doo-wop song, as Page says, similar to "Poor Little Fool," Benny King–type songs, and perhaps '60s girl group Rosie & the Originals, who get a name-check on the sleeve of the first pressing.

In something of a recurring theme, a novel drum beat from Bonham caused the song to evolve in a different direction, and coupled with the band's idea of not taking the song too seriously, what resulted is a pure 1950s melody and lyric stitched to reggae, an effect that comes mostly from Page's dub-like guitar part, given that both Bonham and Jones are not exactly playing ball, nor is Robert for that matter. At the time, reggae was all the rage in the United Kingdom, intensified by the genre's biggest band, Bob Marley & the Wailers, beginning to spend a lot of time in London due to their signing with Chris Blackwell and his Island label.

The odd title for the track derives from the joke, "My wife's gone to the West Indies." "Jamaica?" "No, she went on her own."

Bonham's massive drum sound was achieved by placing three mics at a distance from his kit, resulting in a goodly amount of echo and bleed, most enjoyable on the bare fills where Bonzo made smart use of pregnant pauses. Bonham was recorded in a large semicircular glassed-in conservatory area with a wooden floor and wooden ceilings, reviving his turn in the foyer at Headley for "When the Levee Breaks"). Page's solo is amusingly underachieving, underscoring the song's aimless, no-hurry vibe.

Jones (who tinkles the ivories on the track, on top of his linear bass line) is no fan of "D'yer Mak'er," but Robert liked it so much he wanted the band to issue it as a single in the United Kingdom, an idea that was scotched in the spirit of saving face on the band's no-singles policy (by now in place on their home soil only). Despite it reaching the Top 20 in the United States, the song was never performed live in its entirety, the guys known to be thin-skinned about negative press and fan reaction to both this and "The Crunge." Page, for his part, downplayed the song's reggae feel, recognizing that you have to live it full-time to come across as authentic.

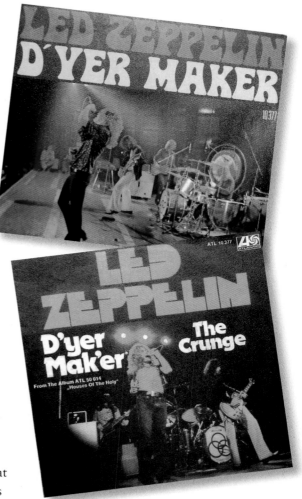

OPPOSITE: Robert liked "D'yer Mak'er" so much he wanted the band to issue it as a single in the United Kingdom, an idea that was scotched by manager Peter Grant in light of the band's no-singles policy in the UK. Plant and Grant are seen here goofing in New York City, May 7, 1974.

# NO QUARTER

JONES/PAGE/PLANT/7:02

With "No Quarter," Zeppelin evoke the brooding majesty of "Dazed and Confused," taking the listener on a long and dangerous journey of menace and doom. The song's origins go back to the Headley Grange sessions for the fourth album, where it was played slightly faster.

The sense of a psychedelic bad trip is enhanced by the song's prevalent underwater keyboard sound, achieved by Jones processing his Hohner ElectraPiano through an EMS VC53 synthesizer. Also creating the sense of foreboding are Bonham's huge drums, played slow and linked by busy high-hat work. Jimmy plays aggressively distorted and Robert's chorus effect vocals meld with the keyboard melange for additional warbly, watery atmosphere.

Each distinctly heard musical part serves the song's lyric, outlining a resolute trudge by soldiers of yore through a blizzard, against the "winds of Thor," and past howling "dogs of doom" and the mocking devil himself. A couriered message is alluded to, but the titular warning is that no mercy will be proffered or expected by either side once battle commences.

Throughout, gorgeous appointments soundtrack the epic trek, including an uncommonly jazzy solo from Jimmy, and a tour de force of musical textures from Jones, including synth washes, synth soloing, Moog Taurus pedals, and an atmospheric electric piano solo. All the while, Bonham's drums and splashy crashes have never sounded better. The band recorded "No Quarter" at Island with Andy Johns engineering. Johns also conducted the mix at Olympic (of note, Johns told me that to get the buzz out of Jimmy's guitar he used a technique similar to that used for "Black Dog," namely a couple of compressors and direct injection into the mixer). The thick sound was due in part to Jimmy slowing the entire song down using a vari-speed pitch control, a device best described as an early analog ancestor to Auto-Tune.

"No Quarter" became a perennial live favorite (played a half-step higher, to D minor), with John Paul Jones getting a rare moment in the spotlight as a pianist, along with demonstrating his other duties on this most seriously moody of *Houses of the Holy* tracks. Live, it could stretch to half an hour, with Jones offering portions of classical pieces as the crew really went to town with lighting and fog effects. The song was included both on the album and in the theatrical release of *The Song Remains the Same*. Additionally, Page and Plant named their first duo album after the track, somewhat ironically, given Jones's annoyance at not being asked to be join the project.

OPPOSITE: Gorgeous appointments adorn the epic "No Quarter," including a tour de force of musical textures from Jones and an uncommonly jazzy solo from Jimmy.

# THE OCEAN

**BONHAM/JONES/PAGE/PLANT/4:31**

Given the lack of a real heavy metal rocker on the album, it's a bit surprising that "The Ocean" was somewhat denigrated by critics, who smelled an underwritten, arguably unfinished song. True, Bonham's performance isn't much, the recording is quite raw, and perhaps the pace is a bit lumbering. But one might conjecture that without "The Ocean," *Houses of the Holy* would have been in for an additional avalanche of complaints, because, indeed, the album could use a thumper.

And fortunately, the band do buff it up a bit by tampering with time, turning in something akin to a 7/8 (or 15/8, depending on how you count) by dropping a beat on the opener and ersatz chorus (even if the verse is unarguably a stacked and blocked 4/4).

Lyrically, the central idea is that the ocean is fans at the band's shows (hence the dedication to them live). Really, it's surprising the band didn't have more songs about the live experience—anytime they did press, much of the conversation was about touring, with a dearth of introspection on the records. Of course, that would have been too ordinary. The metaphor is reinforced by the idea that the "houses of the holy" are in fact the arenas and stadiums wherein this ocean of humanity gathers. Plant also muses about singing for his own fulfilment, singing for free, singing about the mountains and the sunshine, and singing to the new girl who had won his heart, three-year-old daughter Carmen.

One provoking touch is the questionable harmony late in the sequence, purposefully pushing the boundaries of melody to give the advanced listener something to ponder. Page intimates that the idea is also utilized on "Dancing Days" and "Misty Mountain Hop."

Additional appointments are Bonham's count-in, letting us know that this is take five (although some conjecture that he's talking about the fifth album), and, at about 1:37, a ringing phone, plausible because it was recorded at Stargroves, Mick Jagger's house. Furthermore, there's an a cappella section and an old-time shuffling rock 'n' roll jam of an exit, essentially a different song, where a doo-wop gang vocal (Plant, Jones, and Bonham) serves as the album's second reference to the '50s rock that first captivated the band members.

OPPOSITE: Lyrically, "The Ocean" is a metaphor for fans at Zeppelin's shows. It's surprising the band didn't have more songs about the live experience—anytime they did press, much of the conversation was about touring and playing live, with a dearth of introspection on the records. Berlin, March 19, 1973.

SIDE

# 1

**Custard Pie**
**The Rover**
**In My Time of Dying**

SIDE

# 2

**Houses of the Holy**
**Trampled Under Foot**
**Kashmir**

SIDE

# 3

**In the Light**
**Bron-Yr-Aur**
**Down by the Seaside**
**Ten Years Gone**

SIDE

# 4

**Night Flight**
**The Wanton Song**
**Boogie with Stu**
**Black Country Woman**
**Sick Again**

Recorded
July–December 1970, January–March 1971,
May 1972, January–February 1974
Ronnie Lane's Mobile Studio, Headley Grange,
Hampshire, UK, Island Studios, London
Rolling Stones Mobile Studio, Stargroves, Berkshire, UK
Olympic Studios, London

Release Date
February 24, 1975 (US, Swan Song SS 2-200; UK, Swan Song SSK 89400)

Produced by Jimmy Page
Engineers: Ron Nevison, Andrew Johns, Eddie Kramer,
George Chkiantz, and Keith Harwood

RIAA Certification: 16x Platinum
Top Billboard Position: No. 1

1975

PHYSICAL GRAFFITI

# PHYSICAL GRAFFITI

**ROBERT PLANT**
lead vocals,
harmonica,
acoustic guitar

**JIMMY PAGE**
electric and acoustic
guitars, mandolin

**JOHN PAUL
JONES**
bass, organ, acoustic
and electric pianos,
Mellotron, mandolin,
clavinet

**JOHN BONHAM**
drums, percussion

**IAN STEWART**
piano on "Boogie
with Stu"

Lord knows I've defended *Physical Graffiti* many times as the greatest album of all time, calling it an "aircraft carrier" of a record, which I think captures the majesty and might of this collection of disparate pieces arranged to create a seamless, sophisticated whole defying deconstruction. The synergy among *Physical Graffiti*'s parts is so remarkable that only a scholarly audio detective could find reason to compartmentalize the sounds and songs featured here. Ergo, I'm not going to wax any further with hollow adjectives.

Now, to dwell on its doubleness for a moment, I'd like to add that despite having four sides, this is a record with no filler, no weak spots, and an ebb and flow of inspired creativity throughout—a fractured mirror of directions, revealing sparkly, blinding, glinting, and soft light variously throughout. Yea and verily, in terms of double trouble, I would yank the chain of *London Calling* nipping at the heels of *Physical Graffiti*, but nothing else—not *Exile*, not *The Wall*, not "The White Album," and certainly not *The River*, *Mellon Collie and the Infinite Sadness*, or *Quadrophenia*. Let's not even mention *Tusk*.

Not a point to particularly love, but a point of curio: ain't it interesting how disc one of *Physical Graffiti* is one hit after another, and record two, no hits? And can ya dig that album cover? Not by Hipgnosis this time, but groundbreaking all the same, with die cuts revealing through tenement window a tornado of life and culture. It's a visual metaphor for this record's sensual overload only. Which is not to say Robert's words of wisdom paint any pictures of the urban experience. Rather, he's untethered to any specific time or to the topical. Top-loading with a wraparound inner featuring letters spelling the title through each window. A sleeve for each record featuring windows overflowing with loud humanity. Solid credits. The name of the band carved in stone front and center. The packaging was enough to garner a Grammy nomination for its designers, Peter Corriston and Mike Doud, with 96 and 98 St. Mark's Place in New York City's East Village, the tenements pictured, becoming a silent monolith to a time when rock gods walked the earth. (Rock 'n' roll side note: the tenement steps were later the site of the Stones' video for "Waiting on a Friend," Corriston having designed the cover for that single's album, *Tattoo You*.)

Issued February 23, 1975, *Physical Graffiti* would be Led Zeppelin's first record for their new house label Swan Song, preceded by Bad Company's self-titled debut and *Silk Torpedo* by Pretty Things. Upon release, Zeppelin cemented their place in the pantheon of rock's best, a position previously claimed with the fourth, but then questioned after *Houses of the Holy*. Effusively received by the press and fans, it would go on to sell eight million copies in the United States while simultaneously dragging all five previous Zeppelin albums back into the charts. It is also Plant's favorite Led Zeppelin album, while Jimmy Page, quite correctly, described it as Led Zeppelin's "high watermark."

With *Physical Graffiti*, Led Zeppelin cemented their place in the pantheon of rock's best. Earls Court, London, May 1975.

# CUSTARD PIE

**PAGE/PLANT/4:20**

Led Zeppelin open their fifteen-song double-album feast with "Custard Pie," one of the eight fully new songs recorded in November 1973 through February 1974 with Faces bassist Ronnie Lane's Airstream-housed mobile unit set up at Headley Grange, Ron Nevison presiding as engineer.

Robert later referred to these eight songs as "the belters," and indeed all of them, save "Ten Years Gone," were at the heavy end of the spectrum, "Custard Pie" fitting that description with its pushing and shoving rhythm, its dirty guitar riff, dirty vocal (Plant had recently had an operation on his vocal cords), and even dirtier lyric.

Speaking of . . . against the spirit of the rest of this mostly modern album, Zeppelin are back to their old tricks, pastiching and parodying, paying homage to, and conflating all manner of blues idiom: Bukka White's "Shake 'Em on Down," Sonny Terry and Brownie McGhee's "Custard Pie Blues," Mississippi Fred McDowell's "Mama Don't Allow," Blind Boy Fuller's "I Want Some of Your Pie," and Sleepy John Estes's "Drop Down Mama," which in fact was the working title for this punch-up of an opener. Zeppelin even influence themselves, given the lyric's similarity to that of "Hats Off to (Roy) Harper."

But the music coursing below Plant's lascivious come-on is not blues, Zeppelin having moved beyond ("Boogie with Stu" being the exception that proves the rule, and even there, any blues rules are obscured by arrangement). Despite Page's weave with Jones' funky Hohner D6 clavinet, Plant's swampy harmonica is an additional blues touchstone, turning the song into a joyous jam at the close, Bonham smacking a few crash cymbals for good measure. Enhancing the heaviness are

the stacked, hanging chords at the end of each measure, and the fact that Robert, already gruff and extreme, is a fair way back in the mix. Page emphasizes the song's grit with a solo, the first half of which is crude and brutish wah-wah through an ARP synthesizer, before he dances circular and musical in advance of Plant beginning the next verse.

Never played fully live despite being rehearsed for the 1975 North American tour, "Custard Pie" featured in Page's later solo endeavors, surfacing on the tour for his *Outrider* album and with the Black Crowes. The song was also part of Page/Plant's set in 1996. It remains an FM rock staple to this day, like every other track on *Physical Graffiti*'s first disc.

OPPOSITE AND ABOVE: Despite a mostly modern album, Zeppelin were back to their old tricks with "Custard Pie," pastiching and paying homage to the likes of Bukka White (see page 88) and (clockwise from top) Sonny Terry and Brownie McGhee, Sleepy John Estes, Mississippi Fred McDowell, and Blind Boy Fuller.

# THE ROVER

**PAGE/PLANT/5:54**

As bald-faced a riff rocker in the mold of "The Ocean," "Whole Lotta Love," and "Communication Breakdown," "The Rover" is in fact one of the *Houses of the Holy* outtakes (recorded at Stargroves in May 1972) that would have made that record heavier. Oddly, the song began even earlier, as an acoustic track at Bron-Yr-Aur during the sessions for *III*. Still, it's inconceivable it could have landed anywhere else than right here, stuffed in the middle of *Physical Graffiti*'s side-one terrain, as the record widens and widens toward "Kashmir" before the beginning of the eventual down-winding that is side three.

Robert's lyric is anything but straightforward, however, mixing the restive world traveler, who would have fit fine on *Houses*, with the apocalyptic visions of its predecessor and the girl stuff found on all five records so far. These are presented across three different sections: first, the jet engine roar of the central E-major verse riff, the melodic two parts of the song's ersatz chorus, and then another military-grade aviation riff for a late-sequence break, Jimmy's pull-down bends deftly manipulating pitch.

All the while, Jones and Bonham propel the track with simple, muscular parts, Bonzo accenting with high-hat and bass drum combinations, while Page dances, tentatively, electric, bulked up by phase shifter and additional overdubs, including one of his most organized and memorable electric solos, flamenco in nature and a song in itself. The single-note bass lines beneath the moving guitar riffs during the verses and the bridge foreshadow how many pop and rock hits would be played from a rhythm standpoint in much of the 1980s.

Only snippets of "The Rover" were ever performed live, although it can be heard on bootleg recordings of a rehearsal in Chicago from July 6, 1973, demonstrating many Page licks, Bonham fills, and fiery Jones bass not used in the recorded version, but also its full-fledged thumping heaviness well in advance of *Physical Graffiti*.

OPPOSITE: "The Rover" was a bald-faced riff rocker in the mold of "The Ocean." Alas, these punters queuing for tickets to Zep's May 1975 Earls Court shows in London wouldn't hear the song, as it was rarely performed live.

# IN MY TIME
## OF DYING

**BONHAM/JONES/PAGE/PLANT/11:08**

Like "Custard Pie," "In My Time of Dying" finds the band pounding murky, obscure old blues ideas into something hard, shiny, and weaponable for those new, more demanding rock fans turning fifteen in 1975 and having by now heard a load of Black Sabbath, Queen, Uriah Heep, and Deep Purple. This was a new breed of aficionado for whom Jimmy's early, crude, and appropriating experiments on records like *Led Zeppelin* and *II* just didn't cut it anymore.

The result is Led Zeppelin's snakiest and most thirst-parched sonic journey—a heavy metal classic, even if quite a few minutes are spent on the same windless sea where Sabbath was stranded circa "Megalomania."

But it's an impressive example of one of the half dozen or so things Led Zeppelin did as good as or better than any other band: this creation of an epic that ebbs and flows, eschewing any sense of boredom, building (again) through light and shade, and then resolving in fine fashion à la "Stairway."

"In My Time of Dying" was recorded in February 1974 on Ronnie Lane's mobile at Headley Grange with Ron Nevison on as engineer, making it one of the "new" songs on the album; the mix was performed by Keith Harwood at Olympic. The song, played in open-E tuning, is based on a Blind Willie Johnson tune from 1927 called "Jesus Make

Up My Dying Bed," which itself was adapted from older traditional sources, Charlie Patton and even Bob Dylan having taken it on (Dylan, on his debut album, as "In My Time of Dyin'").

Jimmy's slide is critical to the hallucinatory mood of the song—he was using his trusty Danelectro for the track—but really, it's his stark heavy metal riffing in the panic section beginning at 3:45 that makes "In My Time" one of the heaviest possible Zeppelin tracks of this breed that links overtly to the British blues boom. As well, Jimmy invents a whole new melody, even if the lyric is remarkably similar to its various predecessors.

Robert, who acknowledged that the song "came from the deep south of America," wails in fine blues fashion with his newly gravelly voice, while Bonham takes up the responsibility of making sure things stay interesting, devising a number of devilish rhythms with tricky bits that build on the bass drum and high-hat interplay he used on "The Rover" and more overtly on "The Crunge." John Paul Jones plays fretless bass, but it is really Bonham who garners the most attention, given the balance of power and clarity to his sound here—this is perhaps the best example of his sound done well without any eccentricities.

"In My Time of Dying" is really, from many facets, an improvement on "Stairway"—"Stairway" on steroids, but also more creative, smarter, and wiser, at least from the musical end of things. Much the same can be said about "Kashmir," with both these long songs, and a couple others on *Physical Graffiti*, holding interest through shifts and mood, logically beginning calmly, rising to a crescendo, and then exiting in style, even if Jimmy has since let on that the closing section was more of a jam, and that the band had no idea how to finish the thing.

The actual end of the trip is signaled by a cough and subsequent studio chatter, Bonham asking, "That's gonna be the one, isn't it?" followed by "Come and have a listen then" and "Oh yes, thank you."

All told, a majestic piece of work that reminds us of Led Zeppelin's modus operandi from the beginning, but now with the benefit of much more road traveled and wisdom gained.

After Robert's near fatal car crash in August 1975, he became somewhat spooked by the lyrical content. Still, Zeppelin gamely rose to the challenge of performing "In My Time of Dying" live, and it even lived on in the solo repertoires of Robert and Jimmy.

OPPOSITE: Zeppelin gamely rose to the challenge of performing "In My Time" live. It even lived on in the solo repertoires of Robert and Jimmy. Ahoy, Rotterdam, January 11, 1975.

# HOUSES OF
# THE HOLY

**PAGE/PLANT/4:01**

A nearly indescribably display of melodic hard rock, "Houses of the Holy" supports the heavy premise of *Physical Graffiti* yet manages to be friendly at the same time, perhaps the warmest song on the album. This one came fully formed from the sessions for the album of the same name, not even requiring a remix, given its recording in May 1972 at Olympic with George Chkiantz, and the subsequent mix by Eddie Kramer at Electric Ladyland in New York City while the band were playing summer dates in the United States. One still hears Bonham's famed squeaky bass drum pedal throughout, which is more of a talking point than a distraction.

Lyrically, the track fits the preceding album's MO, with Plant once more exalting the concept of the concert venue as a place of the gods, good and bad, where romance is always possible and where one can let go, drugs and sex both being fair game. A secondary venue is the movie theater, which almost serves here as a more innocent version of the more intense and potentially corrupting concert experience. There's a reference to "Satan's daughter," which some have taken to represent woman in general, or a groupie more specifically, but I don't buy that Robert later sings *Satan and man*, which is often quoted.

Despite its being so much of the *Houses of the Holy* oeuvre, the track was left off the album apparently because of its similarity to "Dancing Days"; indeed likenesses in structure, tempo, duration, and conservative vocal delivery are apparent. Jimmy's distinct and almost clavinet-like guitar sound is said to have been achieved through use of a Lexicon/Gotham Delta-T digital delay, although some experts chalk it up to accident of mic placement, double mic placement, out of phase guitar pickups, filtering through an ARP 2600 synthesizer, or a simple flanging technique with comb filter effect. There's even the additional assertion that it might have been recorded in the bathroom. There is, however,

a consensus that he used his Fender Telecaster. Ask Jimmy about this and other effects achieved on the fly, and he says, "That's like asking me what I had for breakfast thirty years ago."

Nice touches from Bonham here include his judicious use of cowbell and his straight one-and-three bass drum thump, switching it up at bar's end for some attention to what Jimmy is playing, demonstrating his ability to play with the guitarist rather than the bassist. At close, Jones wanders with his bass line, while Jimmy turns in one of his dirty, free-spirited solos supporting the song's joie de vivre.

"Houses of the Holy" was left off the album of the same name apparently because of its similarity to "Dancing Days." Jimmy turns in one of his dirty, free-spirited solos supporting the song's *joie de vivre*. Earls Court, London, May 1975.

# TRAMPLED
## UNDER FOOT

**JONES/PAGE/PLANT/5:38**

"Trampled Under Foot," kicked off on February 24, 1974, with the working title "Brandy & Coke" after the band had completed "Ten Years Gone," represents another example of Zeppelin managing to rock hard without necessarily using all the tools. Case in point, John Paul Jones leads this one by the nose with his funky, Stevie Wonder–like D6 Clavinet riff (he credits

"Superstition" as an inspiration, as well as Billy Preston's "Outta Space"), with Bonzo's aggro performance enforcing the track's heaviness.

But Jimmy refuses to play second fiddle, strafing the song with gobs of textured wah-wah, figuring in prominently when what is essentially a relentlessly churning one-chord wonder breaks up for some interesting ascending chording. Page also utilizes backward echo, stereo panning, and a degree of reverb that, in some respects, creates a kind of vocal against Plant's performance.

It is left to Robert to remind us that Led Zeppelin began life as a transformative blues band, turning in vocals and lyrics inspired by Robert Johnson's 1936 classic "Terraplane Blues," while also channeling James Brown, his grunting and groaning egged on by Bonham. Both songs equate a hot rod of a car with a hot woman (as does "I'm in Love with My Car," issued later the same year by a band suggested as a new and improved model of Led Zeppelin, namely Queen). Robert has said his lyrics were written in about a half hour as the band was recording the music. He speaks of dashing off to his bedroom, penning feverishly behind a locked door that was subsequently smashed in because the band thought he was "up to no good."

But this is really a John Paul Jones song. Clearly not satisfied with providing just a memorable central riff, the maestro rises to some sophisticated chording for the solo, on which he adds a second Clavinet track put through a wah-wah low in the mix. Jones also plays traditional electric bass on the track, which, when this song was taken to the stage, he had to cover with bass pedals. "Trampled Under Foot" was performed on every Zeppelin tour from 1975 up to and including the band's last show on July 7, 1980, in Berlin.

"Trampled Under Foot" is experimental and yet simple enough that we can hear the band's torrid, tight performance that turns it into a heavy rocker despite what it's supposed to look like on paper: a driving song built on keys, prescient of what the band would do on *In Through the Out Door*, which in turn would pave the way for full albums by Genesis and Rush in the 1980s, not to mention things like Van Halen's "Jump."

"Trampled Under Foot" was widely issued as a single, backed with "Black Country Woman," achieving No. 38 on the Billboard charts and like roughly half the album's tracks, becoming a classic rock radio staple.

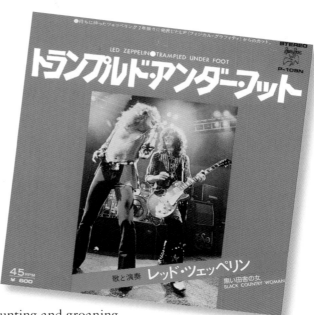

OPPOSITE: Jones leads "Trampled Under Foot" by the nose with his funky, Stevie Wonder–like D6 Clavinet riff. Bonzo's aggro performance enforces the track's heaviness.

# KASHMIR

**BONHAM/PAGE/PLANT/9:41**

Like an M. C. Escher staircase, "Kashmir," one of Led Zeppelin's most revered songs, ascends, taking the four band members with it into an exotic and rarified realm visited by few others. At minimum, what we get is an improbably chaperoned excursion to the Himalayas, via Morocco, where the spirit of this song was and still is eternally fired, along with the band's trip to India, where these melodies and the song's orchestration also reside. Plant's lyrics were penned mostly in southern Morocco, where he holidayed after the 1973 US tour, driving from Guelmim to Tan-Tan on a single-lane road that seemed infinite.

At eight-and-a-half minutes, "Kashmir" (working title "Driving to Kashmir") is a sweeping track of breadth and ambition, even more considering the slow tempo expertly harnessed and controlled by Bonham, who never overplays and makes every sparse hard-hitting fill count. Look for the reverse grace note on the bass drum every second measure. Plant, in fact, credited John and this least adorned of beats for the first spark, the opening bit of writing as it were, something generated at rehearsal that became Kashmir through "a touch of the East and a little bit of cholera on the arm."

The song was one of the new tracks recorded with Ron Nevison presiding, but the song's construction, most notably the gathering of the lyrics, stretched back three years.

Growing out of a demo by Page and Bonham, Page's repeating ascending chord pattern evokes a trudge through desert sands, as Robert reinforces the image with timeless, ancient lyricism, an effect also reinforced by the alternate D-A-D-G-A-D tuning Page utilized for "White Summer," "Black Mountain Side," and the instrumental that gave name to the band's new record label, "Swan Song."

The final touch was inventive Arabic orchestration from Jones, parts that formed complex countermelodies to the hypnotic advancement of the simple riffing, which, simple as it is by itself, interacts polyrhythmically in 3/8 against bars of 4/4 and 2/4. Plant was thoroughly intimidated by the task of finding his place inside that math, claiming to have been almost in tears as he confronted the difficult phrasing challenge and the enormity of the song's drama. In a sonic twist that perhaps plays up the desert haze of the imagery, Bonham's kit rather than the guitar is phase-shifted, courtesy of Nevison, who applied an Eventide Instant Phaser PS-1010. As if to underscore the song's enormity, the band used session string and horn players from a Pakistani orchestra in Southall, London, to fulfill Jones's vision, although John Paul himself played Mellotron Mark II, heard most prominently at the bridge's G minor and A chords.

All effects are subtle, and the arrangement measured and sensible. And like all choice Led Zeppelin epics, all within sturdy framework of four riffs the band summits a hill and descends the other side, panorama unfurling. At this point, Robert's formal and flowery lyrics have melted away and he can only implore, "Let me take you there."

"Kashmir," cited by Jimmy, Robert, and John Paul as a favorite recording, went on to become a concert favorite, played nearly every time through the remainder of the band's touring life, right up to and including their last show, July 7, 1980, in Berlin—a credit both to the band and the fans who supported such a slow drip of an abstract tale.

OPPOSITE: Cited by Jimmy, Robert, and John Paul as a favorite recording, "Kashmir" went on to become a concert favorite, played at nearly every show through the remainder of the band's touring life. Concert footage shows Page donning his Danelectro for the performances.

RIGHT: Jimmy again turned to his trusty DC 59 Danelectro, for live performances of "Kashmir."

**Ahoy, Rotterdam, January 12, 1975.** *Gijsbert Hanekroot/Redferns/Getty Images*

# RECORDING *PHYSICAL GRAFFITI*
## "WHAT TIME IS CHARLIE GETTING HERE?"

Having already cut his teeth with the Who and Bad Company, Ron Nevison suddenly found himself manning the board for the biggest band in the world. He would help whip into shape all eight of the new tracks for *Physical Graffiti*, completely unaware that there would be anything else.

"Right—I didn't actually know at the time it was going to be a double album," Nevison said. "I had just finished Bad Company's first album, and I was scheduled to do the *Tommy* film. I had done the *Quadrophenia* album with the Who. Zep had a habit of using the engineers at whatever studio they were going to as long as they were a decent engineer. I mean, they didn't take one guy with them for everything. If they went to New York, Electric Ladyland, they would use Eddie Kramer. If they were in London, Olympic, they would use this guy.

"It's interesting, they're not particularly fussy about their sound," he continued. "With them, it's all about vibe. No one ever kind of said anything to me about the drum sound or the bass drum or the guitar sound or the vocal sound that I provided them—it was all okay. Guitar players will fuss over it and get very into it. I don't remember that. I do remember when we were cutting the tracks, Jimmy Page coming in and pulling down the guitar track immediately. And at that time I thought, oh, he's embarrassed by what he played. But as I came to kind of produce, I started to realize he was doing what I do—I pulled down the scratch guitar track to make sure the drum track is solid, and so it will make it easier to put the guitars on later. He knew exactly what he wanted. That's the biggest strength. As producer, we don't always know exactly how to get there, but we know what we want, and we know what we don't want. And so getting there can be a trial and error process.

"I usually do albums start to finish," Nevison explained, "tracking, mixing, overdubs, everything like that. They would hire me, I cut the tracks, do the overdubs, make the album, the whole thing. A little different on the *Physical Graffiti* album. I was just a lowly engineer. I probably didn't make more than a hundred pounds a week when I did that album. And eventually, they just pulled out old tracks from *Houses of the Holy* and whatnot. Plus I didn't do the orchestral stuff and the mixing.

"They already had five albums and I don't remember there being any discussions about what their future might be like, or who they were compared with. They were always unique, always their own thing. You know, the interesting thing about them was that John Bonham, he just played the guitar riff. If you listen to Zeppelin, you hear him; he plays the guitar riff. And most drummers just lay time down and play with the bass player. Instead of laying down a 4/4 feel with a bass player and letting the riff kind of wander through that, whatever riff Jimmy came up with, he played that riff—and he helped create a very interesting and unique sound."

But despite Zeppelin's fecund creativity, Nevison recognized that Zeppelin was based in the blues.

"Everything to do with the musicality, well, 90 percent of it, was Jimmy Page," Nevison asserts. "I'm not saying that Jonesy didn't contribute—he certainly did—but I think Page did everything from the inception of all the riffs to presenting it to the singer, to having him write melodies and lyrics and all that kind of stuff. And, being the producer, it was all him. He was the genius, pretty much like a Townshend was the genius of the Who. Very different styles of course, but the blues aspect of it . . . you know, Jimmy was not a blues guitar player, but Jimmy had been through the blues wars. Like a Jeff Beck and all those guitar players lined up from Mayall and all the other groups."

There weren't any parties or anything thrown during recording, but that didn't mean there wasn't "partying."

Nevison recalled: "We were in Headley Grange, and it was the house I also recorded the first Bad Company album in. It was a house that we rented and took all the furniture and put it in the garage or something, and we just rolled up the mobile and started recording. There was nobody there. It was just myself, my assistant, Ron Fawcus, and the roadies. So there were like five of us and then the guys in the group. And I remember they didn't let anybody come over—no women, no anything. And we were holed up there for weeks."

Nevison: "Headley Grange . . . was a house that we rented and took all the furniture and put it in the garage or something, and we just rolled up the mobile and started recording. There was nobody there—no women, no anything. And we were holed up there for weeks."

"They're all sober at the beginning of the day," chuckled Ron when asked about Zeppelin's proclivities with substances. "You know, when I worked with Pete on *Quadrophenia*, he would start drinking a bottle of cognac at noon, and when it was empty was when we finished, like ten o'clock at night. That's the way it was in England in those days. You'd just work and break up for dinner, and then 'Charlie' would turn up. I found out later who Charlie was. Charlie wasn't anybody. Charlie was cocaine. 'What time is Charlie getting here?' I'm thinking, 'I never met this fucking guy, Charlie. Who is he?' So with Zeppelin, I just started going home at midnight and locked up the studio, because they were waking me up at four o'clock in the morning and we weren't getting anything done. So I talked to management and said, 'You know, it would be better if I locked up and went home.' And they said, 'I agree with that.'"

But then Nevison had to bow out, which just might have had something to do with the infamous liner note credit on "The Rover": "Guitar lost courtesy of Nevison. Salvaged by the grace of Harwood."

"Now, of course this [credit] came out six months or nine months after I finished working with them," Nevison began. "But the curious thing is, it's on 'The Rover,' which I didn't record. So somebody, maybe one of the engineers, said, 'Nevison must've done that' or something. But I did not record 'The Rover.' It was part of the recordings that were done."

"But here's the thing," he continued, thickening the plot. "I didn't get to finish it, which is a shame, but I had to leave the project. They had me for a certain time. For the fall of '74, I believe it was, and then in January I was supposed to start on the *Tommy* film, which was like a whole year project. And with Zeppelin, sometime during the fall of '74, we went out to the studio, to the house, and we were supposed to start cutting tracks, and Jonesy had some type of problem. Now I've later heard that he quit the group. But I don't know how credible that is. I was just told that he had a personal problem, right? And so we just hung around for a couple of weeks and just . . . I don't know what we did, but we recorded a bunch of songs, Elvis songs and stuff, just messing around. And I got the feeling that they were expecting him at any time, but he never turned up and we finally had to go home.

"The reason I'm telling you is that there was this delay and then I had to [leave the project]. And I remember them calling me up pissed-off and screaming at me like, 'You motherfucker, fuck you, you fucking . . .' And you know, what can I say? That might be why they said I lost a guitar. I guess nobody had ever quit Led Zeppelin before."

# IN THE LIGHT

**JONES/PAGE/PLANT/8:46**

As we move to *Physical Graffiti*'s second disc, darkness falls, slightly more intensely than it did with "In My Time of Dying," but more intensely nonetheless. Before the titular light breaks late in the story, this is arguably the creepiest song in the Zeppelin catalogue. Even in its final state—what with Jones' ominous drones, Plant's anguished wails, and, once the band shuffles in, Sabbath-like doom—the guys dialed back the creepiness from that of the tabled original version, called "Everybody Makes It Through" (available on the 2015 expanded edition, and also known as "In the Morning" and "Take Me Home.")

Lyrically, the song is not another *Physical Graffiti* track about crossing over to the other side, but rather advice for seeing one's way through trauma, embracing change, realizing that the road traveled should be a hopeful place. Still, the music starts depressed and hopeless, incongruous with the advice on offer, advice that seems to take hold only after Robert's clarion *in the light* mantra announces a lifting of the clouds. It's a provocative construct.

The song's genesis was the domain of Jones, who used it as a synthesizer showcase, but Jimmy rises to the challenge, inspired to add multitracked bowed acoustic guitar to the intro—the final collaborative product recalls the work Jimmy had been doing for Kenneth Anger's *Lucifer Rising* film and the intro the band would craft four years hence for "In the Evening." Later in the song, Jimmy is prominent through two banks of circular doom riffs seconded by Jones while Bonham plods along, staying out of the way, a quality Jimmy was cognizant of producing, leaving proper space for the vocals.

Zeppelin never played "In the Light" live. Despite Robert wanting to take up the challenge—he was a great fan of the track, calling it the follow-up to "Stairway to Heaven"—Jones quashed the idea because he couldn't achieve the synthesizer sound he wanted onstage.

Jimmy's work on "In the Light" recalled his compositions for the Kenneth Anger film, *Lucifer Rising.*

# BRON-YR-AUR

**PAGE/2:07**

The idyllic calm before the gradual easing toward a raucous fourth and final side, "Bron-Yr-Aur" is a short fingerstyle folk instrumental—the band's shortest song, in fact—that was conjured during the Snowdonia woodshedding for Zep *III*. Jimmy intimated at the time that the piece grew out of a short passage he played during "White Summer" in his Yardbirds days. Recording took place in May 1970 at Island Studios, Andy Johns presiding as engineer, with the mix handled by Keith Harwood at Olympic.

The song's lack of production challenged, but its proper studio capture rendered it an easy decision for inclusion on *Physical Graffiti*, especially since nothing else on the record is quite this quiet. Using the same open C6 C-A-C-G-C-E tuning as the haunting "Friends," and similar to the C-G-C-G-C-E tuning on eventual *Coda* track "Poor Tom," "Bron-Yr-Aur" finds Jimmy playing his 1971 Martin D-28, leaving in all manner of fret buzz and a charming recurring rattle caused by the strings' looseness in the alternate tuning. "Bron-Yr-Aur" would be the last solo acoustic piece the band would include on one of their albums.

The title—referring to the rural Welsh cottage visited by the Plant family on summer retreats when Robert was young—rights a wrong, correcting the misspelling in *III*'s "Bron-Y-Aur Stomp." The productive visit that inspired the song almost didn't take place, with Robert pining for the band to go to California's wine country instead, though with much the same goal in mind: resting and writing in a rural environment.

"Bron-Yr-Aur" was performed during the band's 1970 US tour and resurrected for the soundtrack to *The Song Remains the Same*, playing as the band is whisked to Madison Square Garden in limos. Introducing the song live, Robert seemed to intimate that its goal was to celebrate and commit to memory a replenishing place of magical sunrises.

ABOVE: "Bron-Yr-Aur" is a short fingerstyle folk instrumental that Jimmy recorded on his 1971 Martin D-28, leaving in all manner of fret buzz. It's also the band's shortest song.

OPPOSITE: "Bron-Yr-Aur" was used to great effect in the soundtrack to *The Song Remains the Same*.

# DOWN BY
# THE SEASIDE

**PAGE/PLANT/5:15**

"Down by the Seaside" is another logical fit to *Physical Graffiti*'s languid, pensive side three, due to its softness and the fact that, like the song before it, it derives from the 1970 Bron-Yr-Aur writing sessions, where Robert actually played rhythm guitar on it. The song also has a similar assemblage history, namely recording at Island with Andy Johns and mixing at Olympic with Keith Harwood, although the full-band electric version wasn't attended to until the sessions for the fourth album.

The song is essentially framed on a country waltz, Robert affecting a slight southern accent, Page heavy on the tremolo (possibly through a Leslie speaker cabinet), along with continual clean country call-and-response licks, Jones playing a Stonesy Hohner ElectraPiano and Bonham at the bottom, turning in a gorgeous shuffle, occasionally confounding with dropped beats that Bonzo dependably makes fluid.

The song was considered substandard when it was cooked up for possible inclusion on the fourth record, but one can imagine part of that was trepidation of its country rock sound—obviously, the band's fear of weirdness had flown out the window by the time it came to do *Houses of the Holy*. Among so many rock songs, and snuggled into cozy side three, "Down by the Seaside" provides provocative contrast despite the band's reservations, particularly from Jones, who is said to have hated the song.

Debate simmers whether there is a Neil Young *Harvest* influence, or whether the title is a wink to the Canadian's "Down by the River" (not to mention Robert's twangy, nasally, and occasionally falsetto vocal). But it's no secret Robert was a fan, and all four members attended the infamous Crosby, Stills, Nash, and Young show at Wembley in 1974.

The ominous, blustery break at 2:08 finds the band collapsing into an aggressive 4/4 for nearly a full minute, wherein Jimmy introduces an additional (clean) riff, over which he solos. Before we leave it, the band rolls out a second mini-break in which the obvious chemistry between the players meets an almost Byrds-ian apex.

Lyrically, Robert applies a measured cloak of poetic obliqueness over a quiet reminder to depart the rat race (e.g., *See how they run*) and appreciate quietude, nature, and indeed congress with loved ones, singing and doing the twist, as it were. There's certainly much going on, even religious or at least pagan overtones baked into what is really a modest collection of lyrics. Plant doesn't get enough credit for the ideas he can stack up so economically.

Zeppelin never played the song live, but Robert never forgot it, performing it in duet form—and with a pretty much rewritten melody—with Tori Amos on the much-celebrated *Encomium* tribute album issued by Zeppelin's label Atlantic, in 1995.

OPPOSITE AND ABOVE: Debate simmers whether "Down by the Seaside" and Robert's nasally vocal thereon are winks to Neil Young and his song "Down by the River." It's no secret Robert was a fan and attended the infamous Crosby, Stills, Nash, and Young show at Wembley on September 14, 1974, with Zep roadie Mick Hinton (center).

# TEN YEARS GONE

**PAGE/PLANT/6:55**

A track meticulously built of disparate elements, "Ten Years Gone" puts on full display Jimmy's genius for measured, mindful song construction. Usually when a song comes together this way, its disparate passages aren't supposed to mesh so well.

And so we get a loud, pomp rock ballad with an off-to-the-side solo section and a break verging on heavy metal, at which point Robert matches Jimmy, brandishing his newly world-weary voice.

In fact, the man at the mic turns in another of his epic, cryptic, idea-packed lyrics that take the listener to a whole other realm. At the time, Robert explained that the song is about a prefame romantic interest who gave him an ultimatum: the music or her. Robert was wistful about the break, and in the song he's graciously on the fence as to whether he made the right choice, or whether, with more maturity, could have hung onto both. The mature Robert of the song knows there was never a wrong or right answer.

Working in his Plumpton home studio, Jimmy first envisioned this song as an instrumental; probably the song's most remarkable characteristic is that it rolls and roils on an orchestra of guitars and effects (mainly deft reverb, but also some phase shifting and possibly a Leslie speaker). Although it's only subtle and brief of riff, Page mostly utilized washes of chord patterns. There is also a pervasive sitar rhythm track and a sitar come solo time, although Jimmy manages to dampen any Eastern clichés (in any event, this might be electric guitar phased to sound like sitar). In all, somewhere around a dozen guitar tracks are here, yet thanks to the song's sensitive melody and pensive nature, the melange is not overbearing. Even more incredibly, each can be picked out of the sober and sensible mix.

At the rhythm end, Bonham responds to Jimmy's variety of reverb techniques with a fair amount of room reverb and a brief spot of phase shifting. His tom work and sound are subtle or, in a word, quiet, overpowered by so much ride and

crash cymbal. There's also a brief beat inversion coming out of the military snare section and, all told, a looseness to his playing that, again, is sympathetic to Jimmy's meandering, woven, and obscurely jazzy chords.

"Ten Years Gone" would be the odd-man-out mellowest of the newly minted tracks commandeered by Ron Nevison using Ronnie Lane's mobile at Headley Grange, the track having been worked on in January and February 1974. The song would be played live on the '77 US tour and then, briefly, in 1979, Jones playing acoustic guitar, most notably an Andy Manson–constructed triple-neck that included six-string at bottom, twelve-string in the middle, and a mandolin up top. With the addition of bass pedals, he'd take care of his usual end of the bargain, now that he had his hands full.

Zep added "Ten Years Gone" to their 1977 US set list, Jones playing an Andy Manson triple-neck—six-string at bottom, twelve-string in the middle, and a mandolin up top. Madison Square Garden, June 14, 1977.

# NIGHT FLIGHT

**JONES/PAGE/PLANT/3:37**

Zeppelin open an action-packed side four of *Physical Graffiti* with a bright, poppy, and accessible short-snapper made almost self-deprecating by a modest boogie that eventually takes over the song. Jones's keyboard work during this section evokes that of Garth Hudson and subtly we've left the modernity of the verse section for something olden and beholden to the Band and maybe the Stones.

In fact Jones, main writer of the track, is prominent throughout, using a slightly distorted Hammond C3 through a Leslie and adding cloud-breaking organ to the verse section, while his buoyant bass line features an octave leap, lending a nice congruence to Bonham's simple fills and signature high-hat pattern, which actually opens the song (at 2:36, John turns in some of his celebrated open/close high-hat punctuations). Oddly, there's no guitar solo, but Jimmy's parts are interesting enough, given that he's pumped through a whirling Leslie speaker.

Recorded in January 1971, "Night Flight" was a carryover from the Andy Johns/Headley Grange sessions for the fourth album—the mind boggles to think where this might have sat in *IV*'s sequence, or what it might have replaced, if it had made the grade. In any event, this recording date accounts for Robert's hugely powerful and confident vocal, given that 1971 was arguably Plant at his peak.

Plant is also is sophisticated of phrasing here, massaging mouthfuls of inscrutable phrases that add up to, says Plant, a song about a lad being marched off to Vietnam. Enigmatically, neither the music nor the lyrics are sad, thus communicating hope that all will be all right (a darker reading might be duped naïveté).

The band never played "Night Flight" live, but one can hear the band considering it with a punchy, goofy soundcheck recording from Chicago, July 6, 1973. Of note, a bootleg recording of the song that includes additional doo-wop backup vocals during the middle boogie-woogie section, a campy touch dropped from the final version.

OPPOSITE: The mind boggles to think where "Night Flight" might have sat in *IV*'s sequence had it made the grade. The January 1971 recording date accounts for Robert's hugely powerful and confident vocal. Empire Pool, Wembley, London, November 1971.

# THE WANTON SONG

**PAGE/PLANT/4:10**

One of Led Zeppelin's most pointedly heavy metal tracks and another Robert Plant favorite, "The Wanton Song" is all overdrive and electric fire, with Page riffing maniacally and Jones in hard rock unison while Plant turns on a harrowing, distant, hoarse vocal, overwhelmed by the precision of the musical tour de force around him, howling in the night at having his energy and youth sapped by the wiles of wicked womanhood. All the while, it is Bonham who steals the show, with deft bass drum work inside the pregnant pauses where only he and Robert roam, and with lonely snare whacks memorable enough to be considered percussive "hooks."

Named "Desiree" early on, this track was one of the newer numbers caught on tape by Ron Nevison during the Headley Grange sessions, later to be added to and then mixed by Keith Harwood at Olympic. Curiously, Robert once quipped that lyrically "The Wanton Song" was just a newer version of the first song he ever wrote, the biker girl ditty "Memory Lane," back in his Band of Joy days.

The song's construct, said to be instigated by Jimmy at his Plumpton home and then banged together during soundchecks—although Robert contradicts somewhat, claiming it showing up during the recording sessions—is hard-hitting yet instantly accessible. One suspects it must have made an impression on Ritchie Blackmore and his band Rainbow, who penned the amusingly similar "Lady of the Lake" for their *Long Live Rock 'n' Roll* album two years later. In fact, the riff is so innovative and fresh that Jimmy has said he was perfectly happy the song had no chorus, that he could listen to that riff for a half hour and be "riveted and satisfied."

Extra appointments include two jazzy and harmonically sophisticated breaks, with Page utilizing diminished seventh chords. On the first, the band careens back into the riff with one of Page's most pronounced and obvious uses of backward echo. On the second, the break shifts to a strident solo section over which Page features awash in Leslie speaker effect. Again we get the backward echo before we're back for a third verse that sounds downright vengeful, Jimmy pushing himself forward in the mix by way of a subtle wah-wah effect that was not there leading up to the solo break. At 3:33, Bonzo mischievously stops the proceedings with five machine-gun snare whacks, then we're back in business. A huge,

repetitive, and clamoring windup ends the song, after which Robert lets out a painful and tormented howl.

Zeppelin came out of the gates in 1975 playing "The Wanton Song" live in both the United States and Europe but quickly dropped it from their set. It remains one of the band's purest expressions of heavy metal intent, even if the undulating and modulating secondary sections defied such confining classifications.

# BOOGIE WITH STU

**BONHAM/JONES/PAGE/PLANT/STEWART/MRS. VALENS/3:45**

The reason Van Halen as well as all manner of hair metal bands in the '80s figured it was okay to stick songs like this on their albums is that "Boogie with Stu" added a rare stroke of levity to an otherwise heavy affair, same as "D'yer Mak'er" and "The Crunge" on *Houses of the Holy*, and, slightly, "Night Flight" two songs previous.

Much of the track's Zeppelin "smarts" derive from the percussive math, with the frame being uncomfortably faithful to Ritchie Valens's "Ooh! My Head." Hence, one-quarter song credit went to Valens' mother, the seventeen-year-old having been killed fifteen years earlier in the same plane crash that took Buddy Holly. The band had been aware that Valens hadn't received any royalties from his hits. Still, the band's gesture didn't stop Valens' publisher, Kemo Music, from suing four years later, claiming that a sole songwriting credit was more in order. (Ironically, "Ooh! My Head," credited solely to Valens in 1959, had merely been a shifty remake of "Ooh! My Soul," written and recorded by Little Richard a year earlier.) The band and estate reached an out-of-court settlement.

The signature piano comes from Ian Stewart, Rolling Stones tour manager and sideman (even that term sells short his Stones contributions). Stewart's boogie-woogie is pervasive on this 1971 jam session, although Page keeps up with his country blues mandolin, while Robert strums the changes on an acoustic guitar. The discarded Sunset Sound mix features an extra mandolin passage at the beginning that was dropped for the album version; the Sunset mix also features a harsher slapback on the rhythm track.

The spontaneous jam took place as the band was setting up the Rolling Stones' mobile at Headley Grange in preparation for the sessions that would produce the fourth album. An onsite piano, according to Jimmy, was "completely unplayable," and yet Stewart was able to make it work (as he did with "Rock and Roll"). Page was additionally chuffed by the rarity of getting Stewart to record with anybody besides the Stones.

The song, at first jokingly referred to as "Sloppy Drunk," ends with Bonham left alone to his devices. As if boredom overtakes him, he complicates the song's hypnotic stomping hand-clapped and ching-ring rhythm (also said to include a later overdubbed effect created on an ARP guitar synthesizer), stopping just before a breakdown is imminent. Laughter ensues, and after a short bit of continued chatter, we are onto the next track.

OPPOSITE: The signature piano and song title come from Ian Stewart, Rolling Stones tour manager and sideman who was manning the Stones' mobile on the 1971 session.

# BLACK COUNTRY
# WOMAN

**PAGE/PLANT/4:30**

This rollicking acoustic number—working title "Never Ending Doubting Woman Blues"—was recorded in April 1972 in the backyard garden of Mick Jagger's Stargroves mansion, where the band had convened with Eddie Kramer and the Rolling Stones mobile to work on what would become the *Houses of the Holy.* "D'yer Mak'er" was recorded about the same time. Proof of the outdoor session comes at the beginning of the track, when a plane flies overhead and the guys decide to roll with it, in fact, leaving in their discussion about it. According to Kramer, birds can also be heard chirping. Plus . . . is that a ghost at 1:32? Maybe just the birds.

As for the curious working title, Robert's last exasperated gasp at the blues-dripped end of the song had been, *What's the matter with you, mama, never-ending, nagging, doubting woman blues* with the secondary bit dropped for the album version.

There is no bass guitar on the song, and Bonzo's big drums, accentuated by his high-hat work, are placed way back in the mix. Other than that, there's acoustic guitar and mandolin (Jimmy and John Paul, respectively, sitting on barstools on the lawn), plus vocals and harmonica. Jimmy is tuned to open G, giving the song a haunting vibe halfway to "Friends," although any malice is checked by Robert's earthy, broken-hearted blues vocal, the brightness of the recording, and the considerable buoyancy created by Bonham's amusingly incongruent hard rock drumming. It's an interesting track, given that Jimmy and John Paul do not fall upon many blues tropes, and yet the vocal and woman-done-me-wrong lyric are all blues, as is Robert's spirited harmonica.

"Black Country Woman" was used as the B-side to "Trampled Under Foot," issued as a single in many territories. It was played live in medley form with sister song "Bron-Y-Aur Stomp" (and once in full—Seattle, June 19, 1972), and only on the US tour of 1977, John Paul Jones plunking out his parts on an upright bass.

OPPOSITE: Another Rolling Stones connection on *Physical Graffiti*, the rollicking acoustic "Black Country Woman" was recorded in the backyard garden of Mick Jagger's Stargroves mansion, again using the Stones' mobile. When played live, Jonesy plunked out his parts on an upright bass.

# SICK AGAIN

**PAGE/PLANT/4:40**

*Physical Graffiti* ends with one of its many torrid rockers, rumbling along all bulky and complicated like "Black Dog" but more akin to "Out on the Tiles." The song pushes and shoves on note-dense E-minor and A-major riffs and rapid-fire chord changes that refuse to give up, eventually settling into a temporary groove, a bit of an amiable boogie like the non-pop parts of "Night Flight" but harder and more cynical.

Recorded in early 1974 at Headley Grange, "Sick Again" was the final track of the eight new ones that brought the total from the Ron Nevison sessions to about fifty-four minutes. The rest of the album would comprise seven songs essentially previously finished but shelved, six of them getting a Keith Harwood remix to add some semblance of leveling.

With this bitter closing number, Robert laments how young the groupies had gotten, especially in Los Angeles with the so-called "LA Queens." Shockingly to Plant, a married dad, the girl in the song is but fifteen and has had her eye on the prize since thirteen. As he intimated to Cameron Crowe back in 1975, these girls were obviously growing up too fast, which seemed somehow different to the late '60s, when there were measures of equality and innocence to such arrangements.

This is all set to a pile of brutish, pounding rock, with Bonzo going nuts and overpowering everything (note the blown shift at 3:45), the noise made all the more intrusive by the boxy mix of the drums compared to others on the record and further underscored by how far back in the mix Robert's vocal is, not that it's one of his stronger ones anyway.

And if there's periodic noise throughout, the closing jam is practically heavy metal dissonance, as the guys throw everything they've got at it, Robert ominously moaning in harmony with himself. Even Jimmy's slide is nasty, and there's a pick-scrape at the end, followed by a cough from Bonzo, a sensible reaction to the pollution billowing out of this song's tailpipes, not to mention its congruence with the title, which, almost in the spirit of added value, bears little relation to the lyrics. In truth, this sonic maëlstrom all makes sense, for this is the way bands tend to end a long and loud gig—it's like the final windmill chord to *Physical Graffiti*.

"Sick Again" was menacing and combative enough to compete with anything in the Led Zeppelin catalog and was played live on both the '75 and the '77 tours, second song in, as if to shock everybody into paying attention.

OPPOSITE: "Sick Again," Robert's lament on the dropping age of groupies, closed out *Physical Graffiti* with a pile of brutish, pounding rock. The Forum, Los Angeles, March 24, 1975.

**Jimmy attacks the theremin. Earls Court, London, May 1975.**

SIDE

# 1

**Achilles Last Stand**

**For Your Life**

**Royal Orleans**

SIDE

# 2

**Nobody's Fault but Mine**

**Candy Store Rock**

**Hots On for Nowhere**

**Tea for One**

Recorded
November–December 1975
Musicland Studios, Munich

Release Date
March 31, 1976 (US, Swan Song SS 8416; UK, Swan Song
SSK 59402)

Produced by Jimmy Page
Engineered by Keith Harwood; tape engineer Jerry Gee

RIAA Certification: 3x Platinum
Top Billboard Position: No. 1

**1976**

**PRESENCE**

# PRESENCE

**ROBERT PLANT**
lead vocals,
harmonica

**JIMMY PAGE**
guitars

**JOHN PAUL
JONES**
bass

**JOHN BONHAM**
drums, percussion

Circumstances. Even Led Zeppelin sometimes had to roll with the punches. The rushed and chaotic assemblage of the band's seventh album, issued a mere thirteen months after the double-LP *Physical Graffiti* opus, was the result of circumstances usually befallen upon mere mortals.

Given the cornucopia of riches all over *Physical Graffiti,* fans would've found it perfectly acceptable if Led Zeppelin had toured that record for two or three years. But as it turned out, Robert and every member of his family of four (plus Jimmy Page's daughter) were injured—his wife Maureen most seriously—in a car accident featuring a rented Austin Mini on the Greek isle of Rhodes on August 4, 1975. Robert emerged with a broken elbow and a seriously smashed-up foot. Today, frontmen are known to take the stage with such injuries, but in 1975, at the height of Led Zeppelin's commercial powers, it meant a canceled tour.

To keep himself from going crazy, Robert, convalescing in both Jersey in the Channel Islands and in Malibu, wrote lyrics. The band got together for three weeks at S.I.R. Studios in Hollywood and started banging the material together. But then the guys threw themselves a curveball: a self-imposed deadline that had them attempting to record a whole new record in eighteen days before the Rolling Stones were scheduled to take over Musicland Studios in Munich to begin work on what would become *Black and Blue* (although Jimmy requested and got a two-day extension from Mick Jagger).

The result was an exhausting grind involving very little sleep, especially for Jimmy, who had taken the reins, and engineer Keith Harwood. Together they would pound *Presence* together over the course of eighteen- and twenty-hour days. The following year, while mixing the Rolling Stones' *Love You Live* at Olympic Studios in London, Harwood would fall asleep at the wheel on his way home from a session and die instantly when his car hit a tree.

Robert, already depressed at having to be away from his recuperating family, had to do all his singing sitting down, and he would forever be unhappy with the results. Given that it was essentially Jimmy and Robert putting the material together, there wasn't a lot of room left for John Paul Jones to showcase his vaunted arranging and writing skills. Nor would there be a note from him on keyboards, synths, or mandolin, let alone anything crazy like string arrangements. Even John Bonham was less involved, by virtue of coming in late (and somewhat unprepared, or at least unbriefed), and unable to put his personal stamp on the new material, which, in the past, might have already been in the live set for a year or two.

So *Presence* was put together with what almost amounts to a punk rock modus operandi, especially in a world like Zeppelin's. Add to that the fact Jimmy was itching to make a rough 'n' ready hard rock record, pining for the fire from the days of *Led Zeppelin* and *II*, and what you get is a short, brutish, nasty record of rough-hewn rockers, not a keyboard in sight, and one lone acoustic guitar track, deep inside "Candy Store Rock."

Unsurprisingly, the record was somewhat panned, and at triple platinum, it's the worst-selling Led Zeppelin album outside the posthumous odds-and-sods collection, *Coda*. Rescued somewhat from obscurity (and we're talking, relative obscurity—after all, this is Zeppelin), are "Achilles Last Stand" and "Nobody's Fault but Mine," which were at least played live. The rest of the album was ignored onstage, quite out of character for the band.

But hand it to Jimmy. Even though there was no time for evolution, there definitely was an evolution in his guitar work beyond the eight new songs on *Physical Graffiti*. It was a personality that would peek out on *In Through the Out Door* and then really emerge in his work with '80s supergroup the Firm and on his *Outrider* solo album. Not so much elsewhere, not with Coverdale Page, not on *Walking into Clarksdale*, but that smog-clogged, six-string hurly-burly attitude was birthed on *Presence*, and for all the record's imperfections, fans are deeply appreciative the album exists.

Ultimately, *Presence* is a refreshingly spontaneous and simultaneously world-weary record that charms because it is the work of mere mortals coping with the human condition: Robert's accident, Jimmy's continuing fragility, exhaustion and sleep-deprivation, seemingly endless colds and flus, and the self-imposed deadline. All added the sweats to the dream that was Zeppelin, as if the guys were wondering if a nightmare would be more entertaining.

As the rock industry grew by leaps and bounds, one might suspect there existed at least a pinch of self-doubt as to where the band would fit moving forward through a field crowded with good punk, prog, and heavy metal records, many routinely going multiplatinum. The worries would be warranted, for even if Led Zeppelin ruled the rock world as a live draw through the rest of the decade, they would never again make music that attained the levels of genius witnessed over the four sides of *Physical Graffiti* and peppered throughout a back catalog beyond compare.

# ACHILLES
# LAST STAND

**PAGE/PLANT/10:26**

"Achilles Last Stand" is ten minutes of uncomfortably striving heavy metal, with suitably epic lyrics set to a galloping bass that would become the trademark of Geddy Lee, Lemmy Kilmister, and especially Steve Harris, who essentially would rewrite this song fifty times and pioneer an entire genre called power metal based on it. As a smart spot of arranging, this sharp and cutting bass is accompanied by a more traditional bass track, more elliptical and rife with pregnant pauses, simultaneously lying across the gallop and wholly independent of it.

And so there's something forced and contrived about this song, reservations related to the amount of repetition (mainly the military snare exercise and the *ooh-ooh*'s). Then again, the central riff, played on a Gibson Les Paul through a Marshall, is hard-charging and adds to the song's sense of journey. Plus, let's face it, they are beautiful parts, with the most sublime being Jimmy's opening picked *Lucifer Rising*–evocative chord that returns for the haunting close.

As for that strange bass sound, John Paul Jones was playing, with a pick, an eight-string Alembic, resulting in the aforementioned sharp gallop that serves almost as the song's guitar riff. Jones liked the instrument so much he had Alembic's Rick Turner build him a custom four-string bass, which he subsequently played on tour. Aside from this track, you won't notice John Paul Jones much for the rest of the record.

Competing for attention, however, is Jimmy, who records a veritable guitar orchestra, reviving the six-string excesses last indulged in "Ten Years Gone." Here Page uses at least six tracks of axe as well as a vari-speed pitch-control device (Jones was skeptical it would work). Jimmy put much of the overdubbing for this monster track together in one fever-pitched night while everyone else had gone off to some Munich club (the basic tracks had been laid down early in the sessions, November 12, 1975, according to the notes attached to the reference mix). Additionally, Jimmy is particularly fond of his fluid and echo-drenched solo, putting it on par with his work on "Stairway to Heaven."

Again, Robert rises above, this time under considerable pressure and physical pain, essentially touching and torching a travelogue about his travels to Morocco after the 1975 Earls Court concerts with the William Blake he was reading at the

time. Albion is a Blake reference, but it's also an ancient name for what would become England. The Atlas Mountains, which span Morocco, Algeria, and Tunisia, are also referenced, but through a nice twist, the lyric referring directly to Atlas instead, the god who held the earth on his shoulders. Within he also relates his travels in Greece, Spain, Montreux, Jersey, and California, as well as what one internalizes from travel, somewhat akin to his "The Song Remains the Same" lyric.

The working title "The Wheelchair Song" is a nod to the fairly extensive injuries to Plant's ankle, which prompted fears that he might never walk again. But the image of Robert as Achilles is a compliment as well, given that in the myth, Achilles was all-powerful, save for his heel. A further layer of meaning has Robert giving the song its final title because he had reinjured his ankle while hopping back to the vocal booth, which only served to reprise fears that this would be his last stand.

Commendably, "Achilles Last Stand" would be a concert selection at virtually every Led Zeppelin show until the band's end, which says something about the bravery of Jimmy to play a song that can't possibly include all the stacked licks and harmonies he had laced throughout the studio version.

Hammers of the gods. Day on the Green, Coliseum, Oakland, California, July 23–24, 1977.

# FOR YOUR LIFE

**PAGE/PLANT/6:21**

Well on the obscure end of Zeppelin compositions, "For Your Life," according to Jimmy, was whipped together at the studio as the band clamored to make a record in eighteen days, roughly a week less than initially planned due to a late start on the sessions. Judging from the notes attached to the reference mix version, the song was recorded November 20, 1975.

The song's lyric finds Robert bitterly shaking his head at the present-day state of the thirteen-going-on-thirty groupies, referenced in "Sick Again," who were now addicted to coke and emotionally dead. He has also intimated that the withering and world-weary denouncement applies to one acquaintance in particular and also generally to the epidemic levels of cocaine use in LA during his writing and rehearsal visit in advance of the Munich sessions. Adding to Robert's disenchantment with the LA scene were his lack of mobility due to his injury and the fact that the band was well into what would be their nine-month tax exile from England, where if they had returned home, certain portions of their incomes could be taxed at a rate of 98 percent. Adding insult to injury, Robert had to perform his vocals in a wheelchair and Musicland was freezing cold, being in a basement and given that the band were recording just as winter was taking hold. Plant called this a "sneering" track and readily admitted that it was a warning to people around him to start looking after themselves.

In any event, Robert's seemingly deliberately disjointed and blues-mumbled thoughts are set to a loping hard rock track on which Jimmy and John Paul play a fairly eventful and funky riff in unison, while Bonzo's high-hat work is nearly obscured by a continual tambourine track. Incidentally, on the *Presence* sessions John used his Ludwig Silver Sparkle drum kit, which he would replace with a Ludwig stainless-steel set for the 1977 tour, which he pounded throughout the *In Through the Out Door* sessions and up until his last concert on July 7, 1980.

The band gets progressive as the song modulates twice into a set of structured and mostly instrumental jams, even if Robert comes back—although not all the way, given his distance in the mix and his tired voice—to tell a disinterested tale of bad sex.

Jimmy's solo, played on a 1962 Lake Placid Blue Fender Stratocaster obtained from former Byrd and then–Flying Burrito Brother Gene Parsons, is screechy and ordinary, and then pushing the six-minute mark (past the cocaine-through-straw sound effect at 5:30), we're back into another verse. All that's left to ponder is Jimmy's modest suite of guitar licks and tones, including a fair bit of amusing whammy bar. An added bonus comes with the Stonesy adjunct to the riff during the last verse, as well as atonal harmonizing on the verse riff just before Robert starts singing.

"For Your Life" was never presented live during John Bonham's lifetime. However, it was to become, hands-down, the most surprising set list inclusion when Robert, Jimmy, John Paul, and Jason Bonham played their historic London O2 show in 2007.

Bonzo's high-hat work on "For Your Life" is nearly obscured by a continual tambourine track. On the *Presence* sessions, John used a Ludwig Silver Sparkle kit that he later replaced with the Ludwig stainless-steel set he pounded through his last concert.

# ROYAL ORLEANS

**BONHAM/JONES/PAGE/PLANT/2:58**

Second funky hard rocker in a row, but this time it makes sense, "Royal Orleans" being a tale about shenanigans in New Orleans, specifically the Royal Orleans hotel at the corner of Orleans and Royal in the French Quarter. Legend has it the quiet one, John Paul Jones, one night found himself back in bed at his hotel room with a he that looked like a she—"Dude (Looks Like a Lady)" indeed! The *fire preceded water* line refers to a small fire having been ignited in bed from a cigarette, which then had to be doused.

For his part, Jones cops to the entire story being (sort of) true, citing an experience from two years earlier, except that it wasn't a drag queen but a girl, whom he calls Stephanie. And the cigarette was a joint. Jones said that he had fallen asleep and the next thing he knew, the room was "full of firemen." But the band definitely hung out at gay bars, finding the people genuine and enjoying the fact that they didn't hassle the band for autographs.

In the song, the perpetrator is called John Cameron, the name of a session musician back home who was on the same circuit as Jones in his pre-Zeppelin jobbing days. Amusingly, Barry White is name-checked as well. One conspiracy theory has Robert writing the song as a dig at Jones after hearing Jones muse that the vocals are the least important part of a band.

On the musical front, this uptempo funk rocker is punctuated by military snare-patterned full stops and guitar parts intended to sound like horn parts and introducing various colors to the track as the mischievous tale steams along. In essence, it's "The Crunge" made a little more respectable, but not by much, with a party vibe that intensifies once Bonzo's bongos kick in. It could have been much sillier: the companion disc to the reissue features a version with Robert singing what Jimmy calls a "funk vocal," which is more like an impersonation of Dr. John at the bottom of a bottle of bourbon and still croaking at sunup.

"Royal Orleans" was never played live, although it enjoyed release as a picture-sleeve single in France, backed with "Candy Store Rock" (with the billing flipped for the US, Canadian, Italian, Spanish, Portuguese, German, and Japanese issues). Consistent with manager Peter Grant's insistence on treating Led Zeppelin as an album act, at least on home turf, there was no UK issue.

OPPOSITE: In "Royal Orleans," Plant famously detailed shenanigans at the New Orleans hotel of the title—all of which John Paul Jones, to his credit, copped to.

# THE DRAWING BOARD

The art and packaging for *Presence* was the second (following *Houses of the Holy*) of what would be five Led Zeppelin assignments placed in the capable hands of Aubrey Powell, Storm Thorgerson, and their legendary design firm, Hipgnosis. After *Presence*, Hipgnosis would be along for the duration, delighting fans, stirring debate, and doing much to define the Led Zeppelin mystique despite not playing a note on their records.

"Jimmy has it now, but I had the original black object," begins Powell when asked about the eerie talisman that transfixed fans blessed with the good taste to pick up a gatefold LP copy of *Presence* in the spring of 1976. "It was very different, originally. It wasn't twisted, but was very straight and very upright; a solid piece with a flat top. It was made out of cardboard with black velvet on it. I went to Munich, where they were recording, and I was in a hotel room. Jimmy and Robert came into my room, and it was sitting on a table. And Jim said, 'What's that?' And I said, 'It's the idea for your new album cover.' And then I showed him 1950s *National Geographic* pictures with [the obelisk] in every one, and he just went, 'That's it, that's it—that's the power of Led Zeppelin.' Robert said, 'Absolutely. This is awesome.'"

"Storm and I used to sit around at night, just bat ideas around about twice a week until four in the morning," Powell continues, "and we were talking about things that people need. Energy sources that people want, to drive them on. People need dogs, or cats, as something that makes them feel good. . . . And so we originally had an idea about a party where everybody had a black cat. And then we thought, oh, that's silly, we can't do that for Led Zeppelin.

"And then we thought of the black obelisk in *2001: A Space Odyssey*, but we can't do anything science fiction. That's just not appropriate for Led Zeppelin. So Storm said what about something that would be in a very ordinary family situation, that everybody needed? Without it, you couldn't function. You know, a life source that everybody had to touch or commune with. Not a religious artifact, but something that was absolutely intrinsic in order to survive. And so we came up with the black object."

"As I said, the first one was very simple," reiterates Powell, who had the pleasure of seeing one thousand individually numbered replicas ordered up by Swan Song as giveaways for the record's promotional campaign. "And when Jimmy saw it he said to me, 'You know what? Could you put a twist in it, make it slightly less obvious and sort of as though it's of the future, rather than the photographs that are stuck in the '50s?' So we went back and I got our illustrator and designer George Hardie to redraw it with a twist in it. And we painted it totally that black, so it's this completely black object with no definition. And it's intended to be like that."

And the meaning or power of the object? "Nothing—there is no meaning," Powell says. "It's abstract, it's enigmatic, it's a graphic shape—mysterious—and there is no meaning to it. Basically it's an exercise in creating something to be thought about. People would look at it and think whatever they want about it. But the real definition of it is, it's a life source. People without it can't survive. And, that's Led Zeppelin! Without Led Zeppelin, you can't live. And that's what Jimmy liked about it."

And so Hipgnosis set about placing the object among all manner of strangely eerie—and yet on the surface, mundane—life situations.

"The front cover and the back cover I re-created and shot," explains Powell. "Those backgrounds and montages. The front cover, which is of the children with the family, was shot in my studio. And the background of that, I shot at the boat show at Earls Court in London and we montaged the two things together. And then the back cover with the school kids, the young girl and boy, and with a drawing on the wall behind them, that was shot in the schoolroom. But the inside sleeve, all those wonderful sort of dated '50s pictures, were all chosen by us from photo libraries. And it was intended to look like *National Geographic*. There's a very deliberate design process. There was a great deal of thought that went behind these things, with discussions and arguments. Storm and I used to argue like mad [*laughs*]. I mean, really throwing things at each other. But we loved each other as well."

And that was it, says Aubrey, who adds that the Zeppelin guys saw it and they loved it, asking for no alterations.

"Absolutely nothing. But all our clients were like that. It was a huge trust. I mean, again, putting it in the context of the '70s . . . let's say *Dark Side of the Moon* sold what? Fifty-five million albums? There was a lot of money around. We always flew first class, we stayed in the best hotels, we worked with the band. When I was working on *The Song Remains the Same*, they were tax exiles in America, and so they put me up in a suite in the Plaza Hotel for six weeks. And I turned it into a studio so I could create all the artwork for the album cover while I was there, so they could have access to it and say, 'Okay, great, I love that.' It's not like now. If somebody does an album cover, they probably get about $3,000. In those days, it was big business and we were paid significant sums of money to work. We were treated like another artist, like the band members themselves. It was a very privileged position to be in, I'd have to say."

**Madison Square Garden, June 14, 1977.**

# NOBODY'S FAULT BUT MINE

**PAGE/PLANT/6:15**

Essentially, it fell to "Achilles Last Stand" and "Nobody's Fault but Mine," both tracks played live regularly, to carry the roughshod *Presence* album to wherever it was going to go—which wasn't far by Zeppelin standards, at a mere three times platinum.

"Nobody's Fault" is arguably the stronger track—less uptight and more natural while rocking just as heavily. Similar to "Achilles," this one leans proggy, with the inclusion of a triple-tracked, phased Eastern drone-inspired part that ties it, again like "Achilles," to Robert and Jimmy's fond memories of travels and the world music they found on their excursions.

The song's construction found Zeppelin revisiting the band's tradition of adapting, updating, and otherwise Zeppelin-izing an old standard. In this case, the considerable pedigree of the song likely reaches back before recorded music, but at least as far back as Blind Willie Johnson's "It's Nobody's Fault but Mine" from 1927, which Nina Simone semifamously covered on 1969's *Nina Simone and Piano*, where it is credited as traditional. The similarities between the Johnson and Zeppelin versions begin and end with the title and vocal melody, a vague path that can be drawn through the chord changes, and one supposes the theme, but not so much the lyric itself. Page—and most aggressively Bonham, who is big and boisterous throughout—create a steamroller of a hard rocker, both knob-jobbed better here than anywhere else on a record that suffers from what some producers might call "cocaine ears." Spirited harmonica from Robert rounds it out, underscoring the fact that, despite Page's modern riff and what is essentially a mantra oddly stitched to it, this is a dark blues lament from time immemorial.

Lyrically, there have been all manner of theories as to Plant's intentions, from lamenting the band having sold its soul to the devil and now seeing negative outcomes, to veiled admonishment of the band's continuing struggles with drink, cocaine, and even heroin (hence the "monkey on my back" reference). Plant was indeed uncommonly introspective and reflective during this time, especially toying with the guilt of having brought misfortune not only to himself, but his family.

Despite the "Crossroads"-like obscure expressions of doom, the song ultimately came out the other end as a happy times concert classic, aided by the novelty of the huge musical builds to Robert's a cappella near whispering of

the titular admission of guilt. Against this almost comical spot of quiet, Robert elsewhere turns in his strongest vocal of the album, seemingly needing a good kick in the blues to get himself out of his chair and belt it out like he could in the "Black Dog" days. As a bonus, just before the song blows out, Robert gives us one of classic rock's great stutters this side of "My Generation," Bowie's "Changes," and BTO's "You Ain't Seen Nothing Yet."

# CANDY STORE
## ROCK

**PAGE/PLANT/4:10**

Given the echo-drenched rockabilly guitar from Jimmy and Robert's nervy, itchy Elvis impression, it's easy to miss the fact that "Candy Store Rock" is one of the most complex constructions on *Presence*. And it all wells up from Bonham's mathematical, polyrhythmic beat, which is 4/4 but doesn't sound like it, and then goes legitimately off-time as it switches into the various bridge sections. Additionally, Bonham alternates between a normal ride cymbal and accents to the bell, and punctuating the beat with regular crashes mixed a fair way back.

Incredibly, this song was slammed together in about an hour, with Robert piecing together the lascivious lyrics from fragments of Elvis songs he could recall. Plant said that the vocal was inspired by Chicago singer Ral Donner, who phrased, used his vibrato, hammed, and otherwise emoted like an exaggerated Presley. It's a favorite of Robert's on the album, no surprise given he is a huge scholar of '50s rock 'n' roll.

Jimmy is a constant presence, firing off dark blues licks at will, sounding almost surf at times, and even evoking pub rock and Cramps-like rockabilly, most notably at the dangerous flick-knife opening and his hellbound train of a solo, which attacks and then quickly exits the room. And almost as a tribute to Jimmy's skiffle days, there's an urgently strummed acoustic track, the only acoustic guitars on the album. I suspect the fact that this is one of the least covered Zeppelin tracks has less to do with its obscurity or antique-y novelty and more to do with its rhythmic complexity—it's a white-knuckle ride of a song to get right, and yet it's still lacking flash.

"Candy Store Rock" was issued as a single a couple months after the album's release date, but failed to chart in the United States, a first for Zeppelin. Interestingly, though, just as early traces of "Achilles Last Stand" can be founded within jammy live versions of "Dazed and Confused," the roots of "Candy Store Rock" can be heard buried inside live versions of "Over the Hills and Far Away." Only two songs from *Presence* would be trotted out for proper in-full live performances. This throwback of a curio was not one of them.

OPPOSITE: Only two songs from *Presence* would be trotted out for proper in-full live performances. Throwback quasi-rockabilly raver "Candy Rock Store" was not one of them. Day on the Green, Coliseum, Oakland, California, July 23, 1977.

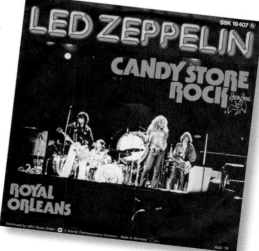

# HOTS ON FOR NOWHERE

**PAGE/PLANT/4:42**

Winding toward the end of *Presence*, things stay just as disarmingly casual and sort of garage-rocking. "Hots On for Nowhere" fits in that "For Your Life" and "Royal Orleans" zone—a seemingly spontaneous song in a funky party-rock zone navigated with more vigor and skill by Aerosmith with "Last Child" from *Rocks*, issued five weeks after *Presence* (and containing its own "Nobody's Fault," not to mention a song called "Get the Lead Out").

Bonham and Jones pretty much follow Jimmy's lead around the circular and swinging riff maypole, confounding the rhythm to keep things interesting. However, it is Robert who delivers the goods, not with his vocals, which push very little air, given the range chosen, but through his large bank of clever wordplay, a series of near aphorisms that add up to a wistful, self-deprecating, and cheery look at the concept of time. As well, the title references his restlessness to get up and get moving.

Which all feeds a theme of the album: Robert with his foot up and taking stock of everything—rock, family, the current phase of his crazy career, the hard drug scourge hitting his band and crew. The most cited line, however, *with friends who would give me fuck all*, is a complaint, specifically pointed at Jimmy and manager Peter Grant, with Robert singing "fluck all" in hopes of staying good with the censors. Still, refreshingly, "Hots On for Nowhere" finds him able to laugh about it all, very much unlike "Achilles Last Stand," "For Your Life," "Nobody's Fault but Mine," and "Tea for One." This indeed is a glimpse ahead at the grownup and reenergized Robert of his prolific solo years.

Musically, the track has its origins in the long, live "Dazed and Confused" jam, in "Walter's Walk" (unreleased at this point and therefore ripe for plunder), and in the *Physical Graffiti* sessions. But the brunt of its construction took place in about an hour in the studio, with Robert penning the lyrics beachfront in Malibu.

A trademark of the track is the recurring break in which Jimmy evokes "Dueling Banjos" on guitar. As well, Jimmy uses his blue Strat and so submits to tempting dive-bombs with its ever-ready whammy bar. Several tones and effects

Robert delivers the goods with "Hots On for Nowhere," thanks to clever wordplay and a self-deprecating, cheery look at life. Here, Robert extends his devil-may-care attitude to an unaware roadie. Madison Square Garden, New York City, June 7, 1977.

can be heard, including loads of echo, but like the rest of the album, all are pretty screechy and rough. If anything, it is Bonham who dominates, not particularly through performance, even if he strikes a nice groove, but through volume, having been placed high in the mix. He also gets to wander, offering an almost skiffle double-time beat for the last verse and throwing in some wall-of-sound triplet fills that seem too much for the modest song (at 4:19 he flubs one). Then again, the track is about not taking life too seriously, rolling with the punches.

# TEA FOR ONE

**PAGE/PLANT/9:27**

A fitting album closer, "Tea for One" represents a pensive drift toward the stillness of the turntable once the tone arm has quietly lifted and swung back and the record has stopped spinning.

It's almost as if the band has it in the back of their minds that this may be the end, and so the only thing to do is write all the way back to the blues roots where it all began. In fact, it's very much the way their last studio record, *In Through the Out Door*, ended, as if to say it was a good idea, but then we didn't stop after *Presence*, so let's do it again just in case.

Conjecture and conspiracy aside, "Tea for One" really belongs at the end of *Presence*, given that it's a traditional slow blues, albeit in C minor, that elevates it at least beyond rote into the realm of the very similar "Since I've Been Loving You" from *III*. In fact, the songs are similar and "Tea for One" breaks a loose band rule to discard songs of a sort already presented. Jimmy was well aware of the songs' similar chordal structures but was more concerned with coming up with a solo that wasn't like thousands of other blues breaks. And across the song's languid 9:27 recline (this is the band's longest blues), he offers many artful passages, even if the approach has been covered.

Oddly, the main "event" in the song is its laconic midtempo opening passage, a funky instrumental amble that collapses into wide-angled blues for the lengthy duration, comparatively a chasm of barely song-written anonymity compared to the curious opening salvo. The band recorded it in a couple of takes, according to Jimmy: one without guitar solo and one with.

Lyrically, the song supports the record's theme of isolation, Robert pining for his wife Maureen, far away due to his work and, worse, still recovering from injuries more complicated than his own. In the more abstract, Robert laments the touring life and the band's nomadic existence as tax exiles. All of this is cloaked in the sentiment of wanting time to pass and seeing it creep slowly by and with dread monotony. The idea has double meaning: sure, Robert wanted time to pass so he could get back to his injured family of four, but he also wanted his damn foot to heal so he could be the footballer and strutting rock lion he once was.

Robert has explained the title as originating from an experience he had sitting in a hotel room in New York City and sipping tea. Of course the proper

OPPOSITE: Plant with his family near their home in Wales, October 15, 1976: Maureen Wilson (center left), Karac (left), and Carmen. Lyrically, "Tea for One" supports the album's theme of isolation, Robert far from home and pining for Maureen.

English meaning of the term as a daily social occasion better suggests a sense of loneliness and homesickness, evoking dinner for one or, more pointedly, a table for one in a restaurant.

In an odd sense, "Tea for One" waves the white flag of surrender—the band's tacit awareness that *Presence* didn't stand a chance of living up to the light and shade of Led Zeppelin at their most virulent, let alone the epic force of the double album stuffed with much of the band's best material and released not a year earlier. So they end the record with over nine minutes of what, in a songwriting sense, is barely more than a jam, perhaps an admittance that the well had run dry after six rushed, contrived, underproduced songs, and that in reality, there was no seventh song to be had.

### SIDE
# 1

**In the Evening**

**South Bound Saurez**

**Fool in the Rain**

**Hot Dog**

### SIDE
# 2

**Carouselambra**

**All My Love**

**I'm Gonna Crawl**

Recorded
November–December 1978
Polar Music Studios, Stockholm

Release Date
August 15, 1979 (US, Swan Song SS 16002; UK,
Swan Song SSK 59410)

Produced by Jimmy Page
Engineer: Leif Mases; assistant engineer Lennart Östlund

RIAA Certification: 6x Platinum
Top Billboard Position: No. 1

# 1979

## IN THROUGH THE OUT DOOR

# IN THROUGH
# THE OUT DOOR

**ROBERT PLANT**
lead vocals

**JIMMY PAGE**
electric and acoustic
guitars, Gizmotron

**JOHN PAUL
JONES**
bass, mandolin,
keyboards,
synthesizer, piano

**JOHN BONHAM**
drums

Led Zeppelin limped into 1979 with John Bonham in the throes of alcoholism and Jimmy Page, always thin and never properly nourished, addicted to heroin— afflictions exacerbated by the band's continued tax exile status and the harsh and hurtful words from the home fans that ensued. But worse, tragedy had struck the Plant family on July 26, 1977, when Robert's and Maureen's son, Karac, died of a stomach virus at the age of five.

So the band entered into the idea of making a new record in just as dire a place as they had with *Presence*. Because of Jimmy's and John's problems, Jones and Plant took the reins and wrote most of what would become *In Through the Out Door*, with Page and Bonham arriving late to the sessions and then lacking the energy to keep up with the vocalist and bassist (although on this record, you might as well call Jones the conductor and keyboardist).

As John Paul told me, "There had been a low point in the band's life towards the end of the '70s. Robert had a car crash and then he lost his son. I mean, everybody was . . . they weren't particularly good times, all around. *In Through the Out Door*, I suppose, was similar, but from a different perspective. I had a new Yamaha synthesizer, a big GX-1, which was the prototype for all the other stuff they made. I just wanted to use it and play with it. And Robert and I ended up at the studio with nobody else there [*laughs*] and we had kind of more or less written the album before anybody else arrived. But then, you know, Jimmy and Bonzo did great contributions on it. And the record sounds good. But then, you know, the technology was good as well, as it was changing all the time."

Hence, Jones is the first songwriting credit on every track, save for novelty song "Hot Dog" (credited to Page and Plant). And the songs he wrote are quite sophisticated—well-arranged and keyboard-heavy—pointing to a band willing to attempt an overhaul of one of the great institutions of the '70s.

Many Zeppelin fans were horrified when they heard the record, complaining that there was very little that one would call hard rock or heavy metal. But then again, the album was a huge success, scoring six times platinum in the States— which was just in the nick of time as far as the industry was concerned. The end of the decade was a strange time in music, with punk imploding and morphing into something called post-punk in the United Kingdom and new wave in the

United States. All manner of hard rock bands were either breaking up or going pop or "pomp rock." The resulting turmoil made 1979 a recessionary year in the business, with all eyes basically looking to three bands—the Eagles, Pink Floyd, and Zeppelin—to save the numbers for the year.

Those bands would indeed do fetching business, but in Led Zeppelin's case, there was fervent discussion about whether they had gotten old and tired and in the way. And yet the record's reputation soon turned around, with ardent listeners beginning to notice that *In Through the Out Door*, by some measures, might be the best-sounding Led Zeppelin record of the catalog. Jones and his music-mad imagination brought an admirable freshness to the project. What's more, it seemed to have sparked Page out of his heroin fog, pushing him to pick his spots and make them count.

Again, one of his spots was the production. Working at Polar Music Studios in Stockholm, Page and engineer Leif Mases got some captivating sounds out of Page and his guitars, out of Jones, and even from Bonham, with these tracks, in the main, parked on frames that no other Zeppelin album can touch.

All told, when it comes to the complexion of the album, its peaks and valleys, sure, there's a joke song and a ballad that Page himself cringes at, calling it "too obvious." But the balance is highly interesting, culminating in a sensuous and sumptuous epic called "Carouselambra," which, fittingly, is a raging "love it or hate it" proposition from the band's secret weapon: Jonesy. In that respect, the song serves as microcosm for the way people view *In Through the Out Door*—whichever side of the divide people might fall on, no one can deny that Led Zeppelin was marching into the new decade willing to be transformed, willing to learn.

Because of Jimmy's and Bonzo's problems, Jones and Plant took the reins and wrote most of what would become *In Through the Out Door*—despite Plant's own recent personal tragedy. Plant and Jones confer with manager Peter Grant backstage at the Knebworth Festival, Hertfordshire, England, August 1979.

# IN THE EVENING

**JONES/PAGE/PLANT/6:48**

The first track on *In Through the Out Door* begins with something very incongruous to the direction the album would take and, indeed, even the song to which it's attached. The drone in E at the beginning of "In the Evening" is a bit of *Lucifer Rising*–type mantra that makes use of the Gizmotron effect, a "hurdy gurdy type of thing," according to Jimmy. Invented by 10cc's Lol Creme and Kevin Godley, the Gizmotron comprised a small bridge-mounted box with key-activated motor-driven wheels inside that effectively bowed the strings. Creme and Godley loaned theirs to Zeppelin, with Jimmy ruing the fact that he's never owned one since.

There's also simulated violin bow-on-guitar sounds using tremolo bar drops and the Gizmotron, as well as Bonham on his live timpanis, playing manic though mixed back single rolls while altering the head tension with a foot-operated tuning pedal. Layered in as well are bass pedals and Jones's GX-1, which Page remembers being called a Dream Machine (Stevie Wonder came up with that one), indicating how important it was in the Jones-led assembly of the album. Page also excitedly noted that the instrument practically turned Jones into a one-man orchestra, allowing the bassist to "come up with whole numbers." Jones sold his GX-1 to Keith Emerson in 1987, who then swapped his own instrument's crude MIDI interface into Jones's. Fewer than forty GX-1s were produced.

Once the song kicks in, well, we don't know this yet, but "In the Evening" is going to be the album's heaviest, most guitar-y, and Zeppelin-like song, driven in part by Jimmy's expansive descending riff, but also by these fresh synth sounds from Jones, who built the song from a framework of just keyboards and drums.

Instantly we hear that Robert's voice has matured into something gruff and world-worn as he opens the song with fragmented thoughts on the temptation of womankind, but then ends philosophically and on the side of going with life's flow, much as he did on the previous album's "Hots On for Nowhere." But here Plant is back in the mix and mumbling, the overall effect being that of a reference vocal using words conjured on the spot.

The Gizmotron returns for what surely is one of Jimmy's most outré guitar solos, commencing at 3:45 and on which he opens each of two passages with an unearthly clang. The band then enters a contemplative moment, a nice counterpoint between two Page guitar tracks featuring deft jazz bass work, before a patented Robert *ooh* announces the next verse of this rocking, midpaced number.

"In the Evening" was played live until the end, opening with Jimmy using violin bow to a strobe light effect. As alluded to, it almost had to be in the set, given that it was the album's most riff-centric song (even if calling Jimmy's screechy wash a riff is giving it too much credit).

Played live until the end, "In the Evening" almost had to be in the set, given that it was the most "riff"-centric song on *In Through the Out Door*. Ahoy, Rotterdam, June 21, 1980.

# SOUTH BOUND
## SAUREZ

**JONES/PLANT/4:11**

Here's a track where you can really hear the sort of tone and production the band got out of Polar Studios. In fact, the band had been invited to record there, Polar's owners wanting Zeppelin to establish the place's reputation. Indeed, the guys had to let owners, Swedish group ABBA, in to do a charity track partway through the sessions. Sadly, there was to be no collaboration.

"South Bound Saurez" cooks upon rhythm piano from Jones, rock-solid rhythm bass (also from Jones), rhythmic coloring from Page, and sublime, buoyant percussion from Bonham. It's arguably the first of four tracks that soundtrack the New Orleans bar scene of the album cover. John Paul is playing tack piano, where tacks or nails are attached to the instrument's felt-padded hammers, thus the sharp percussive effect.

This is one of only two tracks in the catalog on which Page is not included in the songwriting credits, the other also being on this record, "All My Love." Nevertheless, Page's solo is a highlight of the proceedings, and for all the subsequent talk of bum notes (I can't hear any), it's an expert example of Jimmy succinctly capturing a song's joie de vivre and then leaving quickly, respectful of the talents of the songwriters who had taken the reins. With his aggressive playing and dirty, compressed tone, Page is an obscurant match to Robert's pushing and shoving vocal and his valiant expending of energy, even though one leaves with the impression that Robert's voice is on the wane, or at least compromised by recent hardships.

And speaking of vocals, this one has an actual arrangement, come the close, where Robert harmonizes with a multitracked vocal of himself. Inspired at this windup, Jonesy rises to the challenge and plays some honky-tonk worthy of Ian Stewart, while Jimmy fires up a few licks. Jimmy is, in fact, an equal partner on this song when all is said and done, chirping his way through the track, creating dialogue with both Robert and John Paul, while Bonham powers through the rock-sturdy rhythm track, bringing to the table lots of high hat and bass drum.

As for the title, "Saurez" isn't a Spanish word for party, nor is it a misspelling of the French "soiree." It is, in fact, a distinguished Spanish surname that makes the idea of a "south bound" Saurez seem reasonable. Recorded on November 15, 1978, early in the quick and very wintery sessions, "South Bound Saurez" was never played live.

"South Bound Saurez" is one of only two tracks in the catalog on which Page is not included in the songwriting credits, the other also being on this record—"All My Love." It was never performed live. Page arrives at the Knebworth Festival on August 4, 1979.

# FOOL IN THE RAIN

**JONES/PAGE/PLANT/6:08**

Here's the most Latin-influenced song Zeppelin ever wrote, though mischievously, they stuck the Latin title on the song before it. What's more, even though Jimmy is in the credits, "Fool in the Rain" is distinguished by him not appearing until halfway through the second verse, with his twelve-string flourish, under which we hear one of the most note-dense bass lines of the Zeppelin catalog. Besides this recurring bit, it is Jimmy's hairy, sparse but elongated C major modal solo section (augmented by MXR Blue Box octave fuzz effect), where we are reminded of Jimmy's magic, specifically his ability to play simply for the song, but also embrace wild tones when he comes across them. All told, there might not be a song in the Led Zeppelin catalog with less guitar playing.

The song is in 4/4 with polyrhythmic characteristics as well as a triplet feel from the reggae-like riff played in unison by Jones and . . . Jones. This loose definition holds true for the windup section as well. Across this, Bonham plays a form of "Purdie shuffle," a trademark of funk drummer Bernard Purdie, but the clever placement of open high-hat accents is all Bonzo, who is also responsible for the track's memorable timbale work.

Robert's lyric relates a passionate love possibly going south, wholly at odds with the song's festive samba vibe, one that really explodes come the Jones-led whistle break, at which time Bonham plays spirited single-stroke snare rolls and some additional percussion through an overdubbed session. Marimba can be heard as well, apparently played by Jones with both hard and soft mallets. It is said that this most non-Zeppelin-esque of passages was inspired by music coming out of the 1978 World Cup hosted by Argentina through the month of June, just as the band was starting to get some writing together, beginning at the three-week Clearwell Castle sessions in May.

But the deft ambiguity in the lyric—along with the subsequent hope for a happy ending—comes with the line *fool waiting on the wrong block*. Has this fool in the rain comically just gotten the location wrong, or is this, alas, sadly, the wrong woman?

"Fool in the Rain" didn't make the set list for the cherished few shows the band had left—both the piano and the bass were crucial and there was only one Jonesy. Also there's the matter of the rave section, which also needed extra hands, but might have come off a bit silly on stage. Nonetheless, the song was a rare late-career radio hit in the United States, reaching No. 21 in January 1980. A radio edit took the song from 6:08 down to 4:50, cutting out the samba jam. Left in, of course, was the odd sound at 1:05, which some liken to the sound one makes to accompany the hand gesture for firing a gun, thumb cocked, index finger forward.

# HOT DOG

**PAGE/PLANT/3:15**

Having for all intents and purposes put aside light and shade as a governing principle back on *Houses of the Holy*, Zeppelin's new mandate was to underscore and double down on things they hadn't done before. Hence, "Hot Dog," a bald-faced country hoedown well into novelty status.

The song fell out of London rehearsal sessions as the band rattled their way through Ricky Nelson and Elvis Presley numbers to warm up, the song arriving from an original rock 'n' roll place rather than true country.

Jimmy's picked runs are curiously rough, as if he's wrestling them out of the guitar, but then he briefly proves some knowledge of the country and western genre with his Chet Atkins–like solo. Jimmy plays a Fender Telecaster outfitted with a B-bender, a device that allows the player to bend the B string up a tone to C sharp, creating the pedal-steel effect heard in the solo.

Jones is pervasive with his barrelhouse piano playing, and Robert sings a bit of Elvis rockabilly while harmonizing with himself on the chorus. Deep inside the mix are scale walks in the key of D placed on the two, the "and," and the three, but other than that, the song is played quite straight, with Bonham showing up but not exactly swinging.

Lyrically, once again, Robert massages a simple story into an amusing and economically poetic song rumored to be about a groupie named Audrey Hamilton, with whom Plant had hooked up on the 1977 tour. It's self-deprecating like many a country song, and it's the girl who loves 'em and leaves 'em. Robert has downplayed the romance side of the tale, explaining that, generally, it's a song about the Texas state of mind. Interestingly, it's somewhat a redux of the "Fool in the Rain" storyline.

Subsequently included in the set list for the 1980 Over Europe tour dates, "Hot Dog" was also the B-side to the single release of "Fool in the Rain" and the subject of a rare promotional video, although this is nothing more than a pro camera shot of the song played live at Knebworth.

Knebworth Festival,
Hertfordshire,
England, August 11,
1979—Led Zeppelin's
last UK show until
the December
2007 London O2
engagement.

# CONJURING THE BIG EASY

I f the sounds of Led Zeppelin stepping toward the '80s weren't enough to keep fans tittering, the band's cover design team, Hipgnosis, had a few extra tricks up their sleeves. Explains the design house's Aubrey Powell, "Jimmy said to me, 'Listen, I want to return to the roots, the blues roots. I don't want something surreal. I don't want something like *Presence*. *In the Through the Out Door* is a very bluesy album. It's got that kind of rock sound that goes back to its roots somewhere.' And he said, 'You know, there's kind of a New Orleans feel to it, to me, on there.' And I said, 'Let me go to New Orleans and have a look.' So I flew to New Orleans and I photographed all these bars; I came back, and I drew up my ideal bar. It was taken from every single bar you can imagine on Bourbon Street. And I drew them all up and put the characters in.

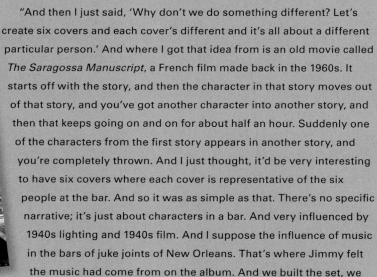

"And then I just said, 'Why don't we do something different? Let's create six covers and each cover's different and it's all about a different particular person.' And where I got that idea from is an old movie called *The Saragossa Manuscript*, a French film made back in the 1960s. It starts off with the story, and then the character in that story moves out of that story, and you've got another character into another story, and then that keeps going on and on for about half an hour. Suddenly one of the characters from the first story appears in another story, and you're completely thrown. And I just thought, it'd be very interesting to have six covers where each cover is representative of the six people at the bar. And so it was as simple as that. There's no specific narrative; it's just about characters in a bar. And very influenced by 1940s lighting and 1940s film. And I suppose the influence of music in the bars of juke joints of New Orleans. That's where Jimmy felt the music had come from on the album. And we built the set, we shot it all, it was great. But looking for hidden meanings, there aren't any."

Yet what a jumping-off point for the imagination. Each character is alone with one's thoughts, but one senses there's lots going on, or that something could happen at any moment. Plus, it's interesting that the idea of New Orleans was evoked. There's a definite weight to place—it's where the band was when Robert heard that his son had died. The fact that some went home with him immediately and some didn't caused major pain, the extent of which is said to be woven into the cryptic lyrics of "Carouselambra."

"I built the set completely in London," continues Powell, illustrating how no expenses were spared when Hipgnosis were on the case. "I mean, it was beautiful, absolutely stunning. Jimmy came down when we were photographing it and he said, 'I want to take this home and put it in my house' [*laughs*]. It was a tragedy we never filmed it, actually. But it was fantastic."

More tricks awaited album buyers once they got the record home and pulled out the inner sleeve—if they were sloppy with their stuff.

"Yes, we had a brushstroke on the cover," Powell says, "and that was a clue, when you got inside, the inner bag, it had a sketch on it. And, of course, for those who realized it, if you put a glass of water on it, it suddenly went to color. That bag was impregnated with different colors, and if you got a brush and wet it, you got all these different colors that came out—the ashtray went red, the glass of wine was green, whatever it was."

But you only found out if you got it wet, or if someone clued you into the brushstroke. "Exactly, exactly," Aubrey explains. "Because when you pulled out the inside, people would wonder, why is there the brushstroke? Well, that creates a color, because it's very sepia-toned. We didn't tell anybody about it. It was intended that somebody would discover it by accident. And we had lots of letters from people saying, 'Is this intended or a mistake? My inner sleeve, you know, I spilt some whiskey on it, and it's all gone different colors. Is this intended?' It's like a magical thing. Some people can say it's cutesy tricks. I don't—I call it deliberate design. It's a piece of art."

As for taking the whole thing and sticking it in a brown paper bag, Powell says, "I went to see Peter Grant and he said to me, 'You're so fucking expensive.' And I said, 'But Peter, we get you so much publicity for the work that we do, it can only be good. And everybody loves it.' He says, 'I could sell Led Zeppelin in a fucking brown paper bag.' And I said to him, 'Okay, so why don't we take the cover we've done and put it under a brown paper grocer's bag, and just put a stamp on it saying *In Through the Out Door*?' He says, 'Done, let's see who wins.' And that's what we did. It came out in the brown paper bag, serrated at the top. It's a brown paper grocer's bag. You could buy apples in it from a store."

Jimmy didn't carry through with his quip about putting the set in his house.

"No, it was all trashed and thrown away," says Powell, "just like any good film set. It was put in a skip and destroyed. Everything—every single thing."

And tragically, without filming it!

"I did suggest this to the band," sighs Aubrey. "Because videos didn't exist. It didn't exist in those days. 'Why don't we shoot this or do something with this?' And they sort of hummed and hawed and said, 'I'm not sure.' But you know, again, there was something kind of creative, I suppose, about doing something like that and just trashing it all afterward, and being left just with the imagery that you'd taken at the time."

# CAROUSELAMBRA

**JONES/PAGE/PLANT/10:28**

If "In the Evening" is the most conventional and guitar-centric track on *In Through the Out Door*, "Carouselambra" might nevertheless be the heaviest and most driving song, given the resolute 4/4 stomp and Page's power chords. Provisionally titled "The Epic," this was one of the few bright spots to emerge from the frustrating Clearwell Castle writing sessions of May 1978, giving the band cause for hope with Robert's emotions still raw after the death of his son Karac. In fact, Robert's return was not a given, and the band spent much of an inactive 1978 fending off rumors that they were splitting.

Across the song's 10:28 (making it the second longest Zeppelin tune, after "In My Time of Dying") are many parts, none progressive on their own, but which together comprise more of an artsy prog rock track than a hard rock monster like "Achilles" or "In My Time of Dying." This is due to the prominence of Jones in the mix, as well as the distinctive and at times almost post-punk parts that often carry the tune.

Robert responds to the challenge of the song's pomp rock vibe with awkward mouthfuls of lyrics that sound somewhat unwieldy, as if all the small words were removed, leaving only the significant ones and a confused listener trying to figure out the aggregate. Robert has intimated that the song is about someone close to him who will one day be able to pick through the dense lyrics and realize that it was about him—or them, as later comments suggested the song was about his relationship with the band and the breakdown of its chemistry. In fact Robert has stated that the latter history of the band can be divined in his words if one pays attention. Part of that history is the death of Karac, and there are some heartbreaking lines in "Carouselambra" that might go to that dark place, also visited, it has been said, in the lyrics of "All My Love," "I'm Gonna Crawl," and 1993 solo track "I Believe" as well.

Helping to obscure the meaning further is the fact that Robert is mixed behind the rumble of the music. As well, the sentences are constructed so oddly that one requires a lyric sheet to figure it out, the type of road map Zeppelin refused to offer outside of *Houses of the Holy* and "Stairway to Heaven." What we have here is a grand bank of words that add up to the most enigmatic and hotly debated lyrics of the catalog.

Plant emerges from the smoke during the shimmering, psychedelic slow section where he turns in some of his best vocals of the album, enhanced by echoes, a perfect effect for such a mysterious, cryptic lyric. Page can be heard using, for the first and last

time in the studio, his Gibson EDS-1275 double-neck, the overall vibe emerging as heat-swelled as that of the intro and outro music to "Achilles Last Stand."

After this, it's back to the '80s, with pots full of percolating synthesizer riffs, long-winding yet simple rolls from Bonham, and Jimmy once again using the Gizmotron to provide texture in the middle of the mix. Robert is situated back in the mix, but there are some oddly anguished harmonies with himself. The combination of uneasy melody and Robert's chilling and admonishing lines makes for a compelling close, especially as he drifts out, leaving only an exotic melange of sounds on slow fade.

# ALL MY LOVE

## JONES/PLANT/5:51

As contentious as the profusion of keyboard songs all over *In Through the Out Door* was, equally disconcerting was the inclusion of a ballad (working title "The Hook") that Page had reservations about, calling it "not us." Indeed, both Page and Bonham, the two poisoned vampires in the band, quietly grumbled about the "soft" direction of the album, vowing to make a hard-rocking comeback next time out.

To be sure, the ballad in question is spare and obvious, there's not much to the arrangement, and the chords to the chorus lack the richness of Zeppelin's usual modus operandi, or even the smart chording of the song's own verse. Page quite perceptively said he was "a little worried about the chorus," and really, one supposes it's testimony to the band's previous seven albums that the ears perk up and recognize something "ordinary" like this as being so out of character.

Lyrically, Robert writes privately to himself, giving the world a rote love song they can play at weddings. But behind closed doors, he's communing with his deceased son while simultaneously addressing how the death affects his relationship with Maureen.

And thus the song is "obviously" substantial beyond its surface. In terms of the ensemble performance, Page plays tactfully, offering sweet high texture, almost session-polite colorizing, while Jones offers angelic and soft synth patterns throughout. Plant's clever phrasings and melodic choices add further shade and dimension, with producer Jimmy choosing Plant's very first take for the album version. Providing more backbone than the track would seemingly warrant, Bonham thumps a rock-solid and resolute beat, winding up bars with big fills and splashy crashes. The effect is as if the song was being recorded at soundcheck.

There's a lushly orchestrated solo section, bits of acoustic guitar, and, late in the sequence, modulation (basically a key change) as the band take it out. Bonham's powerful playing would be amusing if one could for a moment put aside the gravity of the lyric, which is nearly impossible. Incidentally, Led Zeppelin used modulation often, but it never sounded like more of a preposterous pop convention for this band than it did in "All My Love."

An alternate version of the song features an additional minute of jam at the end on which Robert vamps aimlessly, Jimmy brings out his B-bender for a bad solo, and the band wind it up with an over-the-top amount of schmaltz. Proving his good taste, Jimmy knew well enough not to include this as a companion disc bonus track on the expanded reissue program of 2015.

# I'M GONNA CRAWL

**JONES/PAGE/PLANT/5:28**

Featuring Robert's best vocal on the album, "I'm Gonna Crawl" stacks all the lessons Plant soaked up from a life of the blues, most notably here from Otis Redding and the Righteous Brothers. But the song itself is more of a waltz and less of a blues, despite Bonham's stripper pole beat thumping otherwise. Plant was well pleased with the sound Jimmy got for his vocal on this track, also aware that he could be quite unheard and not understood elsewhere on the record. Jimmy, for his part, mused that this is one of his favorite Plant vocals of the entire Zeppelin canon.

And so instead of a blues, it's a torrid ballad with richer melodic bones than "All My Love," the two songs creating a shockingly quiet exit to *In Through the Out Door.* Only Bonham is allowed to play loudly through the album's final eleven minutes, and by default, throughout the entire album. In fact, Bonham makes a pile of noise almost at the very end of the song before crawling off himself for the close of the track. Poignantly, as the curtain draws, there's a final resigned *I'm gonna crawl* from Plant, accompanied by a half-volume chord from Page and then an even quieter wash of keys from Jones, who unexpectedly changes the note, as if creating an expectation for something more.

There would be no more. On September 25, 1980, barely a year after the album's issue, John Bonham was found dead, having choked on his own vomit after a night of rehearsals and a day and night of vodka—roughly forty shots of it, according to the October 27 inquest.

"I'm Gonna Crawl" would have to stand as the band's coda (before the posthumous album actually called *Coda*). Lyrically, the song is almost innocuous, unworthy of notice, and certainly incongruous to the music. But the music is something else, laden with emotion and nostalgia, eerily prescient of the tragic event to come. Jones plays keyboards as if indentured at the gates of heaven, and Jimmy's solo is imbued with blues hurt. And nowhere else on the album does Plant howl the blues like this. But then he just gives up after Bonzo, followed by Jimmy and then John Paul. It's twenty-twenty hindsight, but Led Zeppelin somehow gathered around a finish imbued with meaning, the message being that no one wins in the end—not even Led Zeppelin.

CD

## SIDE 1

**We're Gonna Groove**

**Poor Tom**

**I Can't Quit You Baby**

**Walter's Walk**

## SIDE 2

**Ozone Baby**

**Darlene**

**Bonzo's Montreux**

**Wearing and Tearing**

Recorded
January 1970–November 1978 (overdubs 1982)
Morgan Studios, London; Olympic Studios,
London; Royal Albert Hall, London; Stargroves,
Berkshire, UK; Polar Studios, Stockholm; Mountain
Studios, Montreux, Switzerland

Release Date
November 19, 1982 (US, Swan Song 90051-1;
UK, Swan Song A0051)

Produced by Jimmy Page
Engineers: Andy Johns, Vic Maile, Eddie Kramer,
Leif Mases, John Timperly

RIAA Certification: Platinum
Top Billboard Position: No. 6

CODA

1982

# CODA

**ROBERT PLANT**
vocals, harmonica

**JIMMY PAGE**
electric and acoustic
guitars, effects,
electronics

**JOHN PAUL JONES**
bass, piano

**JOHN BONHAM**
drums, percussion

"The loss of our dear friend, and the deep respect we have for his family, together with the sense of undivided harmony felt by ourselves and our manager, have led us to decide that we could not continue as we were."

That formal and subtly cryptic statement from the Led Zeppelin camp seemed to indicate that Led Zeppelin were no more after the death of John Bonham, though there would be one final album, a rarities compilation that fulfilled Swan Song's five-record deal with Atlantic Records. Originally titled *Early Days and Latter Days*, the more succinctly monikered *Coda* emerged long after Bonzo ended Zeppelin.

"They needed something quickly, to put this out," says Aubrey. Powell of design house Hipgnosis, the implication being that this would not be a marriage of visuals and sounds enthusiastically conceived and considered by the band on one side, Hipgnosis on the other. "They were in no mood for, I suppose, something very intricate," Powell recalls. "They wanted something simple, and something that just summed up the end, I think. And I had seen these extraordinary pictures of irrigation circles from the US, these massive, beautiful, circular rings. And I remember Storm [Thorgerson] said, 'You know what? They look like albums; they look like discs. It would be interesting to put those on the front cover.' And so the cover is much more about a graphic shape symbolic of the record. And when you open it up, inside you've got a whole load of Led Zeppelin photographs, which is kind of a history of the band backwards and forwards.

And because the band was quite desperate, and the management . . . I think Peter Grant had almost given up managing Robert Plant at that time. It was a really uncomfortable period in accessibility terms. Getting everybody to agree on something was troublesome for me. And so it required something simple, not complex, not outrageous. It was more a case of, 'Get it done.'"

Also reflecting that diminished communication, *Coda* appeared on the shelves with no fanfare, very little in the way of advertising or media splash, and nothing in the way of a press campaign.

As for the music itself, well, this wasn't Zeppelin's first visit to the vaults. *Physical Graffiti*, although it wasn't really a fact played up at the time, constituted a first round of pilfering, with seven of its fifteen tracks being rescues from the dusty shelves. So it makes sense that the anchor tracks of

*Coda* would be three fully fleshed-out songs from the *In Through the Out Door* sessions. Meanwhile, "Poor Tom" and "Walter's Walk" were unheard originals from 1970 and 1972, respectively. Rounding things out, there was a John Bonham drum solo, a live take of a debut album–era track, and a frenzied cover of "We're Gonna Groove," adapted from Ben E. King's "Groovin'."

There seems to be a bit of cloak and dagger about how much doctoring was done to these tracks, some of it obscured by erroneous credits and much of it buried until the Internet made information free and easy. There were obvious and admitted edits and guitar tracks added to old live material, as well as much remixing. Most intriguingly, however, given that both Jones and Plant popped into Page's Sol Studios to help out, it's more or less understood that bass and vocals were added in spots, particularly "Walter's Walk," which sounds nothing like 1972 and a heck of a lot like 1978, with vocals by the guy singing *Pictures at Eleven*. As well, there's conjecture that Jimmy called "We're Gonna Groove" a studio track and "I Can't Quit You Baby" a rehearsal track because Swan Song owed Atlantic one more studio album specifically.

In any event, despite the subterfuge over what was new and what was not, the eight tracks comprising *Coda* were presented in roughly chronological order, setting the stage for closer "Wearing and Tearing," through which Led Zeppelin rage one final time before the dying of the light, a high-octane affirmation perhaps, against the somber strains of more legitimate curtain-closer "I'm Gonna Crawl."

Missing were a couple or three mildly interesting things that we eventually heard through reissues. But really, most conspicuous are "Travelling Riverside Blues," "Hey, Hey, What Can I Do," and "Sugar Mama." Deleting "I Can't Quit You Baby" and adding those three would have made *Coda* an album that satisfied even fussiest and most critical fans.

The immediate and indeed lasting philosophical thrust of *Coda* is the tacitly posed debate about how *In Through the Out Door* could've been a very different record, pointedly quite a bit more rock 'n' rolling than what we got. Everything else was just mild amusement for an industry that had moved on to myriad other musics, save for, I suppose, "Poor Tom," which made people chuckle.

*Coda* would be the only Led Zeppelin album not to go multiplatinum, stalling at No. 6 on the US Billboard charts. In the United Kingdom, the album earned a paltry silver designation. Perhaps surprisingly, perhaps not, after the demise of Led Zeppelin, Robert Plant would become the band member with a substantial rock 'n' roll career, with Jimmy popping up periodically on something or another, and John Paul Jones very much becoming the revered cult figure we always knew he one day would be.

# WE'RE GONNA GROOVE

**KING/BETHEA/2:36**

For years, based on the inner sleeve notes of the original LP, fans were under the impression that Zeppelin's torrid cover of "We're Gonna Groove" was a Morgan Studios concoction from June 25, 1969, for possible inclusion on Led Zeppelin *II*. Made sense, given the lack of crowd noise, the locked-down performance, and at times three guitar tracks: two angled and arty high parts plus an amusing and growling clang, often described as a motorcycle sound, generated by a sub-octivider effect (either from an EMS machine or an MXR Blue Box), which can fuzz up the signal and replicate it two octaves down.

But this was corrected first for *The Complete Studio Sessions* and then retained into the reissue program. The base or working take was in fact recorded live at the Royal Albert Hall on January 9, 1970, using the Pye Mobile. Engineering the session was Vic Maile, who manned the mobile for the Who's *Live at Leeds* five months later and produced Mötorhead's *Ace of Spades* before dying of cancer in 1989 at the age of forty-five.

A naughty Jimmy Page added the suboctivider effect for the release on *Coda*, working at Sol Studios (AKA the Sol and the Mill) in Cookham, Berkshire, in February 1982 during an overdubbing, editing, and mixing session, engineer Stuart Epps presiding. Acquired by Jimmy from Gus Dudgeon in September 1981, the studio was also used for Jimmy's *Death Wish II* soundtrack album, both of his records as part of the Firm, plus his solo album, *Outrider*.

"We're Gonna Groove" finds Zeppelin doing what they did often: wholly transforming old rock, in this case Ben E. King's R&B standard, "Groovin'," credited here to King and his partner James Bethea. Perhaps having grown in his thinking, Page credits the newly titled Zeppelin song to the two alone, where really, given the near complete overhaul and bulking of the music, plus the transformation of the beat, he might have added his own name, as he had done repeatedly in the past when performing this feat. Still, both the vocal line and the lyrics are near identical to the jaunty original.

In terms of its structure, the song wasn't a blues to begin with and it definitely wasn't in Zeppelin's telling, sounding more like psychedelic hard rock with its bold and powerful vocal from Plant, its busy and clever bass line from Jones, and

OPPOSITE: The working take for "We're Gonna Groove" was recorded live at the Royal Albert Hall on January 9, 1970. It was a show opener on many 1970 tour dates from January through April, when it was replaced by the "Immigrant Song." Coliseum, Denver, Colorado, March 25, 1970.

the band's patented chemistry come solo time, driven by Bonham joining in and semisoloing along with Jimmy.

The song's performance can be viewed on 2003's *Led Zeppelin DVD* (the show was filmed for TV but never aired), which demonstrates why it was used as a show opener on many 1970 tour dates from January through April, at which point it was replaced by the newly minted "Immigrant Song." However, the DVD version differs in many respects from the LP version, raising questions about how much studio work was done to the LP track—certainly a pile of editing and switching out of guitars.

# POOR TOM

**PAGE/PLANT/3:03**

"Poor Tom" was adapted from a traditional tune at the inspired Bron-Yr-Aur cottage sessions. It was considered for inclusion on *III*, but then shelved. Recorded on June 5, 1970, at Olympic and engineered by Andy Johns, it represents one of the rare cases where, if included, Led Zeppelin would have broken their rule of not repeating themselves, given its similarity to "Gallows Pole." Also, there was already a lot of acoustic music on *III*.

The song features a clever New Orleans shuffle-style drum signature, which seems to inspire Jones to turn in an equally clever bass line, which usually harmonizes in sophisticated fashion with Page's endearing bluegrass riff, performed in the same C6 tuning used for "Friends" and "Bron-Yr-Aur." Jimmy creates a wall of sound with only one guitar track, although granted, it is a twelve-string. There's also an element of reverb or even reverse reverb, aided by room ambience. Inside of Jones's harmonizing with Page, he leaps octaves at will, creating a part so interesting it had to be pushed back in the mix, lest it overwhelm the acoustic jug band playing and Robert's age-old story of a marriage ended with a gun. There's a marked uptick in clarity and richness over the acoustic songs that made *III*, "Poor Tom" bearing the advantage of a remix by Page working at his own studio twelve years later along with the leveling mastering applied across the *Coda* album.

"Poor Tom" bears similarities to the Robert Wilkins original, and the Rolling Stones' cover of, "Prodigal Son," but only in the chord changes and vocal melody, not the lyrics, even if there's a link between a prodigal son and a seventh son. "Prodigal Son" is itself a 1964 gospel reworking of Wilkins's own 1929 song "That's No Way to Get Along," but again, the story told in the original is nothing like that of the Led Zeppelin song (the 1964 track finds the artist billed as the Reverend Robert Wilkins). Additionally, Bert Jansch associate Owen Hand included a song on his 1965 album *Something New* called "She Likes It" that contains some of the same acoustic licks.

In the lyric, Tom dreams of lazing in the sun when he can finally retire from working on the railroad. But his plan is stopped dead in its tracks when he picks up a gun and ends his wife's infidelities. The interesting suggestion is that Tom isn't picking up the clues the usual way, but because he is a seventh son, prone to special psychic powers, he's likely getting the full movie in his head. As well, Tom is poor, because as the seventh son, he's cut out of the inheritance.

As for Plant, our porch-sitting storyteller, not only does he turn in an engaging and thespian folk and blues vocal performance on this murder ballad, he also harmonizes with himself and then gets to play some well-placed, tasteful harmonica (two tracks' worth) that crescendos for the close, the tracks coming together along with unison playing from Jones.

OPPOSITE: "Poor Tom" bears similarities to both the Reverend Robert Wilkins original and the Rolling Stones' cover of "Prodigal Son." Recorded on June 5, 1970, at Olympic, it was considered for inclusion on *III*, but then shelved.

# I CAN'T QUIT YOU BABY

**DIXON/4:16**

The original sleeve notes to *Coda* indicate that this take was from the rehearsal in advance of the band's professionally recorded and filmed 1970 Royal Albert Hall show. However, the 2003 DVD release clears up the fact that it is a performance from the show proper. Knowledge that the show was going to be aired led Page to properly record tracks from which to work later, if he ever chose to. And, of course, a dozen years later he couldn't resist, albeit taking more liberties with "We're Gonna Groove" than with "I Can't Quit You Baby," which is left relatively unaltered.

One might question the inclusion of a live version of a previously released song on *Coda*, and a rote and predictable blues at that (*and* a cover to boot!), but one might imagine that the method to Jimmy's madness was his understanding of how white-hot the band's performance is. The song had evolved from the comparatively staid version on *Led Zeppelin*, into a tour de force, most pertinently for John Bonham, who uses the song for his continued pioneering of his right foot work on the bass drum, along with his continued practicing of triplet fills (and fills in general) that start early and dependably end with a huge crash.

Still, irrespective of whether both were written by Willie Dixon, the inclusion of two similar slow blues on the record seems gratuitous, and again, one wonders why "Sugar Mama" or even the balladic "Baby Come on Home," from the same sessions, didn't make the cut instead.

OPPOSITE: One might question the inclusion of a live version of a previously released song on *Coda*, but the song had evolved from the comparatively staid version on *Led Zeppelin*, into a tour de force, most pertinently for John Bonham. K. B. Hallen, Copenhagen, February, 28, 1970.

# WALTER'S WALK

**PAGE/PLANT/4:24**

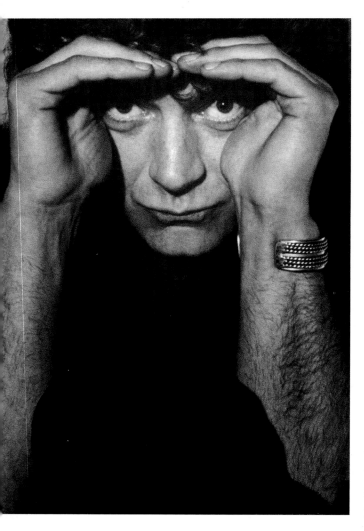

As a kid, after *Coda* came out, when I wasn't paying close attention, I often conflated "Walter's Walk" with "Wearing and Tearing." Decades later, history has borne out why that would've been the sensible thing to do.

Official lore has it that "Walter's Walk" was a rejected track from the *Houses of the Holy* sessions, and the credits indicate that it was recorded on the Rolling Stones mobile at Stargroves on May 15, 1972, engineer Eddie Kramer presiding. And we do know that it's a pretty old song, given that its seeds can be heard in certain extended versions of "Dazed and Confused" live in '72 through '73, as well as an occasional appearance in "The Crunge."

But what we know now is that the song might've existed as a basic track only, or a rhythm track, or even an instrumental track. Because on *Coda*, Robert Plant's labored, echo-drenched vocal was added in 1982, which begs the question: Were his lyrics also written in 1982? They're certainly obscure and philosophical like lyrics the recently reflective Robert was wont to write, and rumor has it that Page asked Robert to write a song about John Bonham's death and Robert gladly complied. Other rumors have the music being recorded during the *Presence* sessions, the vocal done during the *In Through the Out Door* sessions, and the bass played by Jimmy and not Jonesy. Of note, "Walter's Walk" does indeed rear its head during *Presence*, because the secondary or post-verse riff in the song is also the secondary riff in "Hots On for Nowhere," played comparatively half-time in the latter.

Also pegging the song to the later period is the fact Jimmy plays like the labyrinthine, pollution-choked player he would reveal himself to be from *In Through the Out Door* through the Firm and onto his *Outrider* solo album. And that's not a dig—remarkably, he really only found his trademark sound—*this* trademark sound—in 1978. Even if the blood and guts of "Walter's Walk" existed as early as 1972, the guitar sounds are pure *In Through the Out Door*. And presumably nothing had changed about this pure and human part of Jimmy's persona, as expressed through his fingers, by the time he was playing mad scientist all over Led Zeppelin rarities in his own studio in 1982. In other words, it would make sense that a song built from the chassis up in 1982 would sound like an *In Through the Out Door* outtake.

And that's why, as an angry metalhead of nineteen, not really thinking about it, it always felt like there were four outtakes from the band's last album on *Coda* rather than three. "Walter's Walk" with "Wearing and Tearing" were two of Led Zeppelin's heaviest metal tracks of all time. And of the two, "Walter's Walk" was the ass-kicking winner, a tank trundling at full throttle through the desert haze and over dunes, fired by Jimmy's heat-swollen playing.

I even have a hard time picturing this soft and ambient yet powerful Bonham drum track as circa 1972, finding the presentation pure *In Through the Out Door* as well. Whatever it is, it's driving and simple and authoritative, a sturdy frame upon which Page can go nuts, which he most certainly does, beginning at 2:19 and then a minute later through to the close, where the band create one of their most impressive sonic firestorms, pushing Robert to the sideline where all he can do is shake his head and put down his mic.

OPPOSITE: Even if the chassis of "Walter's Walk" existed as early as 1972, the echo-drenched vocal and guitar sounds are pure *In Through the Out Door*. In fact, we know Plant added the vocal in 1982.

# OZONE BABY

**PAGE/PLANT/3:35**

"Ozone Baby" was a Page showcase, thanks to his use of a Telecaster B-bender possibly the same one being played here at the ARMS benefit, London, September 20, 1983.

"Ozone Baby" is one of three *Coda* tracks finished for inclusion on *In Through the Out Door*. And of this trio of songs from 1978, "Wearing and Tearing" is the clear bodice-ripper, "Darlene" the old rock 'n' roller, the weak link, and as a result, the closest fit to the rest of the material. But "Ozone Baby" is a curious one, combining rock drive with a link to the past, perhaps to 1970s Rolling Stones, given the Keith Richards swagger of Jimmy's riff, along with some cleverness and complication that takes it into a "Carouselambra" zone.

There's not much to the lyric, Robert basically telling a woman with stalker potential (a childish, airheaded "ozone baby") to go away. But there is a dark, typically cryptic turn toward the end, congruous with how doom seemed to lurk behind every corner of Robert's lyrics after his family tragedy in 1977. Also notable is Robert's bit of harmonizing with himself, and at one point, the penultimate *my own true love* bit utilizes a vocal harmonizer effect.

But "Ozone Baby" is really a Jimmy Page showcase, from his circuitous riff through to his variety of tones come solo time, aided and abetted by his use of the B-bender used in a similar chord-bending manner here as on "All My Love."

Had it made it onto *In the Through the Out Door*, this would've been the only song besides "Hot Dog" without synths, Jones being more than busy enough with his grace-noted bass licks in the verse along with his enjoyable walk for the chorus.

# DARLENE

**BONHAM/JONES/PAGE/PLANT/5:04**

Never content with old rock 'n' roll just being old rock 'n' roll, John Bonham makes sure, as he did on "Candy Store Rock" and even "Poor Tom" earlier on this record, to come up with an uncharted beat, over which everyone else can do their thing. Sure, Jimmy picks a riff with pregnant pauses modern enough, but then Robert throws himself into an old blues and almost girl-group lyric and vocal, while Jones plays never-ending barrelhouse piano.

"Darlene," one of the Polar Studios songs (recorded November 16, 1978), lines up well with the likes of "South Bound Saurez," "Fool in the Rain," and "Hot Dog" in terms of tracks that would have contributed to *In Through the Out Door*, being bouncy and nostalgic at the same time.

Opening with a brief but powerful guitar-driven intro, the song quickly gets down to its pop rock—or pomp rock—half-time verse, but then what serves as the chorus rocks a little harder, before we're back to the recline of a verse filled with Robert moaning about Darlene in her tight dress. Robert's reference to "a pink carnation and a pickup truck" might be a direct quote from Don McLean's "American Pie," but Plant and McLean are likely both wistfully thinking about Marty Robbins's image of "a white sports coat and a pink carnation," and the expectations a girl like Darlene would have of her suitors.

Jimmy's solo is elliptical and elegant, playful and gleefully noisy. Jones follows with one of the best pure piano solos of his career and everybody meets for a grooving swing. The song then takes yet another unexpected left turn into pure boogie-woogie, which doesn't stop Bonham from throwing in huge and muscular fills. Jimmy and Jonesy solo together as the song jams its way toward the fade. One can only begin to imagine the old rock 'n' roll knowledge that went into this one, along with the in-jokes from deep within the record collections of each of the guys.

With "Bonzo's Montreux," recorded at Mountain Studios in Montreux, Switzerland, on September 12, 1976, Bonham comes up with something novel as he did probably twenty times before.

# BONZO'S
# MONTREUX

**BONHAM/4:15**

As Ron Nevison said earlier on, John Bonham tends to play Jimmy's riffs. Well, on "Bonzo's Montreux," recorded at Mountain Studios in Montreux, Switzerland, on September 12, 1976, Bonham writes his own riff—or he's playing to a riff he hears in his head.

Why Montreux? Well, it was just another crazy chapter in a rich band's life as tax exiles. Jimmy and John were there trying to make Bonham's long-held wish come true: to record for the band an all-drums track, engineer John Timperly capturing the experiment on tape.

In any event, Bonham succeeds in being musical (bass pedal squeak notwithstanding), coming up with something novel like he did probably twenty times before. Here the frame of his "song" is a toggle, a dialog, between snare and bass.

Jimmy was suitably impressed to have the thing dressed up, having John throw on extra drum and percussion tracks (timpani, timbales, congas), sprinkling it with a little audio pixie dust in the form of synthesized vocals provided by Page himself. As well, Jimmy managed a steel drum effect by manipulating his recently acquired Eventide Clock Works harmonizer (which works with a keyboard controller, and for this composition was used with the high feedback setting). The timpani provide the first hint of melody and then the steel drum effect adds a little more, in a fusion direction.

Backward echo was used as well, but ultimately, with respect to the attention spans of potential listeners, "Bonzo's Montreux" would live or die on John's percussive "hook." On the sleeve notes to the album, Jimmy credits the playing on the track to the "John Bonham Drum Orchestra," allowing himself a credit for "electronic treatments."

All told, "Bonzo's Montreux" is "Moby Dick" without the strummers, and whether it really can appeal to listeners other than drummers is up for debate. The point is, John knows this, knows the bar is set high, and he's trying his darnedest to write a song on the drums.

# WEARING AND TEARING

**PAGE/PLANT/5:27**

Closing our last Led Zeppelin album of a mere thirty-three minutes is a blast of hard rock that finds the band answering their punk critics with a hand up saying, "We can still rock." But that's as far as I'm going to cross into hyperbole, because "Wearing and Tearing" isn't particularly punk, nor is it crazy heavy or hard to play or any of that. But it's an impressive melange of semi-extreme sounds working in mischievous concert—a hot mess of boomy drums; earthy, even muddy guitars; and vocals from Robert that are much the same: bassy, hoarse, and obscured by echo, plus desperate, manic, and thrashing.

The song was slated to be issued as a single in time for the historic Knebworth live shows and was indeed talked about by the guys as a rejoinder to the punks who thought they had cornered the market on energy. Page himself, gratuitously, had seen the value in the new music, citing the Damned as impressive. The guys even had the idea to issue it under a pseudonym, just to see how it would compete if the punters didn't know it was Zeppelin, not that that was going to fly for even a minute. In any event, issues at the pressing plant scotched the idea.

Lyrically, to match the song's thundering attack, there's the pent-up energy, sexual at first, then vaguely somehow action-oriented or impulsive, but then shifting to darker themes, possibly druggy ones, culminating in an escape to the country to clean up. A secondary or tertiary meaning might involve a striving to try to understand the motivations and frustrations of punk rockers, and how

Zeppelin might never buy the punk ethos because they came from a different generation. Page has intimated as much, indicating that the song expressed something to the effect that "We may be big rock stars, but we've got problems too that we're trying to figure out."

To reiterate, however, "Wearing and Tearing" is by leaps and bounds the most aggressive song recorded at Polar Studios during the *In Through the Out Door* sessions, this one coming late in the short burst in Stockholm, on November 21, 1978,

perhaps as a pendulum shift toward the slamming rock Bonham and Page weren't seeing enough of the previous week.

Things take a malevolent turn at 4:58, when the band indeed conjures a punk head of steam, Robert shoving his way into the middle of the fray, pogoing and screaming *Medication!* like a raving young punk, all four members piling on to create one last wall of sound before going silent forever.

As Robert, Jimmy, John Paul, and John expressed through the sonic violence of "Sick Again," they agree resolutely to lock horns and turn it up, sending their fans into the Zeppelin-less 1980s with a bluster of stacked electrics every bit as visceral as the seething sounds first heard through "Good Times Bad Times" and "Communication Breakdown" back in 1969. And with this gesture, this sequencing of "Wearing and Tearing" last, perhaps we can infer the notion that if hard choices had to be made within the band between light and shade, winning out every time would be the rock 'n' roll magic and drama of overdriven guitars played at unsafe speeds.

"Wearing and Tearing" is by far the most aggressive song recorded during the *In Through the Out Door* sessions. Things take a malevolent turn at 4:58, when the band indeed conjures a punk head of steam. Knebworth Festival, Hertfordshire, England, August 11, 1979.

# LOOKING BACK

With *Coda* being a career retrospective, essentially encompassing 1969 to 1982, and given its status as, indeed, the band's coda, it's fitting to end somewhat as we began back on the first album: with some additional well wishes from rockers who were contemporaries of the band or immediately influenced by Led Zeppelin—or, in some cases, both. The importance of what Robert, Jimmy, John Paul, and John created throughout their astonishing run shines through these words.

**Yardbirds drummer Jim McCarty:** "Think About It," "Tinker Tailor, Soldier, Sailor," "Dazed and Confused," obviously—they all came from heavy blues riffs, along with "Smokestack Lightning," which Jimmy actually sort of simplified. He used to do so many of these blues riffs very cleverly in his own way, simplifying some of them and making some of them more complex. We were a vehicle for what Jimmy wanted to do when he came in. He had pretty free rein, as all the guitar players did, and he pushed the Yardbirds' sound into more of a heavy metal context. He really was the master of the riff.

**Original Judas Priest vocalist Al Atkins:** I used to know Robert; we used to go for a beer together, and sometimes he'd borrow my microphone because he couldn't afford one, if I wasn't playing. We had one mic between the two of us [*laughs*]. It was great times.

Robert's roots have always been blues. He's a very intelligent guy when you're talking to him about the blues stuff. He knows everything about that. You can't argue with him about anything on that subject. One time Alexis Korner was playing on his own at Henry's Blues House, a solo gig he got there, like a one-man band thing or something, and Robert got up and played harmonica and sang along with him.

**Black Sabbath bassist Geezer Butler:** One of the biggest influences was Zeppelin because two of them were from the same part of England that we were from, from Birmingham, and we used to see them in clubs and stuff around town. So we sort of associated more with Robert Plant and John Bonham than anybody else, I suppose, 'cause we were doing the same kind of circuit before we made it. There wasn't competition, just friends. We'd see each other out and have a beer or whatever and just socialize, really. Everybody seemed to be doing their own kind of thing.

**Nazareth guitarist Manny Charlton:** We loved Zeppelin. They were just an extension to what was going on with the guitar bands like the Who, on from the Beatles. It went from the Beatles to the Who and then into that blues boom thing, with Jeff Beck Group. The Yardbirds and Cream, initially, were doing the electric blues thing. But the Jeff Beck Group took it to another level, and then Led Zeppelin obviously did as well. But their first album was basically electric blues songs.

**Cactus guitarist Jim McCarty:** They called us "America's Led Zeppelin," which . . . no idea. It's a mystery to me. I don't know where that came from. It's embarrassing for me. Maybe that came from the label. I don't think you can compare anybody to Led Zeppelin. They're a unique thing unto itself, and they definitely left their recorded legacy.

**Grand Funk drummer Don Brewer:** We played with Zeppelin, as the Pack, in this little club in Boston. Everybody was just raving about Led Zeppelin. I'd never heard of them before and the next thing you know, they're all over the radio and it was like, wow! They were a major influence on everybody for sure.

**Blue Cheer guitarist Randy Holden:** *Led Zeppelin* just came out, but they were doing something entirely different, and I went to see them at their gig at the Whisky [in Los Angeles], which was their first gig in California as far as I know. I liked their album; I thought they got a really heavy sound on the album, but then live they used these Rickenbackers and they're the most God-awful sounding amps I ever heard, which really surprised me.

**Jethro Tull vocalist Ian Anderson:** Led Zeppelin weren't just about being hard rock. Like us, they too had a very folky and acoustic side to them and, curiously, like I was, were also pals with Roy Harper. So there was some cross-fertilization. But Led Zeppelin were a good example of a band who were known for one thing but were not really trapped by it, where a lot of groups really were trapped by a certain kind of success.

**Deep Purple guitarist Steve Morse:** I saw Led Zeppelin live a number of times in the early '70s and late '60s, and they did a bit of stretching out, definitely some long arrangements and things. And "Moby Dick," the one with the drum solo, that was one of the heaviest guitar riffs there ever was, around that time, I thought. Also one of the cool things back then, I was at the Atlanta Pop Festival where there was Janis Joplin, this new group Led Zeppelin [*laughs*], Dave Brubeck Jazz Trio, Goose Creek Symphony, and Ravi Shankar. It was okay to have variety.

**Aerosmith guitarist Brad Whitford:** I saw them in, I think it was '68, the first time, and yeah, that had a huge influence on Aerosmith and just a huge influence on myself. I think I walked about six inches off the ground for about a year after I saw them [*laughs*]. Jimmy brought the whole concept of sound. The sound of that first record was revolutionary at the time. And now when I listen back, it still holds up. And his, of course, his guitar playing was just so cool. Just so cool."

**Montrose guitarist Ronnie Montrose:** In my book, Jimmy Page is, was, and will always be, the most prolific rock riff writer on the planet Earth. Prodigious output! Of rock riffs, acoustic, electric, recognizable rock riffs. Nobody has ever done that since.

**Ted Nugent, guitarist, and vocalist Derek St. Holmes:** We see Led Zeppelin in Detroit, on a Friday night. And they rocked it; they were great. This is 1970, 1971 maybe. And then we said, hey, they're playing in Toronto the next day, let's jump on the train, go up, we'll see the show. So we get up there, we get over to Maple Leaf Gardens, and it's sold out. Can't get in. So we say, well, let's make it 'round back and we'll at least sit on the curb and watch them come in. We go 'round back, we sit down on the curb, like three little monkeys, me and the two guys I was with. Lo and behold, here comes two limos, they come to the backstage door and it's not opening. It's not sliding up and letting them in. So they got out, and this guy gets out of the car and lights a cigarette and it's John Bonham. And he looks at us and he walks over and he goes, "Man, you've come to see the show?" "Yeah, well, we did, but we can't get in. But we saw you last night in Detroit." And he goes, "Oh man, that's great." Just then the big rolling door starts to go up and those guys start to get back in the cars. He looks at the three of us and goes, "Go on, man—run on in." And he got us in the show. Can you believe it?

Zeppelin at the Lyceum Theatre, London, October 12, 1969.

OVER THE HILLS AND FAR AWAY: **16** ESSENTIAL RARITIES

# SUGAR MAMA

**PAGE/PLANT/2:50**

One of the most celebrated and hotly discussed of the officially released rarities, "Sugar Mama" showed up on the deluxe and super-deluxe reissues of *Coda* issued July 31, 2015. Many purists, in fact, hoped for no expanded version of *Coda*, preferring that the original *Coda* tracks and anything else in the archive be put back in temporal context. Doing so parks "Sugar Mama" way back on the debut, given its recording at Olympic Studios No. 1 on October 3, 1968, when the band was still transitioning to the New Yardbirds.

The song has a deep and complex history—understandable, given its roots as a rote slow blues. There's "Sugar Farm Blues" from Yank Rachell, dated February 1934, followed by Tampa Red's "Sugar Mama Blues No. 2" from March 1934 and "Sugar Mama Blues No. 1" from May 1934. Three years later, Sonny Boy Williamson I issued "Sugar Mama Blues," after which the song sunk into standard rotation throughout the blues world, notably performed by John Lee Hooker and Howlin' Wolf in one form or another.

In Led Zeppelin's telling, however, the song is an uptempo funk number, driven 4/4 by John Bonham in the process of inventing modern hard-rock drumming, complete with bass drum–riddled fills. Plant is powerful, operating in the sweet spot at the upper quartile of his range, as he reels off a lyric that is little more than "sugar mama" ad infinitum. If Plant didn't roll up his sleeves and reengineer the literary side of things, Page's manufacture of completely new music, including melody and chord changes, is enough to constitute the Page/Plant credit, even if the song seems repetitive in its relative paucity of chord changes and literary wisdoms. Refreshing, however, is Page's funk riff, though it admittedly recalls both "Little Games" and "Happenings Ten Years Time Ago" by the Yardbirds, in which case it represents Page drawing from the blues *and* something from the '60s while en route to something new, similar to what he did with "Dazed and Confused."

The production in its final form—cleaned up at Sol Studios, Cookham, Berkshire, on February 19, 1982—is as good as anything on the debut, *II*, or *III*, helped in part by the simple arrangement and drum capture. Although slide guitar, bass pedals, and Hammond organ are mentioned in the performance credit, only the Hammond is obvious; Jones turns in an almost New Wave-y spot of soloing, the modernization apparently accomplished with a harmonizer after the fact, likely when songs were being polished for *Coda*, which makes much use of an Eventide Harmonizer. The recurring descending lick is heavily reverbed and likely put through a Leslie, similar to the solo on "Good Times Bad Times."

Page has confirmed that "Sugar Mama" was in fact remixed for *Coda* and that he was all set to sequence it before "Poor Tom." Calling it "short, sweet, and sappy," he decided to leave it off the posthumous album. This is also why he didn't include it on *Led Zeppelin*, figuring it lacked the rest of the album's intensity, and that when it came to short songs, "Good Times Bad Times" said all that needed to be said.

"Sugar Mama" has a deep history, perhaps beginning with Yank Rachell's 1934 recording of "Sugar Farm Blues." Rachell is seen here at right with fellow bluesmen Sleepy John Estes (center) and Hammie Nixon (left).

# BABY COME
# ON HOME

**BERNS/PAGE/PLANT/4:29**

*"Baby Come on Home" was an adaptation of a Bert Berns track, likely the Hoagy Lands version. Berns (left) was a songwriter and producer who had hired Jimmy for sessions. He's seen here with arranger Garry Sherman at a Van Morrison session in March 1967.*

Unlike the blues adaptations the fecund '68–'69 version of Led Zeppelin was using to form their function, "Baby Come on Home" goes down a soul road and thus never had much of a chance of making it on the debut album. The track was recorded during the same sessions as "Sugar Mama" and was discovered in 1991 on a reel marked "Yardbirds, October 10, 1968." The Olympic Studios No. 1 production, originally mixed at Atlantic in New York, was cleaned up by famed Lotus Land engineer Mike Fraser in Vancouver, Canada, who had been working with Jimmy on the go-for-baroque *Coverdale Page* album.

Originally labeled "Tribute to Bert Berns" by the engineer, the song was given its proper original name when it was cleaned up for its release. Berns, who died in December 1967, was a songwriter, manager, and producer who had hired Jimmy for sessions in the 1960s. Zeppelin's version of "Baby Come on Home" was probably an adaptation of the Hoagy Lands version from 1964, which is credited to "Bert Russell" but also bears the telltale "A Bert Berns Production" credit.

Robert's performance on this slow and sparse, almost gospel-like track is torrid, but it's Bonham who really stands out for his sound and his tasteful resolution of fills at this speed. When he descends on his bass pedal and simultaneously hits a crash, the sound peacefully undulates. Without this grand underpinning, there wouldn't be much of a song at all. Jimmy, filtered through a Leslie, is in fact almost nonexistent, but John Paul is omnipresent with a Hammond. Rare for a Zep track, there are cathedral-vaulted backing chorals.

Years later, Robert was known to view the track with bemusement, rightly thinking it was too left-field for the band, especially before anyone knew what they were about. He thought it was too much like Aretha Franklin or Tom Jones, although it was also in the wheelhouse of Robert's previous act, Band of Joy, and, for that matter, the Band. Viewed another way, it was an exercise in Chicago blues, doomed to chafe against an album focusing on Delta blues, but also at odds with an album built to be guitar-driven and loud, right down to the idea that Jimmy didn't want too many songs on the album lest the physical grooves of the record be too close together, thus constraining the sound.

In any event, the song surfaced for inclusion on 1993's *Boxed Set 2* and *The Complete Studio Recordings* and then in 2008 on *Definitive Collection*. In 1993, it even made the rounds as a bit of a single, reaching No. 4 on Billboard's Mainstream Rock Tracks chart and No. 66 on the Canadian RPM chart. In 2015, it was added to the expanded reissue of *Coda*, where it sensibly lives alongside its sister track, "Sugar Mama."

ABOVE: While Robert's performance on "Baby Come on Home" is almost gospel-like, it's Bonham who really stands out, in part for his tasteful resolution of fills. Without him, there wouldn't be much of a song.

# AS LONG AS I HAVE YOU

**ELGIN/RAGOVOY/8:39**

Boston Tea Party, May 1969. This show produced one of Zeppelin's best versions of "As Long as I Have You."

As with Led Zeppelin's "Dazed and Confused" and "In My Time of Dying," "As Long as I Have You" finds the band spotting something imperceptible to others in somebody else's song and then blowing it up to create a powerful, transformed rock ride.

The subject of this transformation—more like a wanton vandalizing or a razing—is a little-known northern soul–styled song by Bob Elgin (a.k.a. Stanley Kahan) and Jerry Ragovoy; the latter also gorgeously produced Garnet Mimms's 1964 album, *As Long as I Have You*, on which "As Long as I Have You" is the opening track. There's also a lesser-known version from 1965, issued on two separate UK Columbia 45s, one citing the Boston Crabs, the other Junco Partners (yes, the performances are identical). Robert has said that prior to joining Zeppelin, he used to do this song with Band of Joy. Post-Zeppelin, he would do a laid-back lounge-y version with his band the Priory of Brion.

The dark and urgent chord structure of "As Long as I Have You" is to be expected of such Led Zeppelin transformations, but the guys go way beyond, turning it into a proto-metal caveman stomp that could have held its own on Blue Cheer's *Vincebus Eruptum*. Jimmy has his hands full forging riffs out of the original's guitar parts and horn parts while also injecting his own licks as connective tissue.

Led Zeppelin had the song in their set as far back as their first UK tour as the New Yardbirds, but it was most impressively captured for posterity in a soundboard recording during their second North American tour on April 27, 1969, at the Fillmore West in San Francisco. One can enjoy the 8:39 edit or the full twenty-one-minute sprawl, although, strictly speaking, an edit for "nothing but" would take the 8:39 version from 0:00 to 2:00 and from 7:00 to 8:39.

But at 8:39, you get an ad-libbed middle vamp justified by similar sections in numerous Zeppelin live performances of the time (covers and originals), as well as by retrospective consideration of "Whole Lotta Love." The first part finds Robert exercising his blues chops over a naked bass line. At 2:45, Bonzo joins in with a forceful beat while Robert continues, followed by a bunch of Jimmy soloing, occasionally with echo effect. Then there's an uptempo shuffle boogie over which Robert "da da da" harmonizes with Jimmy—unusual.

Despite the superlative quality of the Fillmore recording, there's no right or quick answer as to which is the definitive version, performance-wise. Recordings have surfaced from December 30, 1968, in Spokane, Washington; January 5, 1969, at the Whisky a Go Go in Los Angeles; January 23, 1969, at the Boston Tea Party; April 24, 1969, also at the Fillmore West (possibly the most aggressive performance); April 26, 1969, at Winterland in San Francisco; and May 27, 1969, also from Boston. Presentations vary significantly given that the song was used as a springboard to medley, with Zep taste-testing, variously, the likes of "Fresh Garbage," "Bags Groove," "Mocking Bird," "Don't Judge a Book by Its Cover," "Cat's Squirrel," "I'm a Man," and "No Money Down," although much of these comprise only brief vocal vamping from Robert, practically little more than name-checks.

Eventually, "As Long as I Have You" and the band's myriad other covers were shuffled out of the set as more originals were written for the second album. But it is this track in particular (and arguably "We're Gonna Groove") that represents the most radical Zeppification of an original—a nascent, explosive, live, unself-conscious demonstration of what the band would do across ten to twelve originals that contain at least a kernel of an idea from elsewhere. For that reason, "As Long as I Have You" is one of the great, seminal non-LP Led Zeppelin rarities. It's baffling that the song has not been presented as part of the reissue program.

The title track of Garnet Mimms's *As Long as I Have You* is a gorgeously produced piece of northern soul released in 1964.

# SUNSHINE
# WOMAN

**PAGE/PLANT/JONES/BONHAM/DIXON/JOHNSON/3:06**

The band at New York's A&R Studio in May 1969, a little more than two months after the BBC sessions that yielded "Sunshine Woman." Jimmy later recalled that the song was made up on the spot.

In his usually cryptic or, let's just say, *imprecise* manner, Jimmy told *MOJO* magazine that "Sunshine Woman" was spontaneous, made up on the spot, and that in retrospect it was pretty brave of the guys to act like they were in a rehearsal rather than a BBC session. Maybe so, but the final production *is* fairly formal, including piano overdubs, solid performances, and even a harmonica drifting in and out when Robert isn't otherwise occupied.

For a song produced on the fly, there are a number of nice touches, including barrelhouse piano used very much like a rhythm instrument, somewhat in the manner of "South Bound Saurez." Bonzo makes himself known with persistent bar-crossing snare fills. Jimmy on occasion augments his riff with a little bar-ending lick. But this is a track on which to blow—like a bunch of jazzers, Robert's harmonica solo is followed by a piano solo. After another verse, at 2:37, Jimmy takes the spotlight with support from Robert on "steam train" harmonica before a classic heavy blues wind-up which again, sounds pretty well mapped out.

The song was recorded for Alexis Korner's *Rhythm & Blues* show on the BBC World Service network, along with performances of "What Is and What Should Never Be," "You Shook Me," and "I Can't Quit You Baby," and interview footage. The session went down at Maida Vale Studio 4 on March 19, 1969, with an air date of April 14. The common belief is that the tapes were mistakenly wiped by the BBC and what we hear as the last track on *The Complete BBC Sessions* was rescued from a recording off AM radio. This performance and airing took place in close proximity to other BBC sessions that produced the likes of "The Girl I Love She Got Long Black Wavy Hair" and "Travelling Riverside Blues," both of which bear similarity to "Sunshine Woman," as do "The Lemon Song" and "Moby Dick."

In fact, giving credence to Jimmy's assertion that the song sprung somewhat from the subconscious, Robert borrows, again briefly, from the same two lyrics he does in "The Girl I Love," namely, from "Travelling Riverside" and "Let Me Love You Baby." In *The Complete BBC Sessions* liner notes, this borrowing is articulated in the same manner as it is for the "The Girl I Love," with Willie Dixon and Robert Johnson added to the writing credits. Dixon is credited for the same "when she walks, she shakes like a willow tree" image. Johnson has two references: the "mortgage on my body / lien on my soul" bit plus "teeth shining like gold." Musically, "Sunshine Woman" is close to "The Girl I Love" in the creation of an original hard-rock riff by Jimmy, similar in both songs. Robert's vocals on both tracks reflect a deep knowledge of blues phraseology. The songs also match tempo-wise and are close to "Travelling Riverside Blues," for that matter.

# TRAVELLING RIVERSIDE BLUES

**JOHNSON/PAGE/PLANT/5:11**

"Travelling Riverside Blues" finds the band taking a rudimentary Robert Johnson song from 1937 and completely transforming it, creating a new, elongated, and highly structured riff along with a full-band arrangement. Page pays tribute, though briefly, to some key Johnson licks and phrasings, but Johnson's lyrics serve only as a suggested outline, with Plant also channeling "Terraplane Blues," "Woke Up This Morning," and "Killing Floor" (which Zeppelin was already covering) in the process of adding this song to a half dozen or so Zep classics constructed the same way.

"Travelling Riverside Blues" was played live at BBC's Maida Vale Studio 4 on June 24, 1969, with the band intending for it to be used for radio play only. The song was recorded in mono along with renditions of "Communication Breakdown" and pre-LP versions of "Whole Lotta Love" and "What Is and What Should Never Be" over the course of a seven-hour session apparently arranged more or less on the spot. Tony Wilson engineered, with John Walters taking care of main recording duties.

Unlike on other Led Zeppelin BBC sessions, Jimmy overdubbed a couple of electric solos atop his slide guitar–dominated rhythm track (played on a twelve-string electric), turning the song into an acceptable studio production, at least for 1969. The track was aired as "Travelling Riverside Blues '69" on John Peel's *Top Gear* five days later, along with the other abovementioned numbers, following up a spin of "Honky Tonk Woman" by the Stones and with Peel adding that Zeppelin had just played admirably at the Bath Festival the previous day. In addition to the historic Bath stand, the band was in the midst of their first UK headlining tour, supported by Liverpool Scene and Blodwyn Pig.

Those tuning in to John Peel that day would have heard a confident Led Zeppelin blues-boom rocker. At the bottom end, John Paul Jones can be heard loud and clear, following and extrapolating the melody. Bonham keeps crash cymbal splashes in check, concentrating on rapid-fire interplay between snare and bass drum. His speedy pedal work and grace-noting recalls the faux double bass drum effect of "Good Times Bad Times." Indeed, Bonham seldom touches his toms—one whack early and a few more

during one fill. As for Jimmy's overdubs, the first is a long, highly electric solo; the second is cleaner, sparser, and jazzier.

In this pre–"Lemon Song" lyric, our yarn-spinner is shameless in his repeated tributes to his lemon, squeezed by his sixteen-year-old "rider," his "kindhearted woman" (quoting the title of another Johnson song). One amusing wrinkle has Plant perhaps flubbing a line, at 1:34 singing, "since my baby geen bon" instead of "since my baby been gone."

"Travelling Riverside Blues" was never played live but did eventually find widespread release via a number of Zeppelin reissues, even getting an archival-type video for use by MTV and others to correspond with its first issue on the *Led Zeppelin* box set, for which Page had to obtain permission from the BBC. The excitement over the box set and the general buzz about Zeppelin at the time, along with the MTV play, resulted in "Travelling Riverside Blues" reaching No. 7 on the Billboard charts in November 1990.

Saturday night at a juke joint near Clarksdale, Mississippi, in 1939, not far from the crossroads where, legend has it, bluesman Robert Johnson sold his soul to the devil. Johnson's "Travelling Riverside Blues" serves merely as an outline for Zeppelin's take. Plant also channels Johnson's "Terraplane Blues" and Howlin' Wolf's "Killing Floor," the latter of which would appear as the title of "The Lemon Song" on early UK pressings of *II*.

# LA LA (INTRO /OUTRO ROUGH MIX)

**PAGE/JONES/4:07**

This spirited instrumental hails from one of the many 1969 sessions for *II* (April 14 at Olympic Studios No. 1 in London) and was thus added to the expanded reissue of that album. It's understandable that it didn't make the original album. The happy intro sequence (recurring) offers more of a San Francisco vibe, with John Paul's Hammond also evoking images of the Band or Moby Grape (and maybe even the Partridge Family!), but there's a reggae feel as well, his riff set against counterpoint strumming from Jimmy while Bonham holds down the fort with a confident 4/4. In celebrated Zep fashion, there's an element of playing across the four, landing randomly back at the one. When this theme returns late in the track, they settle in and there's none of that.

Things get even more interesting at the fifty-second mark when the band transitions into what sounds like a tongue-in-cheek tribute to the Who, complete with Pete Townshend acoustic strumming, squalling Townshend electric, and Keith Moon quotes from Bonzo. At 1:26, we're back into the theme, but the heat is turned up, with Jimmy cranking a solo high in the mix.

At 2:07, we get a third all-new theme, a sort of hypnotic, slow stomp over which Jimmy solos further, offering slide, wah-wah, echo effects, and other aggressive noise-making over a minimal melody carried by acoustic guitar, tacitly suggesting the song was worthy enough an

idea to receive guitar overdubs. As the song descends into more of a jam, Bonzo gets adventurous, at 3:14 amusingly performing a faux tom fill on fourteen stomps of his bass drum. This somewhat abstract passage continues through the song's long fade. Once it's all said and done, we've had three completely different musical themes: the opening theme, offered twice, and two additional—almost counterintuitive—themes occurring once each. However, following another Zep theme, the idea of leaving us wanting more, we hear a detectable melodic shift that suggests a fourth musical theme is on the way.

ABOVE: "La La" offers a third section featuring a sort of hypnotic, slow stomp over which Jimmy offers slide, wah-wah, echo effects, and other aggro noise-making.

OPPOSITE: Jones and Page leave the House of Lewis in Boston with manager Peter Grant (right) in May 1969. John Paul's Hammond organ on "La La" provides a San Francisco vibe, evoking Moby Grape—and maybe even the Partridge Family!

# THE GIRL I LOVE SHE GOT LONG BLACK WAVY HAIR

**PAGE/BONHAM/JONES/PLANT/ESTES/DIXON/JOHNSON/3:03**

It's basically because of Robert that "The Girl I Love She Got Long Black Wavy Hair" can't be called a Zeppelin original, for the same reason other tracks fall into this category: there's a direct lyrical reference, in this case the second of four verses, which comes from Sleepy John Estes's 1929 blues "The Girl I Love She Got Long Curly Hair" (not to mention the similar title). Given the song's casual nature, there's the sense that Plant's lyrics are practically a guide vocal, somewhat phoned in, as well as another example of well-meaning Robert paying tribute to an obscure blues song and its writer, and perhaps a bit of a boast that he knows this stuff.

Musically, there are similarities too, but the original is more "Gallows Pole" or "Travelling Riverside Blues," while the Zep redux finds Page inserting a dirty hard-rock riff that bears similarity to "Moby Dick," meaning that there was no way both could have been included on Led Zeppelin *II*. Further on the "Moby Dick" tip, not only is the riff similar, so is the blues mapping. And while "Moby Dick" sounds like Bonzo playing two sets of drums, "The Girl I Love" sounds like one of those multitracks, and not a very adventurous or smooth one at that.

Jones doesn't add much either, sticking close to Jimmy's likewise rudimentary non-chord riff. Come solo time (there are two sets), Jimmy is spirited and rhythmic but essentially turns in the average of all the signature licks we know and love from him. It is left to Robert to carry the track, which he does, assured in his blues phrasing and selling the fact that the girl's parents don't want him hanging around.

"The Girl I Love She Got Long Black Wavy Hair" was recorded only once, at a BBC session on June 16, 1969, in Aeolian Hall Studio 2. Also recorded that day were "Somethin' Else," "Communication Breakdown," and "What Is and What Should Never Be." The session was aired on *Chris Grant's Tasty Pop Sundae* the following week, June 22. When the *BBC Sessions* album was issued in 1997, the song was floated as a CD single, reaching No. 4 on the Billboard Mainstream

Rock Tracks chart and No. 49 on the Canadian RPM Top 100 chart. For the single, the title was truncated to "The Girl I Love," and the credit went to the band and Estes, which matched the credit on the full-length album.

Reflecting Led Zeppelin's drift through the blues songbook and an inclination in later years to get things right, the credit for the track on 2016's *The Complete BBC Sessions* was amended to include Robert Johnson and Willie Dixon, with a citation noting that the song "contains interpolations from 'Let Me Love You Baby' by Willie Dixon and 'Travelling Riverside' by Robert Johnson" (exactly the same citation that appears under "Sunshine Woman"). In truth, there's not much discernable Robert Johnson here, but the nod to Willie Dixon comes mostly from the "shakes like a willow tree" line.

Beyond the modest crediting drama, the most notable aspect of this song is the way it—and, extrapolating, Led Zeppelin—represents a connective tissue between the British blues boom of the 1960s and the likes of Cactus, Mountain, and later Foghat, Bad Company, and even Kiss and Aerosmith, in the early and mid-'70s. In the most basic sense, these bands added electric guitar riffs onto blues- and early rock 'n' roll–framed structures.

Direct lyrical reference to Sleepy John Estes's 1929 blues, "The Girl I Love She Got Long Curly Hair" (not to mention the similar title), resulted in a writing credit. Estes (pictured) was seventy years old at the time Zeppelin recorded the track.

# SOMETHIN'
## ELSE

**SHEELEY/COCHRAN/2:06**

Led Zeppelin's treatment of the rip roarin' Eddie Cochran standard took place during the same sessions that produced a run-through of "Communication Breakdown," the only capture of "The Girl I Love She Got Long Black Wavy Hair," and a trial version of the new song "What Is and What Should Never Be," which was deemed unacceptable enough that the band took another run at it in a second BBC session two weeks later.

This clutch of tracks was put to tape at Aeolian Hall Studio 2 in Bond Street on June 16, 1969. The session was supposed to air June 22 on Dave Symonds's regular *Symonds on Sunday* show, but the host was on holiday that week, so it aired on *Chris Grant's Tasty Pop Sundae*. Also on the show were pop acts Marmalade and Vanity Fair. Grant's "show" was essentially off the cuff, and the host proved his ill fit to the task by conducting a badly researched interview with the band that never aired.

In marked contrast to the band's pulverizing, almost thrash take on Cochran's "C'mon Everybody," Zeppelin's "Something Else" is not driven from the engine room but rather by piano, tambourine, and vocals. Robert's tambourine is relentless, and Jones's barrelhouse piano is persistent to the point that it is he who solos and not Jimmy. Bonzo is just part of the wall of sound, not creating a pocket or a backbeat, but rather joining in with cheery abandon.

Robert's vocal is an exercise in ducking anything high and, in the process, ducking the melody too. For most of the track, he comes off as harmonizing with the music and causes further distraction with his challenging phrasing. A noticeable flub occurs at the 1:20 mark, just after the piano solo; for a split second, you can almost hear the band think about packing it in. Things proceed with a drop in overall volume; one more verse and it's all over, with the song living on briefly in the live set through 1969 and into 1970.

Zeppelin's take on "Somethin' Else" eventually saw release on *The BBC Sessions*, issued November 11, 1997, and again on *The Complete BBC Sessions*, issued September 16, 2016. As for the original, it was released in July 1959. Cochran would be killed in a car accident in England the following April at age twenty-one.

Late rockabilly pioneer Eddie Cochran was a big influence on Page and other guitarists of his generation. The Who, Rolling Stones, Beatles, Jimi Hendrix, and Blue Cheer, among others, all covered him. It's not surprising Zeppelin would record two of Cochran's most prominent tracks.

# C'MON EVERYBODY

## CAPEHART/COCHRAN/2:31

OPPOSITE: Robert challenges Cochran's melody at every turn, but Jimmy piles on the power chords and adds a five-whack coda at the end of each bar, followed by a resolving lick.

Essentially doing a BBC session with video, Led Zeppelin was captured live at the Royal Albert Hall on January 9, 1970, with *II* storming the charts, having reached No. 1 in both the UK and United States. Here they were, knocking out their set before a two-camera 16mm pro shoot, each band member sitting perfectly in the mix.

After a nine-song set culminating in "Communication Breakdown," the band returned with "C'mon Everybody" as the first of three encore tracks, followed quickly by their other Eddie Cochran classic "Somethin' Else" and then "Bring It on Home."

"C'mon Everybody," issued in October 1958, is at least as famous as "Somethin' Else," covered near and far by all manner of heavy metal and punk bands. But one would be hard-pressed to find a heavier or punkier version than Led Zeppelin's wall-banger on this night.

It's not coming so much from Robert, who combines a low-energy, note-ducking strategy with breakouts to his storied yelp, challenging the melody at each turn. Jones helps build the song into a freight train while Jimmy stacks piles of power chords and then, true to his modus operandi, adds a five-whack coda at the end of each bar, followed by a resolving lick.

But it's Bonham who is both the hammer and the anvil. Hats off to the BBC crew for capturing his bass drum so grandly and for their deft recording of his snare, because it is the fulcrum from which Bonzo creates his show-stealing groove with his subtle roll and shuffle technique. Late in the sequence, his catchy dropping of snare beats evokes comparisons with "Walter's Walk" when that song flies off the handle for its energetic close. Bringing to the track unbelievable power is Bonzo's driving of the verse with an eighth-note, faux double-bass-drum pattern, not always, but gloriously right away in the first verse—boom.

Other very lo-fi recordings exist of Zeppelin's take on this rockabilly rebel-rouser, but none exhibit the same intensity.

# WHITE SUMMER

**PAGE/8:23**

It is said that "White Summer" is partly derived from Irish folk song "She Moved thro' the Fair," made recently popular in 1963 by Davy Graham on the album *From a London Hootenanny.*

Typical of Led Zeppelin when it comes to reissuing product, even the mere title of this track comes with baggage, or at least a story. This BBC session, recorded June 27, 1969, at the Playhouse Theatre and aired August 10 on *One Night Stand*, first emerged on the *Led Zeppelin* box set in 1990 as "White Summer/Black Mountain Side," which is what it's always been commonly referred to with respect to live renditions as well. On 2016's *The Complete BBC Sessions*, the song carries the truncated title "White Summer."

The original title is more representative, given that the piece is essentially a live showcase of Jimmy's acoustic guitar skills, presented through two very similar instrumental songs, "White Summer," from the Yardbirds' *Little Games* album, issued in July 1967, and *Led Zeppelin*'s "Black Mountain Side," which has its own complications in terms of writing credits.

In any event, "White Summer" represents one of a few examples of Jimmy bringing what he did in the Yardbirds forward into the New Yardbirds and then Led Zeppelin. Perhaps the best presentation of the piece is the version found on *DVD*, filmed at the Royal Albert Hall on January 9, 1970, if only for the fact that it shows Jimmy playing it on his infamous Danelectro. But the BBC version is nice as well because it's a fairly high-fidelity recording and there's no crowd noise. Bonzo participates in a couple spots too, playing in the circular, raga spirit of Jimmy's early exercise in world music, thumping his high hat while making the rounds of his timpani.

The bits from this eight-minute excursion that one would call "White Summer" are the more frantic whirling dervish–type moments closer in spirit to Indian or Arabic music, with "Black Mountain Side" represented by its distinct and "composed" couple of riffs that link it, arguably, more to the British

folk boom of the mid-'60s. Still, this style of acoustic playing and these melodies—Jimmy used what he called a modal or sitar tuning—overlap with European tradition as well, and it is said that "White Summer" is in part derived from the Irish folk song "She Moved thro' the Fair," made popular by folk boom legend Davy Graham in 1963.

Jimmy was fond enough of his "White Summer/Black Mountain Side" sit-down solo spot that he included the piece on the 1977, 1979, and 1980 tours, and indeed took it forward into his days with the Firm (dovetailing it into "Midnight Moonlight") and the clutch of dates in support of his 1988 solo album, *Outrider.*

"White Summer" features frantic whirling dervish-type moments close in spirit to Indian or Arabic music, as well as a tuning that overlaps European tradition. In 1970, Jimmy was filmed playing the song on his trusty Danelectro. Jimmy included his sit-down solo spot on the 1977, 1979, and 1980 tours and into his days with the Firm.

# HEY, HEY, WHAT CAN I DO

**PLANT/PAGE/JONES/BONHAM/3:53**

TOP: Spanish pressing of "Hey, Hey, What Can I Do," a.k.a."Hey, Hey Que Puedo Hacer."

ABOVE:"Hey, Hey" also appeared on Atlantic Records' budget sampler *The New Age of Atlantic.*

The most legitimate of Zeppelin rarities, "Hey, Hey, What Can I Do" was the only non-LP song the band ever officially released. Showing up as the B-side to "Immigrant Song" pretty much everywhere outside of the UK (in Spain, it was "Hey, Hey Que Puedo Hacer"), the single was issued roughly a month after the launch of *III.* The song has become comfortably familiar through regular radio play over the decades.

Also helping the song become a firm addition to the Zep canon is its inclusion on various compilations over the years, including the *Led Zeppelin* box set in 1990 (the song's first time ever on CD), *The Complete Studio Recordings, Led Zeppelin Definitive Collection,* the 2007 version of *III,* and, most recently, the expanded reissue of *Coda.* A particularly fun one is its appearance on 1972 budget sampler *The New Age of Atlantic* (alongside Yes's non-LP cover of Paul Simon's "America").

"Hey, Hey, What Can I Do" was written at Bron-Yr-Aur and recorded in July 1970 at Island Studios as the band finished up work on *III.* Most of the album was recorded at Headley and Olympic, but Island was the studio of choice for "That's the Way," "Since I've Been Loving You," and this gem, purportedly recorded for use as a standalone single but subsequently relegated to B-side status. Andy Johns engineered the track, with Jimmy producing and formally getting credit on the various seven-inch versions.

Folk song though it is, "Hey, Hey, What Can I Do" nonetheless features a full-on drum track from Bonzo, snares dominating his fills as he takes advantage of the gorgeous sound he got at the sessions. His crash cymbals sustain for miles—as one fades, like clockwork, it's time for another plush splash. Jones keeps up with considerably fat and equally busy bass, also overdubbing one of his signature mandolin lines. Meanwhile, Jimmy strums both languidly and

furiously (come some double-time work), also apparently layering in some zither—certainly late in the track it sounds like zither, but some studious listeners chalk this up to twelve-string guitar. Robert is in fine form, augmenting an uncommonly low-register verse vocal with robust golden-period shrieks. Presented with a wink and a nod is an uncharacteristically ribald lyric, featuring an untrue woman who wants to "ball all day" and "stay drunk all the time." The enraptured male narrator finally decides to pack his bags and leave town.

Despite the production's somewhat haphazard conclusion, it would have made a welcome substitution on the acoustic side of *III*, perhaps in place of either of the two semi-traditional numbers, "Gallows Pole" or "Hats Off to (Roy) Harper." Then again, this feels like a case where, although a song is good enough for inclusion, there are already enough similar arrangements on the album that in the spirit of variety, it was shunted aside.

The band never played the song live, although Page and Plant pulled it out while touring in support of the first of their two albums, *No Quarter*. Simultaneously, the authorized, high-profile Led Zeppelin tribute album *Encomium* featured Hootie & the Blowfish faithfully covering the track.

*Jimmy, seen here in 1970, strums languidly and furiously in turn on "Hey, Hey, What Can I Do."*

# ST. TRISTAN'S SWORD (ROUGH MIX)

**PAGE/5:40**

As a composition, "St. Tristan's Sword" starts with a sparse but novel bass-and-drum groove—Jones jazzy and Bonzo playing one of his signature bass/snare/high-hat proposals—a little "Poor Tom," a little "Over the Hills and Far Away"—directly to Jones. Jimmy joins in with a kind of Southern-rock chicken-scratch guitar. There's a modulation at 1:16, and Jimmy begins a solo in which he extensively, ethereally, elliptically dances around the melody. By 2:11, he throws in a line that harmonizes with Jones's riff, and they are into a second evocation of Southern rock, a brief mid-paced counterpoint. About thirty seconds later, we are back to the original theme.

Bonzo straightens out the beat by 3:14, putting the snare on the one and the three. Jimmy solos again, and there's a sense that the song is turning into a jam, particularly as Jones gets bored and begins looking for something more contrapuntal to what his by-now wayward compatriots are playing. He flubs a note (3:50) against, interestingly, Jimmy, who flubs none, despite this being one of his longest solo tracks of the expanded catalog—then again, given Page's meticulous handling of all this material, one imagines he wouldn't let a guitar flub through. By 4:30, the song has devolved further into a jam space, with both Jimmy and John Paul exploring the melody simultaneously, no safety net in place. Despite the jazzy creativity, Page's soloing throughout reminds us of the song's strong sense of rhythm. Yet another new theme emerges with fifteen seconds left and takes us out.

This Robert-less studio track hails from the *III* sessions, recorded at Island No. 2 on July 5, 1970, with Andy Johns engineering. Jimmy has said it reflects the kind of exercise the band would perform live (echoes of it have turned up in early live versions of "Dazed and Confused," for example) and that they did two takes before moving on. The song was included on the 2015 deluxe reissue of *Coda*. Oddly, it fits there, sounding like the beefy playing Jimmy would perform late in the band's career and less like something so vintage.

Death of
Tristan

The titling of "St. Tristan's Sword" suggests that Robert, with his interest in fantasy and mythology, had intended to put words to it. The story of Tristan, a Cornish knight of the Round Table, and Irish princess Iseult became the subject of the influential Wagner opera *Tristan und Isolde*, which premiered in 1865.

Its titling would suggest that Robert, with his predilection for things Arthurian, might have planned to put some words to it. The story has many variants across many Western cultures, with origins in the twelfth century. Tristan (sometimes Tristram) was a Cornish knight, rather than a saint, and his own sword is not central to most of tales; most accounts have Tristan dying by poisoned lance. The better-known saga of Lancelot and Guinevere is said to have evolved from Tristan's own tragic tale of adulterous love with Irish princess Iseult (or, more popularly, Isolde). The mythological touchstones of the song's title add to the mystery of the song's origins and where it might have gone had the band not set it aside so quickly.

# KEY TO THE HIGHWAY/
# TROUBLE IN MIND
# (ROUGH MIX)

**BROONZY/SEGAR/R. M. JONES/4:05**

Bill "Jazz" Gillum recorded a version of "Key to the Highway" with Broonzy in 1940. This pressing was issued in 1955 on RCA Victor subsidiary label Groove. Gillum was murdered in Chicago in 1966.

This track is another example of Zeppelin acting on their observation that two similar old blues standards can be stitched together seamlessly. The three verses are brief. The first is a three-quarters match to the first verse in most versions of "Key to the Highway," the last is a three-quarters match to the first verse of "Trouble in Mind," and the middle is from neither.

"Key to the Highway" was first recorded as a twelve-bar blues (subsequent versions are mostly eight-bar) with vocals, piano, and drums by Charlie Segar in Chicago on February 23, 1940. Three months later, the song was recorded again in Chicago, this time by Bill "Jazz" Gillum, with Big Bill Broonzy on guitar and Gillum on vocals and harmonica (which features prominently in the Led Zeppelin version). Broonzy's own version, recorded May 2, 1941, is a pretty close match to the Gillum cut, adding some light percussive accompaniment.

The credit for "Key" is given to the first recorder, Segar, and to Broonzy, although the Gillum/Broonzy version is more of a template for Zeppelin's take, the main difference being the jaunty thump bass on the 1940 recording. The song's also been done up by the likes of Little Walter, Eric Clapton, and even the Rolling Stones, who recorded it at Chess in Chicago but never released it.

"Trouble in Mind" was written by jazz pianist Richard Jones back in 1924 and has been covered and continually altered ever since by, among others, Bertha "Chippie" Hill, Louis Armstrong, Georgia White, Victoria Spivey, Bob Wills and His Texas Playboys, and Sister Rosetta Tharpe. Post-Zeppelin, the song has been tackled by the likes of Jerry Lee Lewis, Hank Williams Jr., Hot Tuna, Jerry Garcia, and Bert Jansch.

Led Zeppelin's "Key to the Highway/Trouble in Mind" comes from Olympic Studios No. 2 on June 10, 1970, with Andy Johns

presiding as engineer. The same session produced the somewhat similar "Hats Off to (Roy) Harper." Jimmy discovered it on the end of a studio tape reel, and in 2014, it became a highlight of the expanded reissue of *III*.

One way to look at Led Zeppelin's version of the song is that it adheres to the mandate of the band dressing up old blues songs, but not in the band's usual manner (i.e., electric, bombastic, injected with newly conjured riffs). Here, we get a comparatively slow version with moderately showy acoustic licks (aggressive at times, with lots of fret buzz); dramatic, slow-burn harmonica; and quite showy and emotive vocals from a peak-years Robert, recorded through a Leslie speaker. There are no bass or drums, but there's so much going on with harmonica, vocals, and acoustic guitar that the rhythm section is not missed.

Zeppelin acted on a clever observation: two similar blues standards can be stitched together seamlessly. "Trouble in Mind" was written by jazz pianist Richard M. Jones. Big Bill Broonzy (pictured) arguably cut the definitive—though not the first—version of "Key to the Highway."

# JENNINGS FARM BLUES (ROUGH MIX OF ALL GUITAR OVERDUBS THAT DAY)

**PAGE/5:54**

"Jennings Farm Blues," named for Robert's country retreat in the Midlands, is a heavier, more electric early version of "Bron-Y-Aur Stomp" and a product of the earliest sessions in advance of the *III* album. Identified by the working title "Bar III," the song was fresh, originating during the North American tour dates the band had just finished.

Recorded at Olympic Studios No. 2 on December 13, 1969, and engineered by Andy Johns, the newly named "Jennings Farm Blues" was in fact identified by manager Peter Grant as a possible standalone advance UK single, which would have pleased the Atlantic Records brass immensely, given Grant's no-singles edict discussed elsewhere in this book. But as the band, always nagged by live commitments, got busy on the record, the idea for such a release got scotched.

And so into the first sessions for the third album the band went, cooking up this boisterous countrified romp. Scarcely eight seconds in, Jimmy Page has already piled up three guitar tracks. John Paul Jones enters with a bobbing octave-oscillating country bass line, while Bonham thumps out a 4/4 beat in competition with a wall of sixteenth-note tambourine. Jimmy rises to the folk-rock spirit of the track with a pedal steel–like guitar signature and some finger-picking on top of his rock bed, while the band explores obscure melodic terrain and a tricky beat that reverses itself regularly.

Bonzo gets a massive drum sound, with particularly expansive bass drum, and as the song drones on, he gets more adventurous with his fills. It's odd hearing this fully electric version of "Bron-Y-Aur Stomp" without the vocals, and in truth, it eventually gets a bit tedious. In fact, it becomes obvious that the song wasn't constructed to stand as an instrumental and that, clearly, vocals were going to be added all along.

There are some nice touches, however, such as at 2:08, the first major variant, where Bonham gets positively thunderous and Jimmy rattles off two sets of solos simultaneously. Again, this is a spot where it becomes noticeable that boredom is setting in back at the drum stool, and, in response, Bonzo gets busy. A minute later, we're back to the opening bluegrass-style theme, but everybody's just a little more aggressive. At 3:23, everything stops except John's snare drum, which gets a major case of the rattles.

This juncture feels like a natural stopping point, but then we're back into the theme and the guys take the opportunity to get comfortable with the challenging rhythmic shifts. A little over a minute later, and with a minute left to go, we're into a variant of the muscular wall-of-sound section last heard at the two-minute mark. There are interesting tambourine sounds and some oddball soloing from Jimmy over the last twenty seconds or so before everybody decides to call it a day, each seemingly on his own timeclock.

It's testimony to the band's creativity that the song in its final form would be acoustic, surprisingly less-dressed, with the guys showing the wisdom and discipline to pare it back. On "Bron-Y-Aur Stomp," everybody sounds happy to be playing as minimally as they are, even Bonham, who has set aside what might have been the most powerful backbeat on the *III* album for something elegant, charming, and within the realm of straight timekeeping.

Even with that hat, Robert didn't rate an appearance on the countrified romp of "Jennings Farm Blues."

# SWAN SONG

**PAGE/4:59**

"Swan Song" is an interesting example of what could have been had this idea of Jimmy's not been consumed by the maelstrom of creativity that resulted in the masterpiece that was *Physical Graffiti*.

Page had grand plans for this "Swan Song" concept, mapping out an epic composition in four parts, for which he even had Plant write a suite of lyrics about the seasons. The genesis of the idea traced back to Page working alone at his home studio, Plumpton Place, after which "Swan Song" was explored with the guys at Headley Grange in early 1974. By late February, two sections of the song had been demoed. Beyond their erudite obscurity, it was Jones (who had almost quit the band the previous year) with some brief Entwistle-toned bass licks who distinguished himself on those early demos, although Bonzo also managed some spiffy playing, exploring quite obviously his recurring tendency to play to Jimmy's riff.

Page's acoustic work on the track is simple, ponderous, and almost world-weary, yet once the band kicks in, the song becomes not quite complicated but at least tricky. Parts are kept to a minimum because, after all, there were two entire sections still to be built, along with the addition of vocals and orchestration. Somewhat evocative of "The Rain Song" and "Over the Hills and Far Away," what we have of "Swan Song" points to a classic in the making. Given the extent to which so many Zeppelin songs evolved from idea to final version, it's not so much that "Swan Song" is impressive, but that there are basic arrangements, chord changes, passages, and transitions between passages that clearly, with the usual amount of hand-wringing, could have resulted in a few magic moments.

However, Jimmy, soon to be blessed with an embarrassment of riches (proven by the fact that *Physical Graffiti* became a double), was soon to find his yearning for epics satisfied by "Ten Years Gone," "In My Time of Dying," "In the Light," and "Kashmir," the last of these receiving orchestration that surely would have been difficult to top. But it was "Ten Years Gone" that is said to have directly undermined the completion of "Swan Song," with Jimmy throwing himself into that song's complex guitar layering.

Still, "Swan Song" would not be imagined for naught. Favorable reaction to its title resulted in the name of Jimmy's new record label (and indeed one of the most iconic label logos in rock history).

Jimmy was still thinking of completing "Swan Song" as late as 1976 and then further explored its bits and pieces live, offering tantalizing tastes in his "White Summer/Black Mountain Side" portion of the show on the 1977 tour, all the way through Knebworth and the band's last dates across Europe in 1980.

In fact, working at his home Sol Studios in Cookham, Berkshire, England, Jimmy made use of the idea with his supergroup the Firm. In fact, during the Action into Research for Multiple Sclerosis (ARMS) charity shows in 1983, which marked Jimmy's first live appearances since the retiring of Led Zeppelin, Jimmy and Paul Rodgers revived "Swan Song" as the base for a song called "Bird on a Wing." Renamed "Midnight Moonlight" in the Firm sessions, the 9:13 track would itself be the swan song to band's self-titled debut, closing the record with an epic full-band display that found Jimmy browbeaten in the mix by the drums, a distracting fretless bass, and Paul Rodgers's sonorous vocals, if not exactly his lyrics.

Almost mythic in nature, "Swan Song" would actually outlive Zeppelin. Jimmy made use of it in the Firm and at the 1983 ARMS Charity Concerts, where Page and Paul Rodgers revived "Swan Song" as the basis of "Bird on a Wing." Page is seen here at the September 20, 1983, ARMS show at London's Royal Albert Hall.

Perhaps some sort of preciousness or even reverence about his unfinished masterwork kept Jimmy from including the widely bootlegged track on the expanded reissues of *Physical Graffiti* or *Coda*. Whatever the case, its absence confused and irritated fans. Upon reflection, however, this turn of events only adds to the mystery surrounding the reissue program and continued debates over vague liner notes, where songs should have gone, and how much is left to be unearthed.

# 10 RIBS & ALL/ CARROT POD POD (POD)

**JONES/PAGE/6:49**

Most often referred to as "Carrot," this is a gorgeous instrumental recorded at Musicland in Munich during the dizzying sessions that produced *Presence*. For fully three minutes, it's just John Paul Jones on plaintive, melodically sophisticated piano, which presages the mood he would create on "Ice Fishing at Night" from his 2001 album, *The Thunderthief*. The melody bears similarity to the intro sequence of Phil Collins's "We Said Hello Goodbye," a rarity labeled "Noxious," which is attributed to Jimmy even though it's all piano, and the Who's "Dangerous" (although that's uptempo with a vocal track).

At 3:03, the band kicks in, and we are immersed in gorgeous tones all 'round inside of one of the most plush and enjoyable mixes in the Zeppelin canon, Bonham laying down an effortless, laid-back groove with tasteful fills, Jimmy playing distant electric and overdubbed acoustic. John Paul's piano continues, but he also plays the same Hagstrom eight-string bass used on "Nobody's Fault but Mine" and "Achilles Last Stand." Through the duration, nothing much changes, which is kind of interesting—Jimmy keeps with his two tones, and there is no soloing or new melodic variants, as the band sans Plant collapses into a reclined close.

"Carrot" is so unlike anything on *Presence* that it's hard to see the song being seriously considered for inclusion. However, it sounds like something that might have inspired "All My Love" one record later, with Bonham's playing feeling like the closest match, although Jimmy's passive twanging on that future classic also sounds like it could have been born here.

Many agree the song hasn't gotten the attention it deserves because of the absurdist tongue-twister of a title (one Zeppelin forum theory: the first letters and the *P* as sixteenth letter spell out "TRAC 16"). But ain't it ironic, then, that this track, one made onerous to talk about by name, has no lyrics?

"10 Ribs & All/Carrot Pod Pod (Pod)" features three full minutes of John Paul Jones alone on plaintive, sophisticated piano.

# ACKNOWLEDGMENTS

The author would like to extend a hearty hail and thanks to T. J. Ramirez, who served as consultant and crazy-deep Led Zeppelin expert on this project, even offering input on scaling back some of my more feverish sentences. T. J., a recording artist, music teacher, and all-round excellent explainer, can be reached at tjrmusic.com.

# ABOUT THE AUTHOR

At approximately 7,900 (with more than 7,000 appearing in his books), Martin has unofficially written more record reviews than anybody in the history of music writing across all genres. Additionally, Martin has penned approximately fifty-six books on hard rock, heavy metal, classic rock, and record collecting. He was editor in chief of the now retired *Brave Words & Bloody Knuckles*, Canada's foremost metal publication for fourteen years, and has also contributed to *Revolver*, *Guitar World*, *Goldmine*, *Record Collector*, *bravewords.com*, *lollipop.com*, and *hardradio.com*, with many record label band bios and liner notes to his credit as well. Additionally, Martin has been a regular contractor to Banger Films, having worked for two years as researcher on the award-winning documentary *Rush: Beyond the Lighted Stage*, on the writing and research team for the eleven-episode *Metal Evolution* and on the ten-episode *Rock Icons*, both for VH1 Classic. Additionally, Martin is the writer of the original metal genre chart used in *Metal: A Headbanger's Journey* and throughout the *Metal Evolution* episodes. Martin currently resides in Toronto and can be reached through martinp@inforamp.net or www.martinpopoff.com.

# IMAGE CREDITS

a=above; b=bottom; r=right; t=top

**Alamy Stock Photos:** Front cover, Philippe Gras/Le Pictorium; p2–3, Pictorial Press Ltd.; p7 and 13, Jay Thompson/Globe Photos/ZumaPress.com; p16, Bob Stinnett/Globe Photos/ZumaPress.com; p18, Philippe Gras/Le Pictorium; p32 and 34, Jay Thompson/Globe Photos/ZumaPress.com; p45, Trinity Mirror/Mirrorpix; p49, Philippe Gras/Le Pictorium; p76, PA Images; p84, Keith Morris News; p88, Pictorial Press Ltd.; p144t,b, Pictorial Press Ltd.; p145t, INTERFOTO; p146, Trinity Mirror/Mirrorpix; p164, Pictorial Press Ltd.; p207, Tracksimages.com; p238, Granamour Weems Collection; p265, Pictorial Press Ltd.; Back cover, Philippe Gras/Le Pictorium. **Chess Records:** p43, p47a. **Frank White Photo Agency:** p50, Jay Good; p148, Laurens Van Houten; p209, Laurens Van Houten. **Getty Images:** p1, Chris Walter/WireImage; p15, Michael Ochs Archives; p20 and 22, Jorgen Angel/Redferns; p24, RB/Redferns; p25, Mark and Colleen Hayward/Redferns; p28, Chris Walter/WireImage; p30, Jorgen Angel/Redferns; p39, Robert Knight Archive/Redferns; p40 and 46, Jorgen Angel/Redferns; p53, 54 and 57 Charles Bonnay/The LIFE Images Collection; p59, Michael Putland; p65, Chris Walter/WireImage; p66, Michael Putland; p69, Michael Ochs Archives; p70, Michael Putland; p72, Chris Walter/WireImage; p75, Walter Iooss Jr.; p78, Michael Ochs Archives; p80, Robert Knight Archive/Redferns; p85 and 86, Koh Hasebe/Shinko Music; p89, John Minihan/Express; p92, Robert Knight Archive/Redferns; p93, 97 and 98, Gijsbert Hanekroot/Redferns; p99, Estate of Keith Morris/Redferns; p100, Michael Putland; p101, Chris Walter/WireImage; p106–107, 109 and 111, Michael Putland; p112, Gijsbert Hanekroot/Redferns; p113, GAB Archive/Redferns; p114, Michael Ochs Archives; p115, Gijsbert Hanekroot/Redferns; p119, Hulton Archive; p121, David Redfern/Redferns; p122–123, Michael Ochs Archives; p125, Richard Creamer/Michael Ochs Archives; p126, David Redfern/Redferns; p129, Jeffrey Mayer/WireImage; p130, David Redfern/Redferns; p132, *Daily Express*/Hulton Archive; p134, David Gahr; p136, Jeffrey Mayer/WireImage; p139, Gijsbert Hanekroot/Redferns; p143, Michael Putland; p145b, Tom Copi/Michael Ochs Archives; p149, Geoff Dann/Redferns; p151 and 152, Michael Putland; p154, Mick Gold/Redferns; p156–157, Gijsbert Hanekroot/Redferns; p163, Ian Dickson/Redferns; p165, Gijsbert Hanekroot/Redferns; p167, David Tan/Shinko Music; p168 and 171, Michael Putland; p172, Estate of Keith Morris/Redferns; p175, Michael Putland; p176, Michael Ochs Archives; p178–179, Michael Putland; p185, Larry Hulst/ Michael Ochs Archives; p186–187,

Baron Wolman/Iconic Images; p189, Michael Putland; p190, *Evening Standard*; p194–195, Waring Abbott/Michael Ochs Archives; p198, Ed Perlstein/Redferns; p200, Richard E. Aaron/ Redferns; p203, Terence Spencer/The LIFE Images Collection; p210 and p214–215, Graham Wiltshire/Hulton Archive; p219 and p226–227, Rob Verhorst/Redferns; p229, John G. White/ *The Denver Post*; p230, Michael Ochs Archives; p232, Jorgen Angel/Redferns; p234, Fin Costello/Redferns; p236, Michael Putland/Hulton Archive; p241, Graham Wiltshire/Hulton Archive; p247, Chris Walter/WireImage; p251, Michael Ochs Archives; p252, PoPsie Randolph/ Michael Ochs Archive; p253, Jorgen Angel/Redferns; p254, p256, p260, p261, Charles Bonnay/ The LIFE Images Collection; p263, David Reed/Redferns; p267, Jorgen Angel/Redferns; p269, Michael Ochs Archives; p271, Waterford/Mirrorpix; p275, Michael Ochs Archives; p277, Charles Bonnay/The LIFE Images Collection; p279, Michael Putland/Hulton Archive; p281, Peter Simon. **Library of Congress:** p242–243; p248–249, Bain Collection; p259, Marion Wolcott Post/Farm Security Administration; p273. **Voyageur Press Collection:** p4; p10–11; p17a; p19; p21; p23t,a; p26t,a; p27; p29t,a; p31; p33; p35; p36–37; p41t,a; p42r,b; p47b; p52a,r; p60 and 61; p62–63; p67; p79; p83; p87t,a; p90–91; p95; p96a,b; p102 and 103; p105; p116–117; p133; p135; p140–141; p147; p150; p153; p166; p190–191; p197; p199; p204–205; p208; p211; p216 and 217; p222–223; p233; p240; p253b; p255a,b; p266a,b; p268; p270a,b; p274

# INDEX

"Achilles Last Stand," 23, 124, 184–185

Akhtar, Najma, 99

"All My Love," 210, 220

Allman Brothers, 34–35

Amos, Tori, 165

Anderson, Ian, 245

Anger, Kenneth, 161

Appice, Carmine, 14

Arc Music, 46, 61

"As Long as I Have You," 254–255

Association, The, 19

Atkins, Al, 244

Atlantic Records, 12, 224

"Babe I'm Gonna Leave You," 18–19, 29

"Baby Come Home," 33

"Baby Come on Home," 252–253

Bad Company, 143

Baez, Joan, 18–19

Band of Joy, 35, 253, 254

"The Battle of Evermore," 92, 98–99, 110

*The BBC Sessions*, 264

Jeff Beck Group, 20

Beck, Jeff, 16, 20

Berns, Bert, 252

Bethea, James, 228

"Bird on a Wing," 279

"Black Country Woman," 87, 153, 174

"Black Dog," 26, 76, 92, 94–95, 131

"Black Mountain Side," 28–29, 155

"Black Sabbath," 31

Bob Marley & the Wailers, 135

Bonham, Jason, 55, 189

Bonham, John
alcoholism and, 206

congas and, 43

death of, 221, 224

formation of Led Zeppelin and, 12

other musicians on, 58, 60

Bonham, Pat, 56

"Bonzo's Montreux," 239

"Boogie with Stu," 173

Bredon, Anne, 18–19

Brewer, Don, 60, 245

Briggs, Anne, 28

"Bring It on Home," 38, 39, 61

"Bron-Y-Aur," 68

"Bron-Y-Aur Stomp," 87

"Bron-Yr-Aur," 162

Broonzy, Big Bill, 274

Brown, James, 47, 130–131

Burnett, Chester Arthur. *See* Howlin' Wolf

Butler, Geezer, 244

Cameron, John, 191

"Candy Store Rock," 131, 191, 199

Carlos, Bun E., 58, 60

"Carouselambra," 218–219

"Carrot," 280

"Celebration Day," 65, 68, 70–71, 74

Charlton, Manny, 244–245

Chkiantz, George, 130, 150

"C'mon Everybody," 266

Cochran, Eddie, 264–265

*Coda*, 68, 111, 183, 222–225, 250, 253, 272

"Communication Breakdown," 14, 30–31, 51, 52

*The Complete BBC Sessions*, 257, 263, 264

Corriston, Peter, 142

Coverdale Page, 183

"The Crunge," 118, 119, 130–131, 135

"Custard Pie," 144–145

"Dancing Days," 119, 128, 132–133, 150

"Darlene," 236, 237

"Dazed and Confused," 21, 22–23, 24, 29, 31

Deep Purple, 21, 24

Denny, Sandy, 99

Digby Smith, Richard, 68, 102

Dixon, Willie, 20, 21, 33, 41, 61, 233, 263

Donner, Ral, 199

Doud, Mike, 142

"Down by the Seaside," 164–165

Dreja, Chris, 13

"D'yer Mak'er," 119, 131, 134–135

Earl, Roger, 60

Elgin, Bob, 254

*Encomium* (tribute album), 165, 271

Entwistle, John, 13

Epps, Stuart, 228

Ertegun, Ahmet, 12

Estes, Sleepy John, 144, 262

"Everybody Makes It Through," 161

Fairport Convention, 77, 99

Faithfull, Marianne, 18

Fawcus, Ron, 159

Firm, the, 183, 228, 235

Fleetwood Mac, 96

Foley, Clyde, 87

"Fool in the Rain," 212

"For Your Life," 188–189

Foreigner, 25

"Four Sticks," 92, 96, 110–111, 113

Fraser, Mike, 252

"Friends," 23, 68, 74, 110–111, 162
Fuller, Blind Boy, 144

"Gallows Pole," 80–81, 230
Gay, John, 128
Gerlach, Fred, 81
Gillum, Bill "Jazz," 274
"The Girl I Love She Got Long
    Black Wavy Hair," 262–263
Glover, Roger, 24
"Going to California," 92, 113
"Good Times Bad Times,"
    14–17, 26
Graham, Davey, 269
Grant, Peter, 12, 43, 93, 113,
    191, 201, 224, 276

Hamilton, Audrey, 213
Hand, Owen, 231
Hardie, George, 13
Harper, Roy, 88
Harrison, George, 127
Harwood, Keith, 148, 162, 164,
    177, 182
"Hats Off to (Roy) Harper," 88,
    144, 275
"Heartbreaker," 38, 50–51
Hendrix, Jimi, 16, 48
"Hey, Hey, What Can I Do,"
    67, 225, 270–271
Hipgnosis, 192, 224
Holden, Randy, 245
Holmes, Jake, 22
Honeydrippers, 47
Hooker, Earl, 20
Hooker, John Lee, 250
Hootie & the Blowfish, 271
Hopkins, Mick, 58
"Hot Dog," 131, 206, 213
"Hots On for Nowhere," 200–
    201, 235
"Houses of the Holy," 150–151
Houses of the Holy, 116–
    119, 123
"How Many More Times,"
    23, 24, 34–35, 43
Howlin' Wolf, 35, 46, 250
Huston, Chris, 46

"I Can't Quit You Baby," 21,
    33, 225, 233
"I'm Gonna Crawl," 221
"Immigrant Song," 65, 66–67, 229

"In My Time of Dying," 148–
    149, 161
"In the Evening," 208–209
"In the Light," 23, 161
In Through the Out Door, 153,
    183, 202, 204–207,
    225, 235
Iommi, Tony, 58
"Iron Man," 31

Jansch, Bert, 28–29
Jasani, Viram, 29
"Jennings Farm Blues," 87,
    276–277
Johns, Andy, 77, 79, 82, 98,
    102, 104–105, 113, 137,
    162, 164, 230, 274, 276
Johns, Glyn, 12, 21, 25–26, 79
Johnson, Blind Willie, 148
Johnson, Robert, 47, 153,
    258, 263
Jones, John Paul
career after Led Zeppelin, 225
formation of Led Zeppelin
    and, 12
on John Bonham, 60
on "Stairway to Heaven," 104
on III influences, 77
Jones, Mick, 25–26
Jones, Richard, 274

Kahan, Stanley, 254
Kansas Joe and Memphis
    Minnie, 114
"Kashmir," 23, 29, 124, 147,
    154–155
"Key to the Highway/Trouble in
    Mind," 80, 274–275
King, Albert, 47
King, Ben E., 225, 228
Kramer, Eddie, 41, 51, 150,
    174, 234
Krauss, Alison, 99

"La La" (Intro/Outro), 260–261
Lead Belly, 81
Led Zeppelin, 12–13, 24–26, 31
Led Zeppelin
acoustic work of, 77, 79
album art and, 142, 192–193,
    216–217
formation of, 12
influences of, 12

musicians on importance
    of, 244–246
name of, 13
Ron Nevison on, 158–160
Swan Song label, 88, 143, 155
Led Zeppelin II, 31, 36–39,
    260, 266
Led Zeppelin III, 64–65, 77, 79
"The Lemon Song," 38, 46–47
Lenoir, J. B., 20
Lewis, Dave, 79
Little Richard, 77, 96
"Living Loving Maid (She's
    Just a Woman)," 39, 43, 51,
    52–53
The Lord of the Rings/The
    Hobbit, 55, 87, 99,
    103, 109, 128

Maile, Vic, 228
Manning, Terry, 73
"Many, Many Times," 128
Mases, Leif, 207
Matthew, Ian, 77
McCallum, David, Sr., 23
McCarty, Jim, 22, 24, 244
McCarty, Jim (guitarist), 245
McDowell, Mississippi Fred,
    144
McGhee, Brownie, 144
McLean, Don, 237
Mimms, Garnet, 254
"Misty Mountain Hop," 92,
    108–109, 113
Mitchell, Joni, 77, 113
"Moby Dick," 56, 239
Moby Grape, 73
Montrose, Ronnie, 246
Morse, Steve, 245
Muddy Waters, 20

Nevison, Ron, 144, 148, 154,
    158–160, 167, 177, 239
New Yardbirds, 250, 254
"Night Flight," 169, 173
"No Quarter," 23, 31, 119, 137
No Quarter, 271
"Nobody's Fault but Mine,"
    196–197
Nugent, Ted, 246

"The Ocean," 119, 138
One Night Stand, 268

"Out of the Tiles," 56, 65, 74, 76
"Over the Hills and Far Away," 19, 119, 128–129, 133
"Ozone Baby," 236

Page, Jimmy
backward echo technique, 21
career after Led Zeppelin, 225, 228
formation of Led Zeppelin and, 12
heroin addiction and, 206
other projects, 133, 137, 161, 183, 228, 235
romantic relationships of, 82
Ron Nevison on, 158–160
violin bow effect, 23, 207
writing of, 68, 82, 84
"Paranoid," 31
Parker, Bobby, 56
Physical Graffiti, 23, 68, 119, 132, 140–143, 158–160
Plant, Maureen, 44, 48, 182, 202, 220
Plant, Robert
car accident of, 182
career after Led Zeppelin, 225
formation of Led Zeppelin and, 12
on groupies, 177
other projects, 47, 99, 137, 145, 165
romantic relationships, 44, 48, 166, 213, 220
son's death, 206, 218, 220
writing of, 44, 84, 124–125, 196
Poco, 77
"Poor Tom," 68, 162, 225, 230–231, 250
Powell, Aubrey, 192–193, 216–217, 224
Presence, 118, 180–183, 192–193, 280
Presley, Elvis, 199
Priory of Brion, 254
Purdie, Bernard, 212

Quicksilver Messenger Service, 19

Rachell, Yank, 250
Ragovoy, Jerry, 254
"The Rain Song," 119, 120, 127
"Ramble On," 39, 44, 55
Ramone, Johnny, 31
Redding, Otis, 221
Relf, Keith, 22
Righteous Brothers, 221
"Rock and Roll," 92, 96–97, 110
Rolling Stones, The, 174, 182, 231
Rosie & the Originals, 134
"The Rover," 147, 160
"Royal Orleans," 191

Segar, Charlie, 274
Shaw, Sandie, 27
"Sick Again," 177, 188
Simon & Garfunkel, 51
"Since I've Been Loving You," 65, 67, 73
Small Faces, 41
Smith, Janet, 18
"Something Else," 264
"The Song Remains the Same," 119, 120, 124, 127
The Song Remains the Same, 23, 97, 137, 162
"South Bound Saurez," 210
Spence, Lewis, 103
Spirit, 101–102
St. Holmes, Derek, 58, 246
"St. Tristan's Sword," 81, 272–273
"Stairway to Heaven," 19, 92, 101–103, 104–105
Stewart, Al, 28
Stewart, Ian, 96, 173
"Sugar Mama," 20, 33, 225, 233, 250–252
Sullivan, "Big Jim," 19, 29
"Sunshine Woman," 256–257
"Swan Song," 155, 278–279
Swan Song label, 88, 143, 155, 224
Sykes, Roosevelt, 47

"Tangerine," 82
"Tea for One," 202–203
"Ten Years Gone," 144, 166–167

"10 Ribs & All/Carrot Pod Pod (Pod)," 280
Terry, Sonny, 144
"Thank You," 39, 48
"That's the Way," 67, 84
"Think About It," 23
Thorgerson, Storm, 192, 224
Timperly, John, 239
"Trampled Under Foot," 152–153, 174
"Travelling Riverside Blues," 225, 258–259

Unititled (IV/Zoso/Runes), 92–93

Valens, Richie, 173
Van Halen, Eddie, 51

Wallace, Ian, 27
Walsh, Joe, 39
"Walter's Walk," 201, 225, 234–235
"The Wanton Song," 170–171
"Wearing and Tearing," 225, 234, 235, 236, 240–241
"We're Gonna Groove," 225, 228–229
Wexler, Jerry, 12
"What Is and What Should Never Be," 39, 44–45, 264
"When the Levee Breaks," 92, 114
White, Bukka, 88, 144
"White Summer," 155, 268–269
"White Summer/Black Mountain Side," 268
Whitford, Brad, 246
Who, The, 260
"Whole Lotta Love," 23, 38, 41–43, 131
Wilkins, Robert, 231
Williamson, Sonny Boy, I, 250
Williamson, Sonny Boy, II, 61
Willis, Arthur, 87

Yardbirds, 12, 22, 73, 82, 128, 250, 268
"You Shook Me," 20–21
Young, Neil, 165
"Your Time Is Gonna Come," 27, 29

Inspiring | Educating | Creating | Entertaining

Brimming with creative inspiration, how-to projects, and useful information to enrich your everyday life, quarto.com is a favorite destination for those pursuing their interests and passions.

First published in 2017. This edition published in 2022 by Chartwell Books, an imprint of The Quarto Group 142 West 36th Street, 4th Floor New York, NY 10018 USA T (212) 779-4972 F (212) 779-6058 www.Quarto.com

Chartwell titles are also available at discount for retail, wholesale, promotional, and bulk purchase. For details, contact the Special Sales Manager by email at specialsales@quarto.com or by mail at The Quarto Group, Attn: Special Sales Manager, 100 Cummings Center Suite 265D, Beverly, MA 01915 USA.

10 9 8 7 6 5 4 3 2 1

ISBN: 978-0-7858-4180-7

Library of Congress Cataloging-in-Publication Data available upon request

Acquiring Editor: Dennis Pernu
Project Manager: Alyssa Lochner
Art Director: Brad Springer
Cover Designer: Silverglass Design
Layout: Silverglass Design

Printed in China